Hm
1261
.B85
2010

2699282 115

STORIES *of*
TRANSFORMATIVE
LEADERSHIP
in the
HUMAN
SERVICES

D0162001

*With love, to Patricia Beresford, who keeps me honest and helps me play (SB),
and Eone Tolliver, my mother and first teacher (WT)*

STORIES *of* TRANSFORMATIVE LEADERSHIP *in the* HUMAN SERVICES

Why the Glass Is Always Full

STEVE BURGHARDT and WILLIE TOLLIVER

*City University of New York (CUNY)—Hunter College School of Social Work
and Partners in the Leadership Transformation Group, LLC*

Nyack College
Wilson Library

Los Angeles | London | New Delhi
Singapore | Washington DC

Copyright © 2010 by SAGE Publications, Inc.

All rights reserved. No part of this book may be reproduced or utilized in any form or by any means, electronic or mechanical, including photocopying, recording, or by any information storage and retrieval system, without permission in writing from the publisher.

For information:

SAGE Publications, Inc.
2455 Teller Road
Thousand Oaks,
    California 91320
E-mail: order@sagepub.com

SAGE Publications India Pvt. Ltd.
B 1/I 1 Mohan Cooperative
    Industrial Area
Mathura Road, New Delhi 110 044
India

SAGE Publications Ltd.
1 Oliver's Yard
55 City Road
London EC1Y 1SP
United Kingdom

SAGE Publications Asia-Pacific
Pte. Ltd.
33 Pekin Street #02-01
Far East Square
Singapore 048763

Printed in the United States of America.

Library of Congress Cataloging-in-Publication Data

Burghardt, Stephen.
Stories of transformative leadership in the human services : why the glass is always full/Steve Burghardt, Willie Tolliver.
    p. cm.
Includes bibliographical references and index.
ISBN 978-1-4129-7016-7 (cloth)
ISBN 978-1-4129-7017-4 (pbk.)
    1. Leadership—United States. 2. Human services—United States.
I. Tolliver, Willie F. II. Title.

HM1261.B85 2009
361.0068′4—dc22   2008045848

This book is printed on acid-free paper.

09 10 11 12 13 10 9 8 7 6 5 4 3 2 1

Acquisitions Editor: Kassie Graves
Editorial Assistant: Veronica K. Novak
Production Editor: Brittany Bauhaus
Copy Editor: Melinda Masson
Typesetter: C&M Digitals (P) Ltd.
Proofreader: Victoria Reed-Castro
Indexer: Diggs Publication Services
Cover Designer: Janet Foulger
Marketing Manager: Carmel Schrire

CONTENTS

FOREWORD

Students are going to like reading this book. So will the seasoned practitioners and managers who grapple with the daily challenges of work in social agencies.

It's both about how agencies work and how to work the system. Although *working the system* can be for personal advantage, Steve Burghardt and Willie Tolliver take a broader perspective, exploring how organizational life can be made more meaningful and productive for all those associated with its work—staff, clients, and others.

Traditional application-oriented books are likely to begin with descriptions of theory and then move on to demonstrate how concepts and conceptual frameworks can be used to shape action in specific situations. Not this one.

The pages that follow begin and end with situations. The authors have chosen to tell stories about how change occurs through the interactions of colleagues and others in the workplace. Storytelling is an ancient art, often used to clarify values, choices, and actions taken (or not taken). It is a way of both passing on wisdom and learning from the experiences of others. Stories permit readers to enter a presented situation *as if* they were actually in it and to consider a number of *what-ifs— what* could happen *if* we responded to the situation in one way or another?

A warning: this places an enormous responsibility on the reader. No work situation is likely to be experienced in exactly the same way by all participants. We all bring our past experiences, values, predilections, and aspirations to work with us, and these are mediated by organizational culture and by the histories and dynamics of our relationships with clients, colleagues and to the expectations of others.

If you are using this book as a course text or as for in-service training, you may find your colleagues agreeing or disagreeing on the significance of the specific situations presented or the appropriateness of the actions taken or considered. If you are reading this book on your own, without the benefit of collegial feedback, you'll find the authors' questions and suggested exercises helpful in discovering something about yourself as well as the organizational setting in which you work.

A momentary digression: Most of us have had the experience of window shopping in a mall or on the street. Chances are we may have fleetingly considered whether an article of clothing, appliance, or piece of equipment is attractive, useful, priced-right, or even sensible. And, seeing our own reflections in the glass, we might also have considered how that item might fit us or our life style. A similar dynamic occurs when we read a story or watch a film. We focus on what we are seeing, but also on how what our reflection illuminates about our own aspirations and interests.

The authors describe processes of organizational change and development that are drawn from their combined 40-plus years of experience as community organizers, program developers, academic researchers, and university professors. Those experiences have led them to the point of view that organizational change is everyone's business. But they don't impose that point of view on their readers.

It appears to me that they are after clarity, not consensus—clarity that requires not only looking through the glass, but also at what you see reflected in it.

—*Armand Lauffer*

INTRODUCTION

This book is for people who began their work in human services or public education with a special story, one that started with your heart full and your mind alive to the possibility that the work you are doing actually seems to matter, that the people around you draw meaning and consequence from help offered or service given, that a smile from another is less about happiness in the moment than the beginning of trust—and the beginning, as well, of hard work, late at night, that draws people closer together, not farther apart. Perhaps your story began when you ran that small youth leadership group in an after-school program; or worked with those sleepy, scared kids in your community's domestic violence shelter; or helped fill out forms down at the immigrant center one night a week. Learning from folks whose lives seemed defined by special purpose and who gladly shared their lessons along the way, your extra hours of labor may have left you tired at times but never depleted. If part of your quest as a professional is to recapture and re-create that meaningful experience that brought you to human services or public education in the first place, this is your book.

This book is also for those with a different kind of story. It's for those who once wrote in their college autobiography or ventured in an early social work class or dared to dream that someday they would run their very own agency or school. What kind of agency would your special place be? Would it be open to runaway youth, abused women and children, the mentally ill, the developmentally delayed, the very old, or perhaps the very young? It could be any one of them, and it is "them" for a particular reason: You have witnessed, through your own life experience, their marginalization by someone else, somewhere, in another place at another time. If part of your commitment to social justice finds expression in the form of a well-run agency or a vibrant public school that helps others feel safe enough to take up their own personal and social challenges to live fully in the world, this is your book, too.

And we have written this book for another, more sobering reason. At present there is an empirical shadow forecasting that it is unlikely you will be offered the kind of postcollege executive training you need to make either that dream or that quest a reality. In fact, a recent study on social service executive succession commissioned by United Way of New York City found that less than half of all surveyed social service agencies provided the professional development skills needed to develop future executive staff.[1] Furthermore, perhaps the study's most stunning finding was that 31% of surveyed executives "resist professional development because they think it, on balance, a threat to employee retention."[2] Almost a third of social service executives would rather underskill their staff members than provide them with the tools that would make them more marketable . . . and better equipped to improve their agencies.

Such findings help explain another threat to effective public and nonprofit management. Carol Munson, among others, has identified that the business demands of managed care and the fiscal constraints of a less generous welfare state have increased human service agencies' hiring of MBAs and other, more business-oriented professionals for top agency positions.[3] However, the United Way findings suggest that the executive-level entry of non–human service professionals across the social service field may be less a cause for professional concern than a symptom of the above lack of consistent preparation for what today's social service executives, middle managers, and supervisors do. After all, corporations spend $60 billion a year on training, 61% of which is spent on management/executive training.[4] It may be less the MBA degree and more the ongoing preparation for what it takes to become a successful manager or executive that turns agency boards to other fields for their future leadership. As reported by the United Way:

Learning [for human service executive training] is exclusively on-the-job and informal, and . . . many non-profit professionals deem that appropriate. . . . [Furthermore] front-line staff feel they were good at their jobs and had the skills to perform them well, but that they lacked management training that would take them to the next level of organizational leadership and fulfillment of their career aspirations.[5]

The dilemma wrought by one's hopeful past and our daunting present is that such tensions, embraced rather than denied, can create the foundation for that dilemma's powerful, positive resolution. As MIT's Edgar Schein's research demonstrated, the anxiety created between "what is" and "what can be" is necessary for ongoing learning.[6] And it is this learning that is at the heart of how cutting-edge organizations grow and change in today's globalized, fiscally challenging world. Such organizations, as Michael Austin and Karen Hopkins illuminate, have embraced a "learning organization" culture that turns the anxiety of what people aspire to and the conditions under which they work into an opportunity for systems improvement, adult learning, and collaborative problem solving.[7]

Equally compelling is the clarification by Austin and Hopkins that such agencies do not simply appear overnight or after an in-depth strategic planning intervention. Agencies with learning organization cultures are being created by individuals whose distinctiveness is not their brilliance or business degrees; it is their willingness to embrace the dynamic challenges to learn while they work and work while they learn. As Austin and Hopkins clarify:

Research shows that it is more common to see learning and subsequent improvement or change taking place in individuals or small groups or teams than as a coordinated effort across the organization. . . . Most case studies of successful learning organizations show that learning begins with a small group or team (i.e., one supervisor and a work group or unit) that develops a learning culture and gradually spreads this culture across and up the organization.[8]

This powerful insight illuminates a central theme of *Stories of Transformative Leadership in the Human Services:* If you are actively committed to your own lifelong learning, you can be part of the creation of a learning organization culture, too, regardless of the position you hold. Given patience and perspective, early dreams can be found in what you do throughout your career, without waiting for others to make them come true.[9]

That said, while dreams may come true, the work itself will never become easy. There is a daunting reality to public and nonprofit work that is distinctive from work in the private sector. William Bell, now chief executive officer of the Seattle-based Casey Family Programs, reminded us of this distinction when he was head of the New York City Administration for Children's Services. Having been forced to cut his $2.1 billion budget by almost a third while remaining committed to creating the best practices in child welfare, he reflected on what most leadership books fail to recognize about human service work. Holding up a *New York Times* bestseller, he said, "Last night, trying to get some inspiration, I turned to one of those leadership books. . . . It had five stars from a few Barnes & Noble reviews, was easy to read, and made sense . . . commit to your staff, learn to listen to everybody, keep focus." He paused for emphasis. "But such books always include meetings with a team made up of product developers, market analysts, and sales staff out to build up their market. *Their crisis* is always about how to get a larger market share or some business strategy for expansion that's light years from my world." He gave a mildly sardonic smile. "When the book ends, they've doubled their market share, created five- or six-figure bonuses for the execs, and taken a final retreat down in the Caribbean to celebrate." He placed the book on his desk. "I'd like a book that comes from my world." He paused again. "A world where there are no financial bonuses, where we may be expected to shrink our market, not expand it. Do you really think our success should be measured by having more children in foster care?"

Bell's insight was a powerful motivator for this book. Social service executives, public school educators, and municipal health care leaders work with very different resource constraints than do their private sector counterparts. No one in social services ever flew down to former General Electric Chief Executive Officer Jack Welch's retreat in the Bahamas for a week of strategic planning, market forecasting, and tennis. People in the human services count paper clips more often than stock options— a lot more often, in fact—and no one working with kids at risk or isolated adults ever got rich.

Bell's challenge—and that of the many students, practitioners, and activists with whom we have worked over the years—was clear: Tell the stories that cast not shadow but light and in which the struggle to find meaning is realized more often than not, not through financial incentives but through a return to the values and beliefs that inspired us all to enter this work. There is richness everywhere you turn in human services, if you know how and where to look for it. Furthermore, there are agencies being led, right now, by people with vision, excitement, and lessons to share who measure up to the Jack Welches and Lee Iacoccas of the world. Some of those leaders are executives who learned, often the hard way, what it takes to move from front-line teacher or social worker to supervisor and then to manager handling a $5 million budget. Some of these leaders work at other levels of an agency or a school: They mop floors, prepare mailings, and answer phones. Occurring in the middle of a crisis or in a 5-minute conversation with their boss, their lessons seem to show up by accident . . . but when they happen often enough, there may be more design involved than unlikely coincidence.

Our final challenge in writing this book was that most leadership and management books, especially in human services and education, are written primarily for fellow academics and intellectuals. They are analytic and conceptual, using case studies to deductively illuminate theory.

However, most practitioners, whether social workers, supervisors, or elementary school teachers, *while just as intelligent,* learn inductively—that is, they learn theory from case studies. In fact, research has demonstrated that more generative and resilient adults are far more likely to use narrative stories to maintain perspective and purpose than they are to use analytical frameworks based on theories or concepts alone.[10] If the challenge confronting human services is to begin developing an organizational culture capable of reflection, critical thinking, and problem solving as they adapt and change to the world around them, the people involved, first as individuals and then in small teams working outward, must have readily available skill sets and leadership frameworks that they can use as everyday tools—tools that serve as lessons and guideposts to their own internal growth and external achievement.

Therefore, given how most of us learn, we decided that we would meet these challenges in a new way: first by telling stories and then by tying those stories to theory. Parts 1 and 2 of this book tell two stories about management and leadership in the tumultuous, intercultural, extraordinarily rich world outside the private sector where millions and millions of good people work every day. Grounded in the facts of everyday life across the human services, it is a different kind of fiction, based on everything we have learned that is real.

The first story takes place in an agency that you might recognize. Facing a fiscal shortfall, people are working hard, often too hard. Things break down; staff members are stressed out; the program directors get their energy from drinking too much bad coffee and eating too much bad food. In this agency you'll meet a lot of good people, too many of them running on empty.

The second story takes place in a different agency that might be familiar to some of you. As is true of the first agency's staff, not one person is financially wealthy; however, many of the folks in the second agency would tell you they are indeed rich. They work in programs with a $15 million budget that looks like it will be cut. There's a staff of 110, most of whom work well beyond their 35-hour week, and nobody minds, at least most of the time. For them, the glass is neither half-empty nor half-full.

As these stories are designed to be powerful, real case studies of how agency practice actually unfold we follow them with a learning guide to help the reader deepen their value. We are indebted to Michael Austin and Thomas Packard, whose recent synthesis on how to integrate case-based learning into the human service classroom has informed our approach. We have used their focus on a comprehensive and integrated approach to professional skills, leadership frameworks, and the structure and process of community-building to guide our own work so that teachers, students, and individual readers can more holistically apply the lessons of this work to their own ongoing development.[11]

In Part 3, we connect the theoretical dots of community building, social capital creation, and learning organization theory to real people, some of whom are often in the news and others of whom are known only to a few. In support of how readers can use this book as an active learning tool, at the end of each story we have included reflective questions and exercises that one can immediately trace to theoretical issues found in Part 3 (such as community building and learning organization theory).

And so the first story begins. It's about people who began with their own dreams once upon a time.

Acknowledgments

Needless to say, there are more than a few folks to thank for their additions to this book and their support of us both as we labored to bring it forward. At the top are our two dear friends and fellow partners in our training and consulting group, Liz Laboy and Ed Laboy. This book is as much theirs as ours.

Special note needs to be given to the late Michael Mims, a founding partner of Leadership Transformation Group (LTG), whose fierce intellect and genuine passion for the children of our schools and in our communities is still infused within LTG.

We are fortunate to have worked alongside an extraordinary group of trainers and consultants whose passion for their work, professional brilliance, and personal humility have made them trusted friends as well as colleagues: John Aldrich, Clarice Bailey, Alice Baker, A. Kevin Berry, Dolores Brown, Peggy

Brown, Calvin Clark, Angela Cuffe, Ade Faison, Claudette Faison, Alice Fernandez, Liz Fernandez, Gloria Fontanez, Robyn Hatcher, Barbara Hill, Linda Johnson, Marcya Joseph, Jerylle Kemp, Scott Klein, Mohan Krishna, Carmelo Loran, William McKeithan, Tanya Odom, Robert Perry, Evelyn Peterson, Luis Rodriquez, Beth Rosenthal, Emily Rubin, Deborah Sanders, Mary Ann Schretzman, Jacqueline Snape, Denise Torres, Mari Toussaint-Conwell, Dion Q. Turner, Todd Vanidastine, William Vericker, Lorraine Warren, Gay Watson, and Antonio Young have done remarkable work and remain genuine friends. Likewise, we will never forget the legacy of committed work and personal warmth that the late Tom Popowics brought to everything he did with us.

Our administrative assistant, Kamili Franklin, who has suffered through so many of our reports and drafts with kindness and fortitude, has enriched our office with a thoroughness and creativity to her tasks and a warmth and friendliness that makes our working together even better. We look forward to her own book someday.

Over the years, literally thousands of students, trainees, professionals, and community members have enriched our lives with their insights, their commitments to both social justice and personal transformation, and their commitments to keeping us honest and on track with our work. We are humbled by the richness they have shared with us, and we can only hope we have given back at least a bit of what they have given us. This book comes from them, too.

A special group, smaller than the first but still too large to mention all by name, includes the remarkable human service and educational executives, school principals, and staff whom we have directly coached. They have modeled a remarkable tenacity of spirit and willingness to grow, even in the midst of huge external demands and constraints that lie at the heart of this book. It has been an honor to work with them all.

In addition to the remarkable individuals who appear in Part 3 of this book, we are blessed with people who have championed our work in ways that we can never repay: William Bell, Melba Butler, Gladys Carrion, Evelyn Castro, Zeinab Chahine, the late Doris Clark, Steve Coe, Myrna Elliott-Lewis, Aubrey Featherstone, Liz Glass, Robert Gutheil, Beverly Jones, Wendy Junious, Ervine Kimerling, Richard Klarberg, Annette Knox, the late Bogart Leashore, John Mattingly, Beth McGinniss, Kelly McGowan, Stan Mims, Bonnie Rucker, Suzy Sanford, Kathi Way, Mary Wesley Bullock, Anne Williams-Isom, Shondelle Willis, and Linnell Wright advocated for us in ways for which we always will be indebted.

Personal friends and colleagues who either made comments on sections of this work or helped develop our ideas, decidedly for the better, include Mike Fabricant and Anthony Sainz of the Hunter College School of Social Work and Eric Zachary of the Annenberg Institute for School Reform. Danielle Daguilh, working under time constraints as our resident artist, created just the right images for what we are trying to say. Mohan Krishna helped in the final production phase in the classy way he handles just about everything.

We want to acknowledge four exceptional people from Sage Publications as well. First is Armand Lauffer, a special man whose clarity of thought and wisdom of experience have provided us with guidance throughout the development of this work . . . as well as much earlier in life. Kassie Graves, who has shepherded us throughout this project, has used her incisive editorial insights to cohere our ideas, her tenacity of purpose to keep us on the right track, and a singular touch of personal grace to make any suggestion obviously worthwhile. Our copy editor, Melinda Masson, did an extraordinary job in her exhaustive review of our work in ways that have improved it greatly. Both she and Brittany Bauhaus, our production editor, have exhibited a level of professionalism that we deeply admire. It is an understatement to say that we've been lucky to have worked with them all.

On the home front, Pat Beresford and our growing hive of Bs, Lila, Josh, Jen, Lisa, Matty, Dave, Eric, and our newest honeybee, Sara Kaye, have provided some of the personal richness that "balance" and "meaning" are all about. Likewise, in their own special ways, have Frenchy Haynes and the rest of our extended family: Vernice, Jeanell, Cindy, Hollis, and Cheyenne, as well as all those nieces and nephews in New York, Philadelphia, and Florida. Thanks to all for keeping it real, providing support, and making us happy.

The authors and Sage gratefully acknowledge the contributions of the following reviewers:

John Erlich, *Sacramento State University*

Armand Lauffer, *University of Michigan*

Steven R. Rose, *George Mason University*

Ben Shepard, *California State University, Long Beach*

Notes

1. Birdsell, D., & Mazzio, D. (2003). *The next leaders: UNBYC grantee leadership development and succession management needs.* New York: United Way.

2. *Ibid.*, p. 6.

3. Munson, C. (1997). The future of clinical social work and managed cost organizations. *Psychiatric Services, 48,* 479–482.

4. Pfeiffer, J., & Sutton, R. (2001). *The knowing-doing gap.* Cambridge, MA: Harvard Business School Press.

5. Birdsell & Mazzio, *op. cit.*, p. 10.

6. Schein, E. (2003). On dialogue, culture, and organizational learning. *Reflections: The SoL Journal, 4*(4), 27–38.

7. Austin, M., & Hopkins, K. M. (2004). *Supervision as collaboration in the human services.* Thousand Oaks, CA: Sage.

8. *Ibid.*, p. 5.

9. This theme is underscored by the findings of Jim Collins, who researched the difference between great, not good, companies. Among his findings:

   • Larger-than-life leaders from outside the company were *negatively correlated* with taking companies from good to great.

- Compensation packages were not correlated with high levels of success.
- Technology and technology-driven change had "virtually nothing" to do with igniting a transformation inside an organization.

Instead, Collins located an accumulation of small, incremental steps that people worked with, refined, and reworked as they grew to embrace the changes underway. See Collins, J. (2001). *Good to great.* New York: Harper-Collins.

10. McAdams, D. (2006). *The redemptive self: Stories Americans live by.* New York: Oxford University Press.

11. Packard, T., & Austin, M. (in press). *Using a comprehensive case-based examination to evaluate and integrate student learning in social work administration.* Thousand Oaks, CA: Sage.

PART I

The Depletion of Value

1

A BORING ASSIGNMENT

"This sounds about as exciting as watching grass grow," muttered Nick Costello to himself. A stringer trying to catch on with one of the New York papers, he'd just gotten off the phone with Melissa Horowitz, the metropolitan editor at the *Gotham Gazette.*

"I want you to check out the Human Service Alliance," she'd said. "Pete Morrissey, who runs one of the big social service agencies, has been after us for years to see life on the inside of their organizations. He's complaining we don't see how hard it is to keep things afloat. He says business models don't fit what they have to deal with."

There'd been a pause on the phone as she responded to one of her reporter's queries. "We've heard that cutbacks are hitting agencies hard over the next 5 years, given this economic downturn. It can't hurt to take a look at what they're up to."

"I'm happy to take your assignment, Ms. Horowitz, and I appreciate your call. But I don't see the hook you're looking for. There's a story every month or so on what's happening to the poor."

Nick had hoped he didn't sound indifferent, but it would be the kiss of death to his journalistic career if he turned in a 5,000-word article that had been written a hundred times before or, even worse, was boring.

The editor had laughed. "No, no, I don't want that kind of 'needed services for the poor' piece. I'm after something different. This alliance isn't some grass-roots operation doing their normal advocacy thing. It's made up of executives; the players in social work, mental health, health; and even some educators. They're trying to see if they can set up an operation like the National Association of Manufacturers. My contact said they've got to get people to see that what makes them tick isn't the same as big business, even though they run operations that are just as large.

"If that's what they want, then let's find out how they really manage. Morrissey said he got his people to agree for us to look inside. Hell, his place had $50 million in contracts. That's no fly-in-the-water storefront. So I want to see how they really run things, what's so different between them and a profit-making company. You get to sit in on their meetings, see how they make decisions. I want to know the 'who, what, how, and why' of their management structure. Look at their decision making, how they work as a team when faced with hard decisions. See in what ways they do and don't compare to GE or Microsoft"—she'd laughed again—"besides the money. It may take you awhile, but then we'll know. Are you interested?"

"Of course I am," Nick had responded untruthfully. "You said it may take awhile. Can I put in for per diem and expenses?"

Hearing the affirmative, he had relaxed a bit, as had the worry lines around his eyes. Freelance work had aged him since he'd hit 30 a few years ago. *I may end up bored but not broke,* he had thought.

Looking back 2 months later, Nick had to laugh at his reluctance. He'd had no idea at the time that the most boring assignment he'd ever been given would turn out to be one of his best.

2

HALF-EMPTY? HALF-FULL?

"Welcome to our world," smiled Pete Morrissey, as he invited Nick Costello to sit in on an Alliance members' breakfast meeting. Pete had debriefed Nick over the phone the day before on what the Alliance was up to. Its long-term goal was to raise enough money for both a lobbying firm in Washington and a significant advertising/public relations campaign that could make the Alliance's nonprofit cause better known. From there it hoped to attract private and public support for its work. The breakfast group was a subcommittee of five members working on what kind of marketing campaign they wanted and how much it would cost.

A local gourmet coffee shop's breakfast treats were neatly spiraled around the mahogany table in a small, attractive room off Pete's executive suite. The shiny leather furniture had the worn, baggy creases of frequent use. Pete invited Nick to join the four others selecting from the bagels, muffins, and fruit in front of them. Nick decided to go last, making sure he didn't take too much.

"We rotate these meetings at each of our places," said Frank Churchland, extending a beefy hand whose grip gave iron a weakened meaning. "This way we share the costs, even when they're small. As you'll see, it all adds up."

A large heavyset White man who ran one of the largest mental health facilities in the state, Frank took a pumpernickel bagel and lathered a generous amount of cream cheese on both slices.

"It's not that we're cheap, just that nonprofits have next to nothing in the way of extras in their budgets. If we buy bagels and cream cheese one time, it means there's a little less for toner for the photocopy machine."

Nick looked over at Frank and nodded. *Please Lord,* he thought, *I hope this isn't going to be a long whining session masquerading as a power breakfast.*

Nick met the others in quick succession as coffee was poured into paper cups. Jorge Pacheco, a Puerto Rican leader of one of the city's largest Catholic child welfare agencies, gripped his hand tightly and nodded warmly, his strong Indian features breaking into a smile. Jason Levy, the only man wearing a three-piece suit, was chief executive officer of a nonprofit hospital. His right hand holding a large bran muffin topped with jam, he used his left to squeeze Nick's arm. They both laughed at the awkward moment, helping Nick relax. Last to greet him was a tall African American woman, Helen Jacques, whose skin was the color of mocha. The head of a medium-sized multiservice agency, she had taken a small plate of fruit and placed it next to a large cup of water. Smiling so much that her eyes seemed to crinkle, she made room for Nick at the table next to her.

Happily, Pete dispensed with formal introductions quickly and got down to business right away. "Melissa Horowitz agreed to let Mr. Costello sit in on our meetings with the proviso that he gets access to whatever he wants. They're interested in telling our story as a comparison between how big business and big human service run things. It's not going to be about what's happening or not happening to our clients."

"That'll be easy," replied Jorge quickly. "Big business sends their new managers to Harvard Business seminars once a year; we send 'em to Lobby Day in the state capital."

He was referring to the annual trek that human service groups in every state make to their capitals regarding the yearly appropriations process. After weeks of preparation, midlevel human service professionals load buses at 5 a.m. with clients, line staff, and volunteers to meet legislators and their staff members to press their case for more funding. People arrive back home that evening around 8 p.m. Not a lot of work takes place the following day.

"Jorge's making an important point, Nick. Human service people don't have budgets for extras, whether it's bagels and cream cheese or training seminars on quality systems improvements."

Speaking deliberately, Jason pressed his fingertips together. "We can't just take those items off as simple business expenses for tax purposes. Every dime is being monitored by some fiscal auditor who wants to know why this bagel's 65 cents isn't being spent on services for clients."

Noticing the didactic turn things were taking, Pete interrupted the discussion. "I think Nick will figure these things out as we just go about our work."

He looked over at the journalist. "How about we go through our agenda, and if there are any questions after each item, you can ask?"

Relieved, Nick quickly responded yes.

The group quickly got down to business. Jorge gave a brief report on Alliance members' expertise in marketing. "Except for Jason and the folks with health care facilities, we've found that nobody in human services knows anything about marketing. Schools are public and not allowed to do that. Nobody in child welfare would be caught dead advertising. What are we supposed to say, 'Come, leave your neglected child with us!'? Multiservice agencies report they have no budgets for marketing, either."

He paused. "Specific programs like after-school or special needs groups spend a few hundred dollars on outreach. Flyers and posters, that kind of thing. No 'Zoom-Zoom' campaigns like Mazda has for its cars.

"So, we need to look to our health care providers for whatever expertise we have."

Jorge paused for a second, seeming to remember something. He smiled mischievously at Helen. "Them and Helen, of course."

The group collectively chuckled, surprising Nick. Obviously composed, Helen said nothing as she sipped her water. Nick made an extra note on his pad. *What expertise did she have?*

"The next agenda item is how much a 3-year campaign would cost."

Pete, a man of quick movements whose hands were rarely still, had no problem moving the meeting along. His finger pointed to the paper in front of him and tapped it three times. Without his smile, the taps would have signaled irritation.

Jason sighed as he reviewed the papers in front of him. "Well, the teachers' union spent $1.5 million on an advertising campaign for better salaries last year alone. Our hospital's advertising budget averaged $700,000 per annum over the last 5 years."

He looked over at Frank, who had his own sheet of paper in his hand. "Frank, what does a lobbyist cost?"

"A state lobbyist used by different trade groups can run between $300,000 up to a million a year for the private sector boys."

He looked over at Nick. "We can't charge members those kinds of union dues, and we can't promise any shareholders it's a worthwhile investment that'll bring us a bigger market share and higher profits later. That Manufacturers trade group has 14,000 members. In this state we're starting with 50."

Pete interrupted. "Look, we went into this knowing we had a fight on our hands. Most of the American public thinks human services are where the slightly less intelligent serve slightly poorer people who ought to be out looking for a real job. Why do you think most Americans think the private sector looks so good? It's because they've been fed a bill of goods on how mediocre we are."

He looked at the rest of the group, his fingers tapping once again. "Given the situation we're in, we have to approach our boards, engage in fundraising, and make this Alliance happen! America has to find out nonprofits and publics are worth it!"

Frank nodded in agreement, his silver hair falling onto his forehead. "I agree, I agree. But we're in trouble. I was just stating what we know. We don't have money to do things that companies can do. I know we've got to take this on, but I'm the pessimist in the group. I find pessimism keeps human services executives and educators in the real world."

He dabbed a small piece of cream cheese from his upper lip as he looked over at Nick, who was busy taking notes. "Nick, let's face it: A lofty mission statement doesn't mean we have lots of money."

Pete felt compelled to respond again, even though he was the chair. "I don't think we disagree, Frank. I know we've got a crisis. But it's a matter of perception. You're saying the glass is half-empty and we're losing drops every day. I'm saying we're half-full and have to work even harder to keep it that way, getting a little more added to the glass."

He paused again and looked at the group, fingers working the table. "Half-full sells a lot better than half-empty."

Nick noticed others nodding in assent.

Helen raised her hand to speak. "Pete, you asked me to be a part of this work group because you said you respect what my agency is doing. So I'm here, even if we're a quarter the size of everyone else around the table. We're going through the same cuts, too. I'm not denying it can be difficult."

She reached down and pushed her empty fruit plate away. "But difficult doesn't mean there's a problem."

The men at the table began to look perplexed as she went on. Even Pete's fingers took a break.

"To tell you the truth, we have a whole different way of talking about things that helps us day in and day out."

Helen picked up her paper cup, now empty. Taking the silver carafe next to her, she poured just enough water for it to be at the midway point. "Half-full? Half-empty? To us, it's neither. For us at South Bronx Multi-Services, the glass is always full."

She took a long drink before placing the cup carefully in front of her, turning it around and around. "Even now."

The men around the table became silent. Jorge looked toward Pete and then over at Jason, who was staring intently at Frank. It was eerily quiet. If playing cards had been on the table instead of bagels, an outsider might have thought it was the final draw in a game of Texas hold 'em, everyone searching for the other's tell. Wanting to break the tension, Nick asked Helen to repeat what she'd just said. She did, as calmly as before. *At our agency, the glass is always full.* Nick now felt as confused as everyone else looked. Her agency had the least money. It was located in one of the poorest urban neighborhoods in America. *Full?* Earlier, he'd noted the intelligent listening she'd been giving the discussion. Giving off neither the nervous energy of the chair nor the guardedness of Jason, Helen's manner had seemed reflective and engaged at the same time. Another thought flickered through the reporter's mind—*Maybe she's an empty suit who got ahead just because she's . . .*—but he quickly repressed it.

The journalist tried not to hide his disappointment. Sitting with some of the most powerful human service executives in New York, Helen was sounding more like one of those New Age mystics spouting abstract formulas that are great at a spa but not much help in an important work group's planning meeting. How could she expect this group of powerful men to take her seriously?

The stunned look on most of the other faces of the work group suggested those members had the same dismal assessment. Pete's face, however, held a different look. Nick looked back at him with surprise. His eyes twinkling with apparent glee, Pete seemed to be trying to suppress a smile and a response at the same time, his fingers back to their old tricks, tumbling merrily against the arm of his chair. *Why on Earth would the Alliance leader actually be smiling happily at such a foolish comment, especially in front of an investigative reporter?* Something else had to be going on.

Nick drew a triple underlining in his notebook, adding question marks to each. He realized he had his work cut out for him.

3

JACK-OF-ALL-TRADES

"I wouldn't let no man talk to me like that! If I was you, I'd . . . Excuse me?"

The attractive young receptionist paused, the sound of irritation spilling from her voice as Nick Costello stood in front of her. "Can I help you?"

Her dark eyes looked past him as if he weren't really there. Her chewing gum snapped once and then again.

"I'm here to see Allison Smith. Jorge Pacheco sent me over."

Nick assumed the executive director's name would catch the receptionist's attention. He was wrong. A broken solar nail as red as her sunburst lipstick had captured her undivided attention.

"Just a minute. Take a seat over there."

She flicked her broken nail in the direction of a stained, orange couch across the waiting room. "What's your name? Mr. Costa? Costowitz?"

She made no attempt to pronounce his name correctly as she speed-dialed Allison's number.

Nick sat down as far from the stains as possible, warily surveying the rest of the waiting room. Painted a dim, gray green, its overhead fluorescent lights missing one long bulb, the room was so drab and faded that the journalist felt even more downhearted. The Alliance work group meeting had ended with a long review of lobbyists' names for future contacts. The only upbeat note was that members had readily agreed for Nick to check out their operations later that week. He'd just spent the morning at Jason Levy's hospital, sitting in with his executive team at their biweekly meeting. Given the meeting's emphasis on cost overruns, the hemorrhaging state of Medicaid reimbursements, and the executive committee's plans for a TV marketing campaign for its top-rated clinics, Nick had had a hard time finding at the medical center a glimmer of the presumably public/nonprofit style that his editor was looking for.

Jason had confirmed his concerns in a private meeting afterward. "Look, we operate in as corporate a manner as GM. I know that. But we're also losing money daily, and we can't just raise prices on a new medical program model like it's a Buick. Health costs are already going through the roof. We have outpatient clinics in a number of social service agencies, including Morrissey's. So I joined the Alliance because I respect Pete and my daily numbers tell me something's got to change. I'm not counting on the Alliance as the only answer. Maybe it's part of one. I've told my board we've got to look at lots of avenues to stem this tide of red ink."

"But that's a service issue, not a management difference. My editor isn't interested in another tail of woe on service cuts or out-of-sight medical costs."

Nick had left the meeting with Jason frustrated. The medical chief had turned him over to the executive vice president in charge of the clinics.

Thinking about the morning as he thumbed through a discarded year-old copy of *Ladies' Home Journal,* Nick at least had appreciated Jason's honesty. He wouldn't have to waste a lot of time trying to find something that wasn't there. The medical executive also had agreed to let him come back and sit in on marketing sessions for the sleep clinic and the hospital's new prosthetic unit. Maybe the organizations he'd visit would fall on a continuum, Jason suggested. Perhaps Nick could write a comparison piece about all of them. Whatever else, the medical director wryly remarked, he was certain his outfit didn't look a lot like Helen Jacques's South Bronx Multi-Services.

The medical center didn't look a lot like Jorge Pacheco's downtown program site, either. The former's gleaming white walls were in stark contrast to the gloomy, musty surroundings in which Nick was now sitting. The bulletin board across the room was overflowing with notices for events, job postings, and federal and state regulations requiring public notice. Except for the latter, half of the flyers were out of date, inviting people to baby showers held a month ago or announcing job fairs long past. *I guess they weren't kidding about counting pennies.* On this bulletin board, one thumbtack did the work of three.

"Mr. Costaw . . . Excuse me?"

It was the receptionist, the unfocused irritation back in her voice. "Mrs. Smith just buzzed. She is running late. She will be out in 10 minutes."

Not waiting for his response, the young woman quickly returned to reading the most recent copy of *In Style* magazine.

Nick got up to get a drink from the water cooler. The receptacle had no cups. Not bothering to ask for one, he returned to thumbing through the recipe section of the magazine. The braised chicken and curried rice with mango looked delicious.

A short, no-nonsense-looking Black woman with dark, half-moon circles underneath her eyes appeared and motioned him to enter the main office. "Mrs. Smith asked me to come get you. Did the receptionist explain what happened? No?"

Her open, expressive face betrayed a moment's frustration. She looked at Nick so directly it almost startled him. "I apologize. We're on our third girl at the front desk in the last 6 months. Seems most of them take the job as their own answering service, not ours."

She sighed, hands on hips. Her arms were thick and strong and fit snugly against her magenta blouse. The woman's stance somehow managed to give off an equitable mix of weariness and determination. "I have no patience for that nonsense. A job is where you *work!*"

She sighed again as she quickly beckoned him to enter the agency's inner offices. "Work. What a concept."

The administrator, who went by the name Regina Courtney, explained that she served under Allison Smith as the site director for programs. Allison was here from the executive offices uptown to review next year's budget and its shortfalls and to begin the strategic action planning process. Jorge had wanted Nick here to see up close how Regina, Allison, and others actually operated as managers.

"We're late because I'm late. I was here last night until 2 a.m. working on a grant for one of our after-school programs. Sex-ed stuff for fifth-grade boys. We've learned that's when you have to start!"

Regina managed a half-smile. "This morning I was doing coverage for our Head Start director. He's been out with a bleeding ulcer. Medication hasn't helped. There was a parents' meeting we just had to have. With those new proposed regulations from Washington on attendance, they were all pretty upset. I had to be there."

The warmth of her smile momentarily removed the fatigue from her face. "So Allison covered for me with morning clinical supervision for our mental health outpatient program. I'd had to cancel two other times on my staff, so she filled in. If new social workers don't get support, they leave. Too many leave too soon as it is."

Nick saw a glimmer of possibility. "So as a manager you're more like a jack-of-all-trades?"

"And master of none."

Regina laughed out loud. "Who can master anything on 4 hours of sleep a night, other than my 22-year-old daughter?"

She went on more seriously. "If you're going to stay in this business, you have to wear a lot of hats. And you have to do a lot of things. Depending on the hour of the day, I'm a clinical supervisor, program director, chief custodian, whatever it takes. All of us managers are. Allison Smith is one of the best of them. That's why she oversees all the programs."

"Allison Smith, associate executive director for programs."

Her handshake was as firm as her introduction. A middle-aged White woman whose large size was nicely disguised by her stylishly draped Eileen Fisher pantsuit, she motioned for Nick to join the three women and one man at the long, rectangular table. "You've already met Regina, a lady who gives new meaning to the term 'no problem'! We couldn't run this site without her. I'll let everyone do their intros."

Her hand swept the table in front of her. "People, this is Mr. Nick Costello. Jorge wants us to give him a no-holds-barred look at how we manage things. He's doing an in-depth piece on that Alliance I told you about."

The blank but open faces in front of Nick suggested nobody knew what she was talking about but everybody would gamely try to remember.

Allison turned to the reporter before they started. "And get some coffee and a jelly doughnut. Nobody survives around here for long without a little sugar high!"

The group members chuckled in affirmation as they began their intros.

Nick took the remaining sugar-covered Krispy Kreme and sat down next to a young, dark-skinned African American woman, her hair beautifully braided in neat rows that fell just to her neck. "I'm Ashira Harris, director of after-school programs. We have 350 kids 'K through 6' at two different schools, funded mostly through foundations and some Board of Education money. And I prefer the chocolate-raspberry."

The multicolored ivory bracelets on her wrist slid down her graceful arm as she delicately picked up the last bite of her pastry.

"Gilsea Carrera, administration and fiscal. I cook the books."

The dark-haired, middle-aged woman with a lilting Puerto Rican accent suddenly looked embarrassed. Her mouth instantly curled down in fear, age lines running into her dimpled chin. "I don't mean *cook* cook. I mean I have to work on getting all the numbers to line up! I only cook at home!"

She looked around the table, her dimples working overtime. "People, help me!"

She quickly gulped her coffee, reaching for her glazed doughnut at the same time. Folks laughed warmly, allowing her defensiveness to melt away a bit. Nick nodded to let her know that he knew she wasn't serious. He put a tiny check next to her name. *Just in case.*

"Matt Modica, head of operations. Me and my guys keep the place running, whether it's toilets overflowing or tile floors to replace."

Dressed in spotless khaki work clothes and a florid purple tie, the White man at the end of the table had an accent made all the stronger by its mix of southern Italy with South Brooklyn. Boasting thick, strong arms that suggested deep familiarity with heavy lifting, Matt had the only plate with three doughnuts. His smile was relaxed, his face open. The pimpled redness around his neck suggested he'd shaved a little too closely that morning.

"Gwendolyn Wilson, director of the homeless shelter. We care for 30 women and their families here."

About 35 years old, attired in a fashionable pantsuit of light green that perfectly matched the frames to her glasses, her straightened black hair pulled tightly into a bun, the lovely African American woman sitting next to Matt caused Nick to blink twice as he took in her almost regal presence. In front of her was a notepad, opened to the middle. Underneath the pad sat a neatly stacked pile of papers about a half-inch thick, which she had just straightened for the third time that morning. "As you will soon learn about me, I run a very tight ship."

She looked around at the group and smiled lightly. "And I *never* eat doughnuts!"

Her colleagues groaned in a friendly manner at what was obviously a familiar comment. Matt leaned closer to her as he took a huge bite of a sugar doughnut, grains of powdered sugar landing on Gwendolyn's notepad. She shook them off in mock horror, slapping the pad against Matt's muscular shoulder. The papers needed to be straightened again.

"Mr. Costello, as you can see, we can have fun. People who work hard in our field deserve a little levity along the way. A touch of sugar doesn't hurt either. Don't mistake this foolishness for how we operate."

Allison spoke with genuine fervor, her blue eyes bright with intensity, her entire right arm moving in a sudden, up-and-down motion. "Matt's on call 24/7. So's Gwen. They'll both show up here day or night. Ms. Wilson will stay with her residents and their children no matter what when her own workers are out . . . family matters, personal plans, what have you. Matt missed a family barbecue just last Sunday."

The custodial supervisor rolled his eyes in mock horror at the memory.

Nick sensed that at last he was on to something. "People are obviously dedicated at your agency. Is that what makes them managers?"

"'Dedicated' can mean a lot of things to a lot of people, Mr. Costello. What got people to this table meant they were able enough and hardworking enough to do what has to be done for our clients. What you see at this table are people with at least 12 years' experience, with an average of about 20.

"But that's only half the story. The other half is nobody here works less than 50 to 60 hours a week."

Allison's face had an almost dreamy kind of satisfaction at what she was saying. "Ever." The last word sounded like a mantra.

"You'll see why as we go over the agenda."

She turned slightly to direct her comments to her staff. "The first item is shift coverage. With the recent turnover among line staff and social workers this month, we are short on coverage. So Regina will speak on her latest plans. Second is the anticipated budgetary shortfall given cuts in after-care funding. Gilsea and Ashira will speak on what we've been working on. That item will take awhile, so be prepared! Third is what we can do to shorten the length of stay of our homeless families. The city wants a faster turnaround time. They threatened funding losses if we don't comply. So . . ."

"The city drives me crazy," Gwendolyn interrupted. "How can we stay on top of families when I can't fill social service job slots and my home finder staff has to do service plans rather than search for apartments?"

The shelter director was clearly frustrated.

"That's part of what we have to problem-solve today. Like last year, handling staff shortages and budget deficits is this year's 'name of the game.' And we've got to play it, no matter what, if we're going to stay in business."

Allison ran the group with a manner that reminded Nick of his days in the military. Noting her clarity and confidence as she spoke, he could tell that this was a woman who got things done.

"Finally, operations. Matt briefed Regina and me on . . ."

"Ms. Smith! Ms. Courtney! We got a crisis at the front desk!"

The young receptionist had run into the meeting room, clearly frightened. The magazine was still in her hand. "There's this family yelling, and then Mr. Jones, that patient who you said had trouble with his meds, he . . ."

Bent slightly at the waist, the young woman was starting to hyperventilate.

Allison and Regina quickly stood up and headed out of the room, the site director putting a comforting arm around the trembling woman's shoulders as she walked her back to the reception area. "Hold the fort, people!" Allison called back. "This will take a little while. Let's start again in a half-hour!"

"Half-hour? I wish!"

Nick heard Matt's grumbling from across the table. Just then the beeper attached to his belt went off. The operations director quickly checked the number. "See you soon, Mr. Costello. Gotta check on my guys over in maintenance."

Pulling one of the three pens from his shirt pocket as he sped toward the door, he turned and waved Nick toward him. "You can tag along if you want. Allison will beep me when we start. You won't learn much sitting around here."

Nick was happy to walk over with Matt, even if he did wear a purple tie. His friendly, no-nonsense manner seemed typical of how people operated around here. Maybe he was seeing a nonprofit management difference at last.

As it would turn out, Nick had seen a glimmer of much that he would be writing about. It was, he would be surprised to learn, a glimmer of something altogether different from gold.

Critical Thinking

What seems to be the leadership's approach to crisis management? Is there another way in which Allison and Regina could have responded to the receptionist?

4

RUNNING TO CATCH UP

"What the hell happened?"

Matt Modica and Nick Costello were standing in an overheated day care room inside Gwendolyn Wilson's homeless shelter. A huge air conditioner sat idle, water dripping from its frozen coils all over the yellow linoleum floor. A young African American custodian, his perspiring head covered by a black and orange Atlanta Black Crackers baseball cap from the old Negro League, was mopping furiously.

"Don't know, Mr. Modica. The usual. One of the per diems, that new girl, forgot to shut it off last night. System froze up. Hope it's not broken."

"Let Peter know when he comes in. He'll know what to do."

Matt looked at Nick. "Peter Malendez is our evening maintenance supervisor. He starts at 3 p.m. Works a day job over at the construction site on Fulton Street."

He turned back to the young janitor. "Floyd, get some towels on the floor; then add a few of those big pots from the kitchen. I can't get Robert over to fix it before 3 anyway. Our day's up. He's tied up with that boiler inspection."

"I don't believe this happened again!"

Gwendolyn stood in the doorway, hands on hips, a clipboard in her right hand. The clipboard kept banging against her skirt as she stood there. "Now my staff has to traipse over to the park, and it's 93 degrees out! And I can't have the toddlers over there this afternoon. Matt, you sure this can't be fixed right away?"

The defeated tone in her voice foretold his answer.

"Robert's meeting with the inspectors on the boiler. He's been keeping that thing running on rubber bands and glue as it is. Allison's been working with Mr. Pacheco to get a $50,000 board approval for 3 years, and we got a new one lined up at last. I can't pull Robert off with the inspectors here at last. Who knows when they'll return? He's the only one who knows the specs. I'd do it, but the grouting job in our single-room occupancy units'—you know, SROs'—sixth floor is a mess. I had to have Burt and Freddie start all over when I saw the mess they made. Mixed the compound all wrong so the tiles were loose. People have to be able to walk into the bathrooms without falling and killing themselves. I don't think we need another lawsuit, and if our insurance goes up, we're really in trouble."

"I know, I know."

Gwendolyn whacked her clipboard against the back of an already wobbly folding chair. "If Janie had been on top of her per diems, this wouldn't have happened. But her daughter's sick with some kind of flu. She's 13, so she can stay home by herself, but the kid must call her mom every half-hour. Kids'll do that when they're sick."

She exhaled quickly, her unflappable demeanor temporarily replaced by pent-up frustration.

She looked intently at Nick. "There's only so much information a per diem can absorb when they get called in at night. We use per diems a lot, especially for night coverage while we're trying to fill a vacancy. It's not that they're bad. Most are college kids picking up money for books and whatnot. But when they're called at a moment's notice like last night, who knows how awake they'll be? When I was their age, I was out partying four nights a week!"

"How do you manage per diems? They must change all the time."

Nick knew that private sector managers might subcontract, but it was the subcontractor's job to stay on top of his or her people. The managers just dealt with the subcontractor.

"It's not that terrible, really. We plan on needing a whole bunch of per diems every year, so we keep an open ad at the local community colleges and a few local job banks. This way people are always available, even when others move on.

"Then it's the supervisors' jobs to oversee them. They train the per diems on the job, as much as they can. It's not perfect, but it works. Most of the time."

She looked over at the broken air conditioner. "And when it doesn't, we run to catch up."

Seemingly restored, the program director quickly headed out of the room. "Like now."

Matt finished helping Floyd stuff towels underneath the unit. He and Nick walked toward the boiler room. "I don't have per diems. Per diems don't work out in maintenance, period. I'm a lot luckier. I get guys who want their jobs. They stick around as long as they can, a year or 2. Let's face it; they don't have a lot of other options. Where they gonna go without a GED and get paid a buck above minimum wage?"

The operations manager paused in front of a large metal door. "Their problem is skills. They're not afraid to get their hands dirty, but there's only so much they can do without a GED. I keep telling them to get skills on boiler repair, electrical, carpentry, whatever. But they just don't. They hate school too much to try."

Matt's beeper went off. "Damn. The meeting's back on now. I know you're heading back, but I can't go yet. I gotta meet the inspectors, then check back on the tile job. Tell 'em I'm running late. For a change."

He laughed. "They'll understand."

Critical Thinking

Is the system's problem here one of resources? What else could be contributing to all these breakdowns?

5

THE EXTRA MILE

"Welcome to our world, Mr. Costello. No one can say we're trying to sugarcoat things. Except these."

Allison Smith smiled as she took a large bite from one of the leftover doughnuts. Its late-in-the-day stickiness gave off an overly sweet smell that reached Nick from across the table. He was there with only Allison and the site director, Regina Courtney.

"Our resident 'Doctor of the Dozens' and all-around cuss artist, Mr. Brown, got himself in a lather when one of our new families' 6-year-old got in his business. When he goes off his meds, he sees all children as little devils. That's the bad news. The good news is he exorcises them just by swearing a blue streak."

"Why is that good news? Heavy-duty swearing in front of children can't be good for them."

"Of course not. What I mean is swearing's just words. We've got other folks in our single-room occupancy residence who get violent when they go off their meds. That never happens with Mr. Brown. Once we've had a chance to explain that to our homeless families, they know to give him a wide berth if he or any of the other SRO people are acting odd. But sometimes a new family learns the hard way. It doesn't happen too often. Besides, he only goes off meds once or twice a year. Look, that's the nature of the disease. We can't control for that. Would that we could."

The site director stood and walked over to a small table at the very back of the room. "How about some coffee? I made it earlier today. Shouldn't be too bad."

She poured two cups right away, handing the first two to the agency deputy executive director.

Feeling a bit tired, Nick said yes. "A little milk, no sugar. Thank you."

He met Regina halfway and took his cup. He was disappointed to see the coffee had the brackish look it gets when a brewed cup is past its prime.

"I'm gonna lose control if this meeting doesn't get going soon. How many times . . ."

Allison caught herself, except for the irritation. Her body radiated the same frustration Nick had witnessed momentarily in Gwendolyn Wilson; only here it registered more powerfully, her shoulders hunched downward with a weight that seemed suddenly familiar. Nick could tell her upset went way beyond his presence. Her fingers tapped nervously on the table as she took a large swallow from her cup. "Gwen's figuring out where the toddlers can go for the afternoon. You said Matt is playing host to our overdue boiler inspectors and then gets to be Bob Vila in the bathroom."

She paused to add a packet of NutraSweet, stirring quickly. "Regina, where's Gilsea?"

"She's reviewing the numbers again so they look OK."

Regina glanced nervously again at Nick. "I think Mr. Costello unnerved her. Or rather her comment about cooking the books did! She's been angry with herself since."

Nick flinched as she added three packets of sugar to the afternoon brew. "I calmed. . . . I talked to her for a while, and she's OK. Be here any minute."

She quickly swept up the inevitable spill from the packets and deposited it in her cup.

"For what it's worth, I never thought she meant she was cooking your books. Anyone who really was would never say so!"

He looked over at the two managers as Allison, without looking, shared her doughnut with the site director, who wordlessly accepted it. Nick would be checking out the finance officer later. He decided to go down another avenue. "I see you two wrapped that incident up as fast as possible and got back here right away."

Regina looked at her fingers. Each pink nail was neatly tipped at a half-inch with what were obviously a salon's best efforts. "My love of 'prompt' got me these."

She waved her glossy manicure in the air. "We start on time so rarely around here that I was biting my nails down to their cuticles. Talk about wanting to kill!"

She and Allison laughed in unison. "Since social work school taught me that neither homicide nor cussing are part of supervision, I fell back on nail biting to keep me in check whenever we'd start late. Or better put, start later. Much later."

Regina took a long drink from her 2-hour-old coffee, tried to hide her grimace, and put her cup down.

Allison interrupted. To Nick's surprise, she had a genuinely warm look on her smiling face, her eyes bright again. "Actually, that's what I first noticed about Regina—what was it—15 years ago?"

Regina blushed, nodding in agreement.

"Regina is one of our agency's walking success stories. You see, she was one of our first residents when we opened our homeless facility. I was working as a social work supervisor, running a group on financial management, budgeting, that kind of thing. Regina was the only participant who showed up on time."

She smiled again. "Every time.

"I knew she was special then. She had her high school degree and was working on her associate's when she arrived at our door."

"So why were you at the shelter?"

Regina's reply was matter-of-fact. She'd clearly spoken about this topic before. "Oh, that's simple. My husband and I had two children under the age of 3. Then he died. Had a good job as an auto mechanic. No health insurance, though, so he rarely went to the clinic. Heart attack. His family was from down South, my mother was in a nursing home up here because of a stroke, and I wasn't going to leave. Rents being what they are, in 4 months I ended up here on February 16, 1988. I think it was the coldest day of the decade. I didn't know it at the time, but it turned out to be a very good day."

"It was a great day for me, too. Well, the next week was, when you got to the group. When I saw how motivated you were, I didn't mind going the extra mile. Everything I expected from you happened. You've become an inspiration."

"That inspiration thing is a two-way street, Mr. Costello. Allison did so much for me; I couldn't let her down. I may be a role model to some of the young ladies, but Allison Smith was always mine. If she was going to work to find child care for my kids, if she would sit late in the day at the clinic with my boys so I could go to class, then I was going to study harder.

"I got a job here after a few months, thanks to Allison. Worked as a per diem at night on the weekends. My mom came home from the hospital and could take care of the kids. If things were quiet after 2 a.m., I could get my studying done. Made for a long week, I'll tell you."

She turned toward Allison with a look of two parts gratitude, one part fatigue. "If I'd known this lady was getting me into a permanent 12-hour-a-day lifestyle, I might have gone into banking instead. If Allison doesn't slow down soon, I still might!"

"Sounds like you have a reputation as a workhorse." Nick addressed the executive.

"Emphasis on the horse, of course. The way I eat around here, I'll be in a size 24 before you know it."

Allison's off-handed humor pleased Nick. For all the hard work, she wasn't pretentious. "Seriously, when people like Regina come along, why wouldn't you work hard? So many come through here, whether in foster care programs, the homeless shelter, or older people with mental problems in our SRO. It's our job to work with everyone, but more often than not you get disappointed in what happens."

Her hands never stopped moving as she spoke, emitting tiny circular motions of enormous energy. She pushed a strand of hair away from her eyes as she went on. "Some people are too stressed to notice; some don't care, period. So you invest where you can make a real difference.

"So I expected great things from Regina, and the more she fulfilled them, the more I found myself willing to go the extra mile. She's succeeded beyond my wildest dreams."

Allison went on with pride in her voice. "After 10 years of night school and more lost sleep than a career deejay, she got her BA *and* her MSW."

Nick saw the equivalent pride on Regina's face. "Now, as a certified professional in this field, she gets to join me in the stable full time, with all the other workhorses."

"Which makes me certifiable."

The two women laughed again, Nick joining in.

"So what do you two do to relax? All this work and stress has got to get to you. When's the last time either of you had a vacation?"

"I de-stress on weekends. Clean the house and get the laundry done. Sunday night I cook for the week. Stews, lasagnas in the winter; lighter stuff in the summer. That relaxes me. Good energy food. I'm a salad-a-day woman from May on. If I ever cut out the daily doughnuts and nightly nachos, I'd be a size 14 in 3 months."

Allison shrugged. "But that's not gonna happen anytime soon. Maybe when I take my Barbados vacation."

"You were going to Barbados last year. Didn't happen."

Regina's voice was stern.

"How could it? You got a case of walking pneumonia, if you'll recall. What was I supposed to do? Let you handle staff coverage from a hospital bed? Besides, your idea of a good vacation is a 3-day road trip to South Carolina. Last time you went in April, you were in your car more than on the beach!"

"Hey, at least I took it!"

Nick could tell that the two women had had this conversation more than once. "Mr. Costello, people like Allison and me aren't real good at planning vacations—I'll admit that. But we fit in 'R and R' here and there. I take a 3-day weekend whenever I can, when grants aren't due. Allison does the same. Hey, it helps that we love what we do. People need us; we make a difference. How many people can say that about their work?"

"Not me!"

The site's financial officer came rushing into the room. "Sorry I'm late. I know we have a lot to do."

Gilsea Carrera put her books down as Allison and Regina opened inch-thick manila folders. "I'm ready to do it."

Nick looked at his watch. 5:30 p.m. His dinner plans would have to wait. He excused himself momentarily from the room to speed-dial his girlfriend. "Hi, Meredith. Can we change dinner to 8:30? I'm running late."

— Critical Thinking —

In what ways do the two senior people take care of themselves? What, if anything, seems to be missing? Is there anything problematic about how they handle vacation time?

6

CLIPPING COUPONS

Allison Smith looked over at Nick Costello. "So Mr. Pacheco said we had to be completely open with you. I have no problem with that. But when it comes to personnel and budgets, how about off-the-record or deep cover, whatever you call it?"

"You mean change the names and disguise the agency? No problem with this part of the meeting," Nick quickly agreed. The three women in the room looked relieved.

"I don't know what we're going to do."

Gilsea Carrera, the agency's financial chief, looked down at the spreadsheets in front of her. "With the cuts in the mental health program, we'll be down $86,000. We're going to have to lay some people off in the SRO."

She looked as upset as she did earlier in the afternoon.

"Wait a second, Gilsea; we might have other options."

Allison turned to Nick. "We nonprofits operate with three major fiscal problems you're not going to find in corporate. First, most of our funding from government falls in the 'restricted' category. That means we have to use it exactly as we say we will. So unless we can be really creative, learn the art of relationship building, and plan ahead, we have no money for a homeless staff line to be used for, say, the SRO. If we were a private company, we could just take line staff dollars from our high-selling widget department and put 'em into staff lines for a new product line of yo-yos to jump-start it. We can't do that here without a lot of time and energy spent on planning and diplomacy."

Nick saw Allison look warily over at her financial officer again, who was looking down at her spreadsheets. "And I mean a lot."

She paused and drained her coffee cup, causing Nick to inwardly blanch. The woman obviously had a cast-iron stomach.

"Second, we get a 'rate' payment from government agencies to pay for things. We get this much per client for a staff line, this much to pay for food, this much for purchasing baby blankets for kids in the shelter. If we don't stay on top of sales at Wal-Mart or Costco, our kids will go without. There's no running over to Linens 'n Things while we save on something else. The rate price is the rate price. We have to plan ahead, a lot."

The last word seemed to be emphasized in bold.

"I wonder how many $50 million businesses have to clip coupons like us?" Regina Courtney chimed in, slightly defusing the tension building in the room.

Allison nodded in agreement as she went on. "Third is when we get paid."

Nick noted but couldn't quite follow a further irritation behind her words. *If this is the way things run normally,* he thought, *what is there to be irritated about?* "My husband, who used to work for one of the Big Three car companies, says a corporation expects and gets payment within 30 days, 60 max."

"The last time that happened here you could buy a hot dog with mustard and sauerkraut for 50 cents!"

The folks around the table all laughed at Regina's comment. It seemed that lightening the mood of a room was an unwritten part of this site director's job description.

"The state pays us within 2 years of a contract. The city? It's about a year, sometimes 18 months. The feds? At least there it varies. Foundations are better, usually. Depends on the grant."

"How do you make your payroll?"

Nick was genuinely surprised at what he was hearing.

"At first, it was 'make or break' all the time. But eventually, you get enough grants, enough state and city funding, and the money comes in. That's why our executive director is always out working with foundation honchos and government officials. But by the end of the year, each rate and every line item has to account for itself. We have a little creativity along the way, but the books have to balance out, program by program."

She looked over at the financial chief. "That's where Gilsea comes in."

"There's a line in any budget called 'OTPS' that goes for basic agency costs outside of personnel. Pays for overhead on the buildings we run, that kind of thing. But that's rarely more than 8% or 10%. Not a lot to play with."

Gilsea sighed again, an octave lower. Whatever her other talents, Nick could tell she was a champion in the "sigh" department.

"The really big boys get around some of this with their hundred-year-old endowments. Back in the 1800s and early 1900s, rich people put real dollars into their favorite charities. Sometimes in their wills they left them valuable real estate. They get to use the interest from $50 million or $100 million that newer agencies like ours can't. If it weren't for Mr. Pacheco's incredible skills in fundraising, we'd never be as big as we are. Our executive director is amazing when it comes to locating new money sources."

"But they come with the same restrictions."

Gilsea shook her head at the site director. "I wish we could play 'big business' for a while. Then we wouldn't always be playing 'musical chairs' every time a cut took place in some program. It seems like we're always in trouble somewhere."

Allison looked over at the financial officer. "So that's what we're doing now. Musical chairs. 'Chair 1' is the homeless services budget; 'chair 2' is mental health; 'chair 3' is child welfare. We're trying to see who gets to keep their seat."

Nick was amazed. Allison headed back to the coffee pot. She filled her cup with gusto, grabbing another NutraSweet along the way. Why she mixed dietetic sugar into her coffee while eating a large chocolate-covered doughnut mystified him, but she was not the first he'd seen on that special diet plan. He quickly refocused his attention as Allison fixed her financial officer with what seemed like a glare.

"Gilsea, based on last quarter's projections of line turnover, where does it look like we have some play in the wheel? Any monies to move around?"

Gilsea looked at her spreadsheets again. "I was looking at our spending over the last 3 months. We've kept food costs down by $2,000 because the food bank over at City Harvest . . ."

"Gilsea, that's just a little savings from free food. What about those custodial line items in our mental health program that we knew would be open after Ralphie and Jose left? What happened to transferring that money to our SRO operational lines? The city might be open to that."

"I called our city mental health contract officer, but they didn't call back."

The financial officer shuffled her papers again, her dimples working overtime.

"Of course they didn't call back. Who does? It takes five calls for them to know we're alive, eight to get a response. Didn't you have Miki call for you?"

Nick learned later that Miki was Gilsea's assistant.

"Miki hates using the phone; you know that. I called again last week, but they still refused to call me."

The financial officer was digging in her heels.

Noting her defensiveness, Allison paused and drank again, using the moment to shift the tone of her response. "I think we'd be OK if we use the custodial line monies that have been open for 3 months to pay our operational lines. Then we could use that money for a 'clinical support' line. That way nobody has to go, right?"

Nick could tell she wasn't really asking.

"I don't know about that, Allison. I have to speak with people over at homeless and mental health . . ."

Allison reached into her thick folder and took out a long, yellow sheet of legal-pad paper. "Back in February, we agreed this was going to be an issue to plan for. Gilsea, I'm having a hard time understanding why it didn't happen."

Gilsea looked at Allison, then Nick, and then Allison again. Her lower lip started to tremble. "I have been planning! We are saving monies in food and other items. It's not my fault when people don't call back!"

Her voice was rising noticeably. "It's not my fault we're down over a hundred-thousand dollars! I work hard at this! I went to Costco at night myself for that big purchase for our toddler program to make sure the supplies were good!"

Regina quietly asserted herself between the two women as Allison frustratingly leafed through her folders, shoulders hunched forward even more. "Hey, ladies, let's bring it down a notch, OK? We don't need to go down that road again."

By the looks on everyone's faces, this was clearly a well-traveled path between Allison and Gilsea. "Gilsea, can you and Miki take the next day to get permission from your contract officer? If we get this handled by *mañana,* nobody has to get laid off. We can handle the budget one more month."

"I don't know if it can be a day. What if our contracts person is on vacation?"

"Gilsea, just call her supervisor."

Allison's tone was as flat as the coffee and just as bitter. "You know the assistant commissioner as well as I do. She's gotta cover emergencies."

She drained her coffee cup again. "Like this one's become."

The hard-driving deputy executive director immediately regretted her last words as Regina belatedly signaled for her to stop, her large eyes pleading for quiet that came just a little too late.

Gilsea stood up and grabbed her spreadsheets. Her eyes brimming with tears, she looked at the surprised journalist. "Since this is off the record, Mr. Costello, think about this. Just because people work with the poor doesn't make them nice!"

Nick looked around the table. The financial officer was almost in tears. The circles under the site director's eyes had grown darker. The deputy executive director looked like she wanted to rip her inch-thick folder in two. All three looked exhausted.

The journalist had had more than enough for one day. Nick looked at his watch. If he left now, he could get to his dinner date with Meredith with 10 minutes to spare.

"Nick, can you wait just a minute?"

It was Allison, who was checking her watch. Without a word to her boss, Regina had stood up and was following quickly to speak with Gilsea, who had left the room.

For the first time that day, Nick found himself sighing in frustration, too. "A minute" around here was good for a half-hour at least. He leaned back in his chair, anxious to find out what she wanted, trying not to hope too hard that it would be quick.

His slender hope evaporated. Jorge Pacheco, his beige suit jacket slung over his shoulder, strode into the room, a wide smile across his face.

Maybe Meredith would be free for dinner tomorrow night.

7

THE ASSEMBLY LINE

"Nick, glad you're still here! We've got plenty for us all."

Jorge Pacheco held a white plastic bag, a Chinese menu securely stapled to its handles. "Down the block is some of the best Chinese take-out in the city."

The executive director began removing steaming cardboard containers. "There's veggie tofu, green string beans with garlic, a little moo shu pork for the nonvegans, and enough noodles to keep even Allison happy."

He tossed the agency's second in command a pair of chopsticks. From somewhere at the end of the room, Allison Smith had located paper plates. She obviously had expected her boss's arrival, chopsticks and all.

"I make it my mission to make sure Allison eats one healthy meal a day."

He smiled warmly at her. "As you may have noticed, Allison Smith is firmly in command of this ship when I'm not around."

Jorge ladled some brown rice onto his plate. "Since her primary fuel is black coffee and chocolate doughnuts from 8 a.m. until at least 5, I've promised her husband she'll get one balanced meal a day at the office, whether she likes it or not."

He smiled again, looking in the direction of Gilsea Carrera and Regina Courtney's recent path. "I know her staff appreciates it.

"A hypoglycemic Allison Smith is the last thing this agency needs!"

"Very funny."

Allison tried not to act perturbed. "Look, Nick, in one way we're a lot like big business. The Number 1 is Mr. Outside; the Number 2 is Mr. Inside. Or, in this case, Mrs."

Nick Costello turned to Jorge. "Does that work for your staff?"

"Has to. The board is happier that way, knowing we have eyes on both greater fundraising capacity and keeping the ship afloat. I can't do both—nobody can—once you get bigger than a couple of million dollars. There's just too damned much paperwork at that point—and somebody has to be in charge of that, period.

"I'm proud we're at $50 mil and growing. I get a lot of the public credit, but I'd be the first to tell you that without Allison running things inside, we'd be nowhere the agency we are. You think we'd get refunding year after year if we didn't meet our units of service? That, my friend, is because of Allison Smith."

Nick felt himself getting lost in the jargon. "'Units of service?'"

He looked at Allison. "Is that what Mr. Pacheco meant by all that 'paperwork'?"

"You better believe it."

Allison dug into a huge mound of sesame noodles. "This is another huge mistake people make comparing us and business. I figured it all out years ago in discussions with my husband, Mike. In the private sector, 'units of service' are the number of products a company sells or number of hits it gets on a Web site. The tension in the private sector is making sure you have a market to buy all those products or make all those hits. A lot of sweat can go into that happening: Too few products, you lose your market to a competitor; too many, you lose your shirt in overproduction. Management's job is to expand the market on the one hand and, on the other, make sure you get all those widgets delivered on time. That's why they're supposed to get paid those big bucks."

She quickly stabbed at the noodles again. "In the nonprofit and public world, we don't operate that way. In some ways, the guesswork of the market is taken care of. We don't have to do market trends on how many homeless there will be. Someone else does that, usually in policy debates between the advocates and the politicians. Then legislation gets passed, and money is allocated to take care of the problem. But we all work off the numbers we say we can handle. For example, our 'market' of 50 is homeless beds to fill each night. Across the city, other agencies are taking care of their share of the market too. Some are bigger; some smaller. The city takes care of the rest."

Most of the noodles were gone from the container. "So we don't create a market the way business does. We serve the market that's there.

"Of course, there's never enough money. If the demand for shelter goes higher, it's not like in the private sector where we could up the price for a homeless shelter bed."

She looked at Jorge and laughed sarcastically. "Sometimes it's the reverse!"

Nick was getting confused again. "Slow down here. What do you mean, 'Sometimes it's the reverse!'? With more homeless, you get less money? I don't follow you."

"You better."

Allison's well-known irritability was poking through again. "If the numbers of homeless go up or the mentally ill population increases, the city and state still have to provide for them. But maybe there's an economic downturn that year, so politicians give less for care. So when the money's doled out, each unit of service for a client's care is maybe a little bit less that year. If we want to stay in business, we've got to live with that."

"So you have the market security that the private sector doesn't have but have to get by with a lot less financially in return."

Nick found himself intrigued. "Do you think that's fair?"

"That's only the half of it," Jorge interjected. "A private business is accountable to only one thing: the bottom line. If the company makes profit, great. If it doesn't, after a while it goes out of business. It may be high risk, but at least how you measure the risk is clear-cut."

Jorge passed Nick the tofu dish. "Our accountability is so much messier! Allison oversees 15 other managers. How do you measure 'success' with a homeless person? If they get housing but not a job? If a mentally ill person takes her meds but never leaves her room? If a child is returned to his biological mother who's been out of drug rehab for only 3 months?

"The truth is, different contracts are looking for different measures of 'success,' and we have to give it to 'em: so many visits to a biological mom's home, so many GED lessons for the homeless parent. Each unit of that 'success' fits in a service plan, and each service plan becomes the prime way we show we're creating 'good product.'"

"So a service plan is like the completed automobile on an assembly line in your husband's car company?"

"That pretty much captures it." Allison nodded. "Just remember, though, we're not going to make more and more cars and get a bigger and bigger profit. It's our job to manage making that 'service plan car'—only some of the car parts are missing because they stayed in bed to sleep late. Or perhaps the worker doing the finishing touches on that 'car' decided she didn't like that job and walked away. You try to manage that!

"Why do you think I work the long hours I do? Me, Regina, everybody around here does overtime, all the time. Without overtime pay, of course."

Allison was clearly proud of her work schedule.

"So if the assembly line keeps rolling along but clients don't show up or workers leave, how do you get those service plans done?"

"My managers know I expect them to stay on top of their supervisors. Regina's got to keep her programs going. So she trains her supervisors on what needs to get done with each service plan. Then they train the people in their units. The city and state sends them to mandated trainings as well. Overall, things get taken care of."

Nick sensed there was something else. "But today I witnessed lots of breakdowns on everything but service plans. People late for meetings, air conditioners freezing up, handling turnover, people frustrated with each other and leaving the room."

Nick hoped he wasn't offending Allison, but his journalist's eye had seen too much turmoil to let it pass.

Oddly, the deputy executive director wasn't upset at all. "Hey, I've been in the field 25 years. All that stuff you call 'breakdowns' I call an average day in the life of a social service executive."

She paused, a flash of distant memory crossing her face. "People like me and Regina know from turmoil, way, way back."

The brief sadness in her face deepened the furrowed lines above her eyebrows. Just as quickly, they were gone as her boss brought everyone back to the subject at hand.

"Mr. Costello, we live with underfunding, every year. For us it's quality Chinese take-out, not an expense account lunch at a three-star restaurant."

Jorge was clear and focused as well. "People don't come into this field to get rich. For lots of reasons, they come to help people. Once they find out that help isn't just about being 'nice' but requires that extra hour on the assembly line, the good ones get it. They stay. The rest leave. I don't have a problem with that. Allison's a tough taskmaster, no doubt about it. She's had to be tough all her life. But that's because she cares about the clients. If people can't handle that, then they don't care in the same way."

The executive director carefully wiped his lips. "Better they find out early, don't you think? Better for them; better for the poor they thought they wanted to serve, too."

The tofu, as tasty as it had been, was resting uneasily in Nick's stomach. "But you're asking people to get paid a lot less than in the private sector to work just as hard, maybe harder. Not many people are going to stick around for that, are they?"

"Sure they are! We all get into human services because we have a special gene in our biological makeup. It's the genetic DNA for caring about people. Everybody in this field's here because we're wired just a little bit more than most folks. For some of us, we were that middle child caught between siblings. Some of us came from homes where we were the peacemakers. Doesn't really matter how we got started, even if it comes from way back. The point is that now we put up with all the aggravation because at the end of the day, we've made a difference in people's lives."

"That sounds pretty abstract to me."

Nick thought for a minute to himself. *Saying you "make a difference" when there's so much aggravation and upset might not be much of a difference at all.* He pushed his plate away from him. *Sounds to me like people are a little too personally comfortable with crisis.* Nick's tofu was not sitting well next to the noodles.

"I can't tell you more in words."

Allison looked at Jorge, who nodded assent. "Why don't you come and look closer at our so-called 'assembly line' tomorrow? Regina Courtney's got a 9 a.m. meeting with her supervisors. It's her senior staff weekly report meeting."

The deputy exec looked for a few more green beans in the container. "I think what you'll see might surprise you."

Nick quickly agreed to be there the next day. Ten minutes later he was on the street heading to the subway when his cell phone rang.

It was his girlfriend Meredith. Still at the restaurant, she was steaming. Lost in his own thoughts about all that was being said, Nick had forgotten to call her back.

Personal Reflection Exercise

Allison momentarily reflected on how she had been involved in handling crises all her life, even as a child. She went on to mention that many people in human services seem to have deep personal experience, even as children, in handling others' issues. As a professional, is such a background helpful in working with others? Is it a problem? Or is it perhaps both a blessing and a curse?

Personal reflection: Reflect on your own childhood. What role did you play in your own household as a caretaker?

_____

_____

_____

How have your early roles in your family helped you in your career?

_____

_____

_____

Where have those roles been a hindrance?

_____

_____

_____

8

SPLASHED WATER

Nick Costello arrived for the meeting a half-hour early. His favorite journalism professor had drummed into him that the real meat of a story would more likely be found before and after, not during, an event. He wasn't surprised to find that Regina Courtney was already setting up the room.

"Good morning!"

The site director beamed in Nick's direction. She did not seem surprised to see him. "Did they keep you long last night? When Mr. Pacheco arrives with take-out, it usually means they'll be working 'til at least 10."

Regina paused and then went on, her voice quieter. There was a slight hum at the back of her throat as she continued. "Did they, um, speak about Gilsea Carrera?"

She looked anxious for a moment and then continued. "We're still off the record when it comes to personnel, right?"

Surprised that she was so open, Nick was pleased that an important line of his inquiry could be confronted so early. "Right. I disguise any personnel problem so it can't be traced to your agency. Promise."

Nick seized the opening. "So what's the problem with Gilsea?"

Regina looked forlornly away from her questioner. "There's nothing wrong with Gilsea. She's really, really nice. Works as hard as anyone, cares about the clients. She really did go to Costco last week!"

The urgency in her voice sounded almost pleading.

Nick could tell she was also being evasive. "Regina, you just described New York's Mother Teresa. You're leaving something out."

The site director opened a huge bag and started to place various bagels on a large tray. Her hands banged against the paper as she pulled out three at a time. "It's just . . . an agency as big as ours needs a financial officer who plans ahead on all the big numbers. That February meeting Mrs. Smith mentioned was a long one we had where Gilsea was supposed to forecast ahead how we could accrue more funds, given personnel openings. I've been learning about that kind of forecasting with my own budgets.

"Look, don't get me wrong. Gilsea's good with small numbers. Or, actually, with quality bookkeeping, making sure accounts are straight. Invoicing, monthly bills, that kind of thing. When we were a small agency, that was no problem; we all did a little bit of everything. But she's got to think about the big picture and connect it to her numbers so we can plan today and tomorrow."

Regina sighed, but conviction had returned to her voice. "Gilsea is a great lady. But she just doesn't think like that."

Nick was surprised, both at Regina's honesty and at the problem. When he'd worked for a big advertising firm a few years back, there'd been a kindly but not-quite-capable administrative assistant working for his boss. When it was evident she couldn't handle the new software demands of the job, she was gone in 24 hours. At the time he'd flinched at the coldness of his employer. But Allison Smith seemed like she was cut from the same starched cloth. "So why does your boss put up with this? Mrs. Smith seems pretty clear about what she wants. Why doesn't she, you know, move her on? Let her go?"

Regina looked at him with a shocked expression. "What, you mean fire her? Look, that's pretty harsh, don't you think? It's not like she's worthless."

Hearing her sudden defensiveness, Nick felt himself being drawn into an argument he wasn't making. "Look, I didn't say she was worthless. But when I worked for an advertising firm awhile back, we got yearly performance evaluations. My manager wasn't exactly on target with everything, but the areas for improvement were clear. I knew where I stood and what I had to do to get a raise or a bonus."

"Bonus?" Regina gave a forced laugh. "There's no such thing as a bonus in this field, Mr. Costello! If the work goes well, you're lucky to get a handshake."

She paused to fold the bagel bag and place it in the trash. "As for performance evals, I haven't gotten one in 3 years. I doubt Gilsea has either. When you work the hours we do around here, you have to make choices. 'Am I going to stay on top of those units-of-service records needed for reimbursement, or am I going to spend time on an evaluation that probably won't be used anyway?' Seems like a no-brainer to me."

"But if an employee's not up to the job, wouldn't it be better for everybody to clear the air, own the problems, and move on? I thought Gilsea looked upset and defensive all day. She must know something's wrong."

"I really don't think so."

Regina started to brew a large pot of coffee, pouring half a can of ground coffee into the electric percolator's top. "Gilsea and I are close, but she doesn't think it's a job issue. She thinks Allison just doesn't like her."

"If she's your friend, haven't you told her what you told me?"

"Look, every time I try to, she cries. She cries harder when Allison speaks with her."

She poured a huge gallon container of Poland Spring water into the pot, a large amount of it splashing onto the table. Nick moved quickly to find a paper towel. "I hate it when people cry."

She shrugged as she took the towel from Nick and began to vigorously dry the table. "I'd rather do an extra hour of paperwork than listen to somebody sob. Allison's the same way. We can't stand a staff member's tears. Drives us up a wall."

It was clear from her tone that she and Allison had had this conversation more than once.

Crying as a job protection strategy: Nick was impressed with the approach, if not the outcome. "But doesn't that make everyone around her less effective, too? If she's not up to the job demands, why do they have to be? Why does a line staff have to know her job if a top manager doesn't have to know hers?"

Regina looked at him firmly. "Look, Mr. Costello, it's not that simple. Gilsea is a good woman, a single mom, with two kids in parochial school and a mortgage to meet. If Allison lets her go, then what? Is she supposed to come back here in 6 months as a client?"

Nick felt uneasy at the turn of the discussion. They'd gone from talking about clear job performance problems to expanding the number of homeless. He was here as a journalist looking at management practices, not as the local drama critic. He started to respond. "All I meant was . . ."

"Welcome, ladies!"

Regina's booming voice cut Nick off immediately. He turned and saw three supervisors enter the room, each with thick orange folders under their arms. Two were smiling. The site director's voice had an equal mix of warmth and irony as she went on. "It's only 9:15, and a third of the group's here already. Will wonders never cease?"

Critical Thinking

Regina mentioned in passing that she can't deal with the accountant's crying when her performance is questioned. Is crying acceptable when one's work is being reviewed? How might Regina better respond to her? What is the key difference between the reaction of a professional to a client crying and that of a supervisee?

9

GOOD GROOMING

Nick Costello was impressed. Because of Regina Courtney's thoughtful request for introductions by the group, he found himself in the midst of a mini-United Nations of 11 men and women: Besides Regina (born and bred in Harlem), there were two other African Americans (one born in Brooklyn, the other from South Carolina); a woman from Senegal; two Puerto Ricans (surprisingly, the older born in New York, the younger in San Juan); a woman from Ecuador; a man from Pakistan; two White women (the first a self-described "nice Jewish girl from Long Island," the second a recent transplant from Missouri); and, finally, a formally dressed West Indian gentlemen from Trinidad. All were program directors and assistant directors. The journalist was surprised that most of the top positions were held by the younger people in the room.

It was 9:30. Regina reviewed the proposed agenda quickly. It was the SRO unit's turn to report on recent cases of clinical interest that the other directors could both learn from and provide their own insight on. The site director reminded the staff that because of the journalist's presence, clients should be referred to by their first names and last initials only. The second item was a review of operational systems' problems: the air conditioning, fire safety drills, sign-ins at the front desk when staff took their breaks outside the building. The final item referred to budget matters. Nick was quite aware what this last item would be about. He wondered how staff would respond to the possible cuts.

Angelina Browne, the SRO director, began to speak. The African American woman from Brooklyn and the one older program head, she nervously glanced at her notes as she spoke, slowly and meticulously. She rarely looked up as she spoke, but when she did, she directed her gaze solely at Regina. The case she had chosen to discuss belonged to Harry R., who had lived at the SRO for 5 years. A chronic schizophrenic, he had been discharged from a mental hospital 15 years ago back into his community. Arriving at his new group home at the height of the crack epidemic, Harry was soon an addict. Off his medications that could stabilize his mental condition, he was homeless shortly after that. Only through the tireless efforts of Angelina's outreach team was Harry eventually able to get clean and stable enough to be eligible to stay at the SRO facility. A quiet and solitary presence on the fifth floor of the residence who rarely left his room, he had been here ever since.

Nick took copious notes. *This kind of work in the trenches is underreported,* he thought. *It may not be a management issue, but these people do work diligently for a lot of decent reasons that the rest of the world doesn't much notice.* If he ever got a good handle on their managerial dynamics—which hadn't happened yet—maybe he could work that theme into the newspaper story line, too.

Angelina now addressed the clinical and organizational problems she confronted. A nervous quaver entered her voice, all the more surprising because of what she went on to say. A recent computer literacy program had opened up nearby, and surprisingly Harry had been one of the first attendees. He took to the work with ease and proficiency. The tall program director smiled slightly as she went on. "Our Harry R. is a born computer geek. In no time at all he learned Excel spreadsheets, database entry programs, Web site design—you name it. There's nothing on the computer he can't do!"

Rachel Borenstein, the deputy clinical director from Long Island, interrupted. Nick couldn't tell whether her tone was one of excitement or frustration. "So, Angelina, this is great about Harry after all these years. What could the problem be?"

Angelina seemed to flush momentarily as she quickly looked back at her notes. The quaver, barely noticeable before, became more apparent. "Harry's doing so well on the computer that he never wants to leave the program. His training contract gives him 2 hours a day at their site, but he sticks around for 8. Their computer director likes Harry, but he wants him out of there because he's occupying someone else's spot.

"The trainer thought he had a solution by asking Harry to serve as a tutor, but that didn't work out."

Angelina sighed again. "Harry, as most of us recall, has a hygiene problem. He smells. And because he has a fear of toothbrushes, his breath can knock you out from a block away. So students refuse to sit next to him, let alone work with him."

Rachel interrupted again. "So why not send him to Francine's group on self-care, where he can practice good grooming?"

This time Angelina went on without looking at the young deputy director, the quaver cut away as her sentences grew shorter. "Harry has been to the self-care unit once every 6 months. There's been no change. None."

Her tone was suddenly sharper, a touch of anger at the edges. "None! As I was saying, things are getting intense over at the computer clinic. Harry now has a skill he never had before. But he's getting seriously agitated that he can't stay. For the first time in years, he's talking about not needing his meds. That's a bad sign. If we pull him from the program, he's going to regress in a New York minute. Meantime, the program director has called me and Ms. Courtney to resolve the issue. Until we do, they refuse to take any more of our clients."

She paused and looked coolly across the table at Rachel, her words now razor sharp. "*And that means* residents with other clinical needs can't attend their classes, either."

The reporter saw Rachel's neck turn bright pink, the color quickly working its way up her entire face. She started to speak, her body tightly moving forward. Then she stopped herself, pulling her lower back sharply against the chair.

Regina quickly responded. "So, people, Ms. Browne has a real dilemma on her hands. Help the client, hurt the program. Help the program, hurt the client. Any suggestions?"

She looked to the person farthest from the two fuming program directors, Nigel Melegore, the well-dressed assistant director for health services.

His lilting West Indian accent boomed across the table. "To my mind the problem is quite simple, really. If the man doesn't bathe and brush his teeth, he can stay in his room. Why should other people have to suffer from his carelessness?"

Bonita Sanchez, the older Puerto Rican woman who served as assistant director for mental health services, immediately spoke up. "Mr. Melegore, you can't mean that. Harry R. isn't 'careless.' He's mentally ill. He doesn't put a toothbrush in his mouth because he thinks it's a spike. You wouldn't either."

Nigel recoiled at the thought, his right hand brushing the suit jacket sleeve on his left arm. "Just because a person's mentally ill doesn't give him permission to be filthy."

He went on without pausing, the words rushing from him, the note of condescension unmistakable. "People here get coddled too much. A mental condition isn't an excuse! In the health clinic, our people with diabetes get a strict regimen to follow, or else! If their blood sugar goes up, they know that the wrath of me and my staff follows!"

Nick saw Bonita looking at him, her eyes flashing. She started to speak again. "Mr. Melegore, I think maybe you have a problem, too. When you've been here as long as . . ."

"OK, everybody, let's bring it down a notch, OK?"

Regina seemed as taken off-guard as Nick but far more adept at defusing the tension in the room. "Instead of arguing at each other, let's focus on what can work to stabilize Harry and keep residents attending this valuable program for their job readiness skills."

Led by Regina, a thorough discussion took place over the next 15 minutes. Harry R. would have to attend another self-care group for 6 weeks. If successful, he could go back to the computer program. Regina and Angelina would speak to the computer literacy director. If Harry could be monitored on his hygiene, perhaps he could serve a modified role as an assistant tutor a few half-days a week. The group around the table nodded its assent.

Most of the group, that is. Nick kept careful track of the four people who had spoken most about the case, each of whom was oddly silent. Angelina seemed to be reading from another case record. Rachel chewed angrily on her bagel and refilled her coffee cup, twice. Nigel and Bonita seemed lost in thought, their minds somewhere else. None of them spoke again that morning. Nick underlined his notes carefully, scrawling "fireworks!" at the top of the page.

Little did the reporter know how right he would be. What had happened so far, however, were tiny summer cracklers that simply had got his attention. The real cherry bombs in the room would explode a half-hour later.

Critical Thinking

What seems to be the cause of tension between Rachel and Angelina? Is the disagreement between Bonita and Nigel a reason for them to be upset with each other?

Personal Reflection Exercise

Notice how Regina responded to tension in the room. What did she do? How were problems and disagreements handled?

Reflect on your response to openly expressed disagreement. What is your reaction?

_____

_____

_____

When disagreement occurs, are you comfortable to turn that disagreement into an opportunity for learning? How can differences be expressed without turning different points of view into attacks on the people involved?

_____

_____

_____

10

SALT AND PEPPER IN THE POT

"Thanks, everyone. I knew we could get through those small items pretty quickly. You all have your marching orders on getting those operations fixed."

Regina Courtney was evidently pleased at how quickly her program directors dealt with the systems' miscues of the last few days. Nick Costello also was pleasantly surprised at how quickly the next agenda item had been dispensed with. Regina's brief review of the latest breakdowns was met with concrete problem solving by everyone at the table. While more than a few grumbled about the ancient air conditioning and the lack of time to train new staff on all the daily procedures, people focused on immediate solutions. The general banter in the group told the reporter they were glad to have something concrete to deal with and resolve.

Regina paused for a second, removing a small stack of papers from beneath the agenda page. She stared at the paper as she began. "I spoke with Allison Smith this morning, and there's an unfortunate budget shortfall again due to city cuts in reimbursement rates that have finally caught up to us."

She looked around the table as she went on, a slight nervous pitch to her voice. "The shortfall starts at $86,000, but it may balloon to over $120,000 by the end of the fiscal year. This means Angelina's program is going to lose two staff. She's agreed that it means we lose one clinical staff, one group activities worker."

The look on Angelina Browne's face was grim. Nick now understood why she hadn't been smiling as she'd entered the room earlier in the morning. He also realized that Allison had been at work with Regina far earlier in the morning than he. Did that woman ever sleep?

"I don't know what we'll do."

Angelina's tone was grim. "Our caseload is already so large that sometimes my staff feels like they're on a conveyor belt, just pushing paper. A year ago I had three workers doing the work of four. Now I've got to have two and a half handling it all, with all the clerical work they'll have to do. And all my self-care groups just doubled in size. You can't give that individual attention people need when there's 20 people in a group.

"Somebody like Harry R. can just hide out for an hour and a half and then go back to his sloppy ways."

"Regina, Angelina's got to be frustrated."

Rachel Borenstein, the homeless program director, began to speak. "This is the second time . . ."

"I didn't say I was frustrated," the SRO director broke in. Her tone was as angry as her words were deliberate. "Don't you start talking for me, Ms. Borenstein! I can handle my program without your assistance!"

The pink flush was back in Rachel's face. "What are you talking like that for? I was defending you. It's not . . ."

"I don't need defending! I work out what I have to work out with Ms. Courtney, not you! You've been here less than a year; you act like you run . . ."

"Hold on, ladies, hold on!"

Regina's loud voice cut the two combatants off at once. "We're talking cuts, not personalities."

"That's not fair!"

Rachel's face was now crimson. "All I was doing was offering support as a professional. She"—her finger jabbed across the table at the SRO director—"is the one who became inappropriate! I learned in school that . . ."

"Haven't you learned by now that what you learn in that school and what the real world teaches you are two very different things?"

Yula Carson, one of the West Indian ladies who had been the activities program coordinator at the site for 10 years, thrust her hand forward forcefully across the table. "You people come in here and think you know it all . . ."

"Excuse me, 'you people'?"

This time the interrupter was Edwina Garcia, the Ecuadorian assistant director for foster care services. Her strongly accented voice rose to a high pitch as she went on. "We learn never to call anybody 'you people,' and here you are, throwing that"—she paused, trying to find the right word before going on—"that 'inappropriate' term that some people say is racist. I think we all better look at ourselves if we think . . ."

Nick quickly looked around the room. Most people sat rigidly, as if at attention, their faces immobile. For all the facial rigidity, their eyes revealed a far more emotional picture: shock, anger, fear. The journalist was surprised to see Rachel blinking back tears. What the hell was going on here?

The site director spoke again, her voice suddenly quiet yet firm. "People, people. I want you to listen to me."

She was almost whispering. "We're heading down that long winding road that none of us wants to travel again."

Her voice shot up again, to great effect. "Never."

The room was completely silent as she went on. "We are discussing budget shortfalls and how to handle them. We are not trying to cure the world of its other problems. If you have other issues, I suggest we talk about them elsewhere. But don't bring an attitude; bring a solution."

Her eyes took in everybody in the room.

The papers she had been holding were scattered across the table. She began gathering them up as she concluded, her fingers nimbly caressing their edges into a neater and neater stack. "In an hour I will meet with Ms. Browne and Ms. Carson to review coverage options. At 3 I want to see Ms. Borenstein and Ms. Browne as well."

She looked over at Nick. "Right now I have some debriefing to do with our journalist."

She stood up, reached over to the half-empty bagel tray on the back table, and placed the remains in front of her. "There are a few bagels left, people! Don't forget to take one."

* * *

"Here, Nick, take some of mine!"

Regina placed half of her buttered pumpernickel bagel on a small paper plate and handed it to him. Nick smiled to himself. Growing up in Wisconsin, he'd never heard of a bagel until he came to New York 10 years ago. Today he'd seen this mini-UN group of human service directors devour bagels as if they were their own native cuisine.

Unfortunately, even the bagel selection hadn't united them for long. To Nick's eyes, they needed their own peacekeeping force as well.

"Mr. Costello, what you saw today isn't how we are together, really. You saw how well people pitched in on those systems reviews. People work hard here, and for the most part, we get along."

"Two of your directors certainly don't. To be frank with you, I don't know why Ms. Browne got so defensive when your homeless director spoke. It sounded to me like she was trying to help."

Regina paused before going on. "As a professional to a professional, you don't offer help unless you're asked by a colleague. Angelina wasn't asking."

"Management is all about problem solving. Good management problem-solves with lots of different people. Are you human service folks managing in some new way the rest of the world hasn't learned about yet?"

Nick tried not to sound his own note of frustration, but the combination of meetings that ran too late, systems that were ignored until they broke down, yesterday's tears, and today's anger had left him with a very short fuse. Not to mention that his girlfriend had hung up on him twice last night.

"Look, I'll be straight with you. I hope you'll use this information with sensitivity because we have enough problems without adding another. When people come pay a site visit and meet our directors, they're always impressed. So multicultural! So ethnic! America's melting pot, all under a single roof!"

She sighed before going on. "Don't I wish it were so simple. You see, for every new ethnic and racial group, there are new issues. Lots of West Indians think African Americans are lazy. Too many Africans think they're morally superior to people of color born in the U.S. Puerto Ricans think South Americans are taking over their turf, and South Americans think Puerto Ricans speak lousy Spanish. Our Asian American and Middle Eastern staff think all other Americans are immoral half the time. It goes on and on. So, as you can see, our so-called American melting pot's got more spice in it than it needs! And that, of course, is before we get to the biggest pepper in the pot."

Regina folded her arms across her chest and went on. "I guess I should say salt *and* pepper. Race between White and Black Americans. I am so tired of dealing with this issue my eyes start to close just thinking about it!

"You don't need a long history lesson to see what I mean here. Rachel Borenstein is White. Angelina Browne is Black. Rachel grew up in a middle-class home and got through college and graduate school by the time she was 23. Angelina grew up in housing projects first built in the 1950s. Her mom took in laundry; her father drove a delivery truck for Entenmann's, the bakery, until he had a heart attack at the age of 46. Angelina was the first in her family to graduate from high school, and as smart as she was, college was not an option.

"Once her own kids started in school full-time, she started night school. It was about the same time she started working here as an aide. It took Ms. Browne 10 years to complete her BA, another 4 to get her master's. She graduated with her master's at the age of 48, the same age as Rachel's mother."

"Hey, I'll be honest with you. So far it sounds like a matter of finances, not race. It's not Rachel Borenstein's fault that her father and mother could pay her way through college. She's the one who had to work to get those degrees."

Nick had had this kind of discussion with people for years and wanted to avoid its all-too-familiar path if he could.

To his surprise, Regina looked at him and smiled agreeably. "Hey, for the most part I'm with you. I am tired of this debate, too. But hold on a minute. It gets more complicated."

Sure, Nick thought to himself. *With race in America it always does.*

"With the new homeless initiative by the city a couple of years back, Jorge Pacheco, our executive director, bids and gets a new innovative homeless shelter. Its innovation is a sophisticated behavioral management program for young families that only an MSW who has also studied this kind of clinical work can do. So guess who gets the job? Not Angelina Browne. She's still got another year and a half on that MSW. Jorge hires a 28-year-old whiz kid, making $5,000 a year more on her grant than a woman her mother's age is making running a far larger program on the other side of our courtyard!"

"That still doesn't make it a race issue. More like education and class."

Now Regina was looking frustrated. "Look, Mr. Costello, what part of the planet are you from? Angelina and I have been lifelong friends, so let me tell you a little of her story. Before there were those Brooklyn housing projects, there was a nice neighborhood that Blacks and Whites, working people, lived in. When it got torn up for all those vertical slums, guess who was left? Black folks. Guess why Ms. Browne's father drove a delivery truck? Because he never got past the eighth grade, working in the fields next to his mother and father back in North Carolina. Those fields had once been the family's, but they lost them in a land swindle back about 1900 to the grandson of a plantation owner. Guess what else he had owned? I mean *who?*"

Regina began to be angry, but she contained herself. "I hope I'm making myself clear."

Nick quickly backpedaled a bit. "No, no, I stand corrected. Race and class in America are always mixed together. It's probably impossible to separate them."

He paused for a second, choosing his words carefully. "But in a workplace, you can't walk around living past American history all the time. After all, people have a job to do."

"You're right; you're right! I tell myself that all the time."

Regina began to backpedal herself. "All the time! But it's not easy when some people come in and seem to think that that history never happened at all. We may all be equals, but it doesn't mean we arrived on equal footing, does it? You can't just act like everyone's just alike, blindly, can you?"

"Why not? I think you've got to measure people on what they do, not what got them there. Borenstein had it easier than Browne, granted. But as their director, don't you measure them by their performance—you know, by whether or not they get the job done?"

It was Regina's turn to be defensive. Nick could tell she was regretting having revealed so much about Angelina's past. "Like I said, Mr. Costello, this is a topic that wears me out. There's too much to do around here as it is, whether it's kids in foster care, a homeless family looking for shelter, or poor Harry R. trying for the hundredth time to clean up his act. I basically agree with you."

Nick saw her sigh inwardly, a fleeting look of defeat crossing her face and then quickly disappearing. "People have to put that stuff aside and get the job done, period. That's what I plan to tell my two directors at 3."

She looked at Nick intently again. "I just don't want you writing that we have all this racial tension when it's not really true. People get along. They work hard together."

Nick was measured in his response. "I agree about that: People do work hard."

He purposely said nothing else.

"You said the proof is in the performance, right?"

The site director smiled quickly as she stood up. "If you really want to see how we manage, you've got to look at the work!"

She took out the cell phone clipped to her belt and speed-dialed a number. "I'm alerting all our directors that you'll be dropping in to see us in action. That'll tell you the real truth of how we manage things around here."

Nick looked at his watch. "As long as I can leave by 5 p.m. sharp, I'm yours."

Critical Thinking

Members of this team seem to have difficulty solving problems. What are the causes of the impasse? How would a manager begin to overcome them?

11

GOOD NEWS, BAD NEWS

"First, the good news. I saw day care staff doing great things with their toddlers in the morning. Those ladies could change diapers on two babies while keeping the rest of the kids occupied the whole time. I think they knew every song *Sesame Street* ever recorded."

Nick Costello checked his notes quickly. He was informing Pete Morrissey on what he'd found out so far. "A homeless shelter staff worked hard to get a woman into some housing possibilities. Must have called eight people 20 times. Never gave up. And that computer literacy program was terrific! I saw people excited to try and learn things that could get them jobs. Then I visited a child welfare program. One of the therapeutic foster care program's caseworkers, Francesca Oliva? Her patience with that mother and her two twins was amazing. Dealing with kids suffering with the aftermath of their mother's former crack addiction can't be easy."

Nick smiled. "You said Jorge Pacheco's agency would be representative of yours and most others. If that's so, you have special people working in this field. They may rush from case to case and group to group, but they are committed.

"The day ended when I went into one of your nearby schools to see your after-school program. I found 350 kids all drinking milk and eating cookies before they got down to work. I was amazed that half of them were studying 20 minutes later."

He closed his notebook. "All in all, good, caring people not afraid to go the extra mile for the clients in their lives."

"And the bad news?" Pete asked. Nick was surprised. He didn't seem bothered to ask the question.

"The bad news? Frankly, I've got concerns with the management side. Behind all that good work are too many exhausted people.

A lot of frustrated people handling systems that break down every other day. People so worried about each other's feelings that they avoid performance evaluations."

He paused to check Pete's expression and found him listening intently.

"Management meetings getting interrupted for no good reason. As soon as a client crisis happens, managers handling it instead of their staff. People upset with each other and dealing with it by working harder, as if working late will get rid of the problem."

Nick hesitated for a moment. "And then there's racial and ethnic tensions between your directors. I gotta admit I was surprised to find that one, especially in your field. It may not have been black jelly beans at Texaco, but it sure wasn't something that management had a handle on how to resolve.

"In short," Nick summed up, "you've got good people who try hard and deliver a service as best they can under trying fiscal circumstances that corporate managers don't have to deal with—and would never put up with if they did.

"But I think all these different funding arrangements in public and nonprofit worlds give people permission to not change how they manage things. People could see some cuts coming and make plans, but they don't. A lot of managers give staff permission to act in ways they'd never let their clients—coming late to meetings, crying as a way to avoid new job responsibilities, letting their own anger and frustration get in their way when they try to communicate."

The journalist smiled, slightly nervous at what he'd just said. "Plus, people eat way too many bagels and doughnuts and drink too much bad coffee!"

He paused again. "So much energy is wasted on the wrong things. What they actually value in the day, their time with the clients, is almost an afterthought."

To Nick's surprise, Pete smiled back, his look calm. "Well, Mr. Costello, I think you're finally on to something."

He poured himself a glass of water and then held up the silver Thermos. "Can I offer you some water?"

Nick thanked him and took a sip. "What do you mean, 'on to something'?"

"It's time to visit Ms. Jacques and her shop. She's up in the South Bronx, right near Yankee Stadium. Call her. I think she has a lot to share."

It was Nick's turn for surprise. All he remembered about Helen Jacques was that she was a Black woman with a French-sounding name who spoke some New Age mantra as her approach to management. "You mean the lady with the glass that's always full?"

Pete drained his glass and peered into it. "Yes, Mr. Costello, that one."

He held up the glass for Nick to see. "Who knows? If you think about this glass a little differently, it is full, isn't it?" He paused, serious for just a moment. "I've been trying to keep open lately; I'll tell you. We're in the middle of our own organizational restructuring, and I've been doing some serious thinking."

He stopped speaking for just a second before concluding. "But that's another story. Head up to the Bronx, soon. Helen is expecting your call."

He stood to shake Nick's hand. His grip was firm and warm. "Keep your eyes open, OK?"

PART II

Creating Abundance

12

POPSICLE STICKS

Nick Costello liked the neighborhood near Yankee Stadium. He'd prided himself on getting to know it when he first moved to New York City, years ago. His Wisconsin friends had thought him crazy to move to Manhattan at all. Then his Manhattan friends had considered him slightly insane to venture up to the Bronx. Luckily, an old college friend on scholarship, Luis Maldonado, had been born and bred on 179th Street and the Grand Concourse. He'd made sure his friend Nick got real rice and beans from his *abuela,* Grandma Mimi, the first time he went to a baseball game. He'd been traveling back ever since.

It was 8:30 a.m., and the street was already filled with people. The reporter looked up the long avenue ahead as he walked toward his destination. Street life in the Bronx was so different from the quiet ways of the Midwestern town in which he had been raised! The high energy here had at first unnerved him, but Luis had been a trusty guide, showing him the safety on street corners with kids playing double Dutch, older men slamming their checkers down on makeshift tables of cardboard and empty garbage cans, and younger men tuning the engines on their prized GTOs and vintage souped-up Vegas, each one blasting his car radio to the max. "It's the empty streets you worry about up here, my friend," Luis had confided. "A busy street has an *abuela* on every stoop, with eyes that see everything. If you hear a lot of noise on those blocks, it means the *señoritas* just got their hair done, and the guys have noticed. People from downtown gotta learn that a lot of street noise makes you safe and secure. Show respect and mind your own business, and everybody will love you."

Luis had given Nick's shoulder a squeeze. "Even a guy from Wisconsin."

Nick laughed to himself at the warm memory; Luis's welcome had been given years ago just a few blocks from where he was now. Walking on a commercial strip, he could see both African Americans and Latinos, a greater ethnic mix than before. The reggae blaring from the shops told him a number of West Indians were here, too. *Every neighborhood changes,* he thought, *all the time.* He looked at his feet as he crossed the street, kicking discarded hamburger wrappings away from him. *Except for the garbage and litter.* Luis had explained years ago that streets up here were cleaned less often than those in Manhattan, whether of garbage in the summer or of snow in the winter. Over the years, Nick's frequent visits for *arroz con pollo* with Luis had proven his friend correct.

The reporter looked again at the address on the small yellow Post-it note in his hand. Turning left, he headed up an even steeper block. As the climb began to tax him, Nick became aware that the area was, while not quite as busy, still active. But something was different. Breathing more heavily from the steep climb, he finally noticed. Oddly enough, while there were no metal garbage cans on each corner, there was no litter at all. Two blocks back, those cans were overflowing, and the streets were still a mess. He pulled out his notebook and paused to make his first notation of the day.

A few seconds later, he pushed back a shiny, Logan-green gate and stepped into a small courtyard whose path split off in two directions. Each courtyard path led to a large, nondescript brick building, its windows fully gated on the lower floors and contained on the upper floors by the smaller security gates required by law to protect all small children.

Where the courtyard divided, an older man dressed in workman's khakis was tending to a small patch of land. He was on his knees, gently digging into the ground in front of a huge bush of zinnias. Fully in bloom, their white blossoms gave off a sweet fragrance that reached Nick as he walked forward. Black-eyed Susans and tall sunflowers were also in bloom, while plants with thicker leaves were waiting for the fall.

Hearing Nick's footsteps, the elderly man turned and slowly began to stand, losing his balance only slightly for a moment. He righted himself, took off his work gloves, and extended his hand. "Welcome! Haven't seen you here before, have I? Anybody here this early, you're probably here to see Miss Jacques, right?"

The handshake was strong and sure, the fingers callused. Nick looked into the sparkling brown eyes of the dark-skinned African American in front of him, surprised by the warmth of the greeting but happy to receive it. Tall and thin, the man's posture gave little away to age. A thick, gray mustache encircled his wide smile. Save for his grayness and a few missing teeth along the bottom row, his features otherwise belied his age. Nick responded with his own name when the man introduced himself. "Name's Oliver Trumbull. I'm the first person here in the morning, so I know who's come in already."

He pointed to the overturned dirt and garden tools behind him. "I start the day with my own special kind of therapy as soon as the sun comes up. Nothing like God's earth to clear a man's head."

He leaned over and picked up the trowel, using the tool to point toward the left path. "Go ahead inside. Miss Jacques's there. And so is Miss Samuels."

Nick thanked the gardener and headed up the steps to the building on the left. Pressing the buzzer for entry, he was quickly let inside. As he stepped into the lobby, his eyes widened, unprepared for the bright firehouse-red tones of the walls. Looking upward, he saw the ceilings were slightly off-white in a way that softened the red just enough to make the entire area warm and inviting. The floor, he quickly noted, was linoleum, but its lightly speckled black-and-white design added to the attractive décor.

"Good morning, sir! My name is Gloria Samuels. How can I help you today?"

Nick turned sharply to his right, caught off-guard again. He looked into a modest reception area, complete with telephone banks, computer, and steel-gray desk. Behind the desk sat a middle-aged White woman with thick glasses, a thin smile almost breaking through. Her long, white hair was pulled back in a tight bun, revealing a full face with strong Nordic features. Something about her skin, however, gave Nick pause. It was so pale as to be almost translucent, even ghostly.

"My name is Nick Costello. I'm here to see Helen Jacques."

He checked his watch. "But I'm a little early."

The woman nodded and picked up a pen. She spoke so slowly that Nick sensed the deliberateness of her effort. "Could you please pronounce your name for me again? And if you don't mind, please spell it, too?"

Nick quickly obliged. Again moving with deliberation, the receptionist dialed a few numbers and spoke slowly into the phone. Smiling, she then hung up and turned to him. The deliberation remained.

"Helen will see you in just a few minutes."

She motioned toward the light green couches on the other side of the room. "Please have a seat."

As Nick walked over to the couches, he was struck by the art on the walls. One side was covered with bright African masks from the Yoruba tribe. The yellows, reds, oranges, and blues of the faces were the backdrop to an array of feathers, sequins, and—what was that? Nick looked more closely. Popsicle sticks! The name of each young artist was neatly signed beneath each mask. As the poster board nearby explained, this month's gallery creation was the work of Jacinta Jauquin's after-school art program for seventh and eighth graders. Nick looked over the work carefully. Some of it reminded him of his own tepid junior high school efforts, but many of the masks had a real feel to them, one's fierceness as genuine as another's intense, uplifting spirituality. Ms. Jauquin, he could tell, was a gifted teacher.

"May I offer you something to drink?"

Gloria was standing next to him with a glass of water in her hand. He noticed that the glass was only two-thirds full. As her hand was trembling slightly, he quickly took it from her. "It's a hot, hot walk from the train, Mr. Costello. Very, very hot."

Thanking her, he agreed. The receptionist headed back to her station as the phone rang. Nick sat down and took a long swallow and then another. Momentarily refreshed, he noted that the wall across the way had a series of beautiful American Red Cross photographs of young children, each dressed like an adult at work: judge, doctor, teacher, mechanic, airplane pilot.

He took out his notebook again and started to write. Nice garden, fun lobby. Hell of a paint job. The older gentleman was nice enough, but how does someone in his 70s work here? Where do they get money for such a beautiful garden? Finally, something about that receptionist was off, as polite and professional as she was. He chuckled to himself. And that glass of water wasn't even close to full!

13

SEEKING ILLUMINATION

"Mr. Costello, I hope I am not disturbing you. Helen Jacques is happy to see you now."

Gloria Samuels was calling across the lobby, each word tumbling out with an odd, precise cadence that Nick both appreciated and found slightly unnerving. He stood and walked to the entranceway to the rooms beyond the receptionist's desk. Gloria smiled her thin, awkward smile as she opened the door for him.

Helen was walking toward him, her hand outstretched. Nick reached out, took her hand, and winced. Like Allison Smith, she had a grip of iron. "Thanks for seeing me on such short notice."

"Hey, Pete got me to promise that you could see whatever you want up here. To tell you the truth, you might be disappointed. I think Mr. Morrissey's overstating what's going on in the South Bronx."

She invited him into her office. He found a sunlit room overflowing with plants, every wall covered with original art that was nicely if inexpensively framed. In one corner, an African drum sat next to an Irish lyre. As Nick tried to fathom the cultural connection, Helen went on. "But you'll be the judge of that, I guess. Please sit."

Nick felt adrift, not quite comfortable in his surroundings. He decided to go on the offensive. Perhaps his sparks might create the illumination he was looking for. "OK, Ms. Jacques, let me be blunt. When Morrissey talks about you and your agency, his face gets all flushed, and his eyes start to glow. I don't mean in some romantic sense, but like there's a powerful mystery up here in the South Bronx, and I'm supposed to play Indiana Jones and discover it.

"I've already looked around a bit. You've got a lovely lobby, even a nice garden. That's impressive. But your receptionist acts like she's been programmed. Don't get me wrong—Ms. Samuels was letter perfect in what she said and did. But I couldn't tell if she was a robot, a wind-up doll, or something else. Do you make people memorize a script so things look good?"

Nick was surprised at how aggressive he sounded, but he didn't care. He was in no mood to repeat his trip into Brooklyn.

Helen sat impassively until the reporter finished. "You're not the first person to ask me about Ms. Samuels. Same goes for a number of our receptionists, some custodial staff, all sorts of folks around here. Even Mr. Trumbull, for that matter. But let's stick with Gloria. I promise to answer you, Nick, I do. But first, let me ask you a couple of questions. Was Gloria Samuels polite?"

"Yes, she was."

"Did she take the time to pronounce your name correctly?"

"She even took the exact spelling."

"Did she provide you with the information you needed?"

"Yes." Nick was beginning to get uncomfortable.

"Anything else? Did she cause a problem of any kind?"

"Actually, she was quite thoughtful. Gave me a glass of water without me having to ask."

Nick sought to regain his footing. "Wasn't full, though."

Helen laughed. "Oh, the 'glass is always full' issue! I'll come back to that later."

She paused just long enough to underline her present focus. "Let's stay with Gloria. I do know what you're talking about, Mr. Costello."

"You do? So why the questions?"

He paused for a second. "By the way, please call me Nick."

"And I'm Helen, not Ms. Jacques."

She went on. "Gloria Samuels is a special lady, Nick. She was the first female in her family to be working on her doctorate. At Harvard. Harvard Divinity. She planned to follow in her father's footsteps. Mark Edwards Samuels was a famous pastor in Hartford, Connecticut, 30 years ago. I met him once, a good man. One of the first White Episcopalians to take his mission into the inner city."

Nick looked at Helen closely. *Why'd she mention he was White? Given his daughter's pale, pink skin, wasn't that obvious?* He prayed that Helen wasn't what his conservative friends called "one of those professional Blacks," always trotting out the race card to make other people nervous. If she was, he vowed, his stay here would be shorter than his stay in Brooklyn earlier in the week. Placing two exclamation points in his notebook, he continued to listen as she went on. "Reverend Samuels raised his only child, Gloria, to someday take over his church.

"She would have, if schizophrenia hadn't taken her over first. Full-blown psychotic paranoia about some evil teenagers from Montreal, of all places, trying to abduct her to French-speaking Canada. Would have been funny if it hadn't been so tragic. She ended up on the streets of Cambridge, Massachusetts, instead of in her father's pulpit. Broke his heart."

"I'm sorry to hear that. So I guess that her stilted diction comes from her medication."

"Psychotropic meds will do that, Nick. She takes so much it causes her hands to tremble. But Gloria's learned to compensate. No spilled water for her. Her meds aren't easy, but with them she gets to live a pretty full life."

Nick had read enough about treatment for the mentally ill to not be completely thrown off by the turn of the discussion. Seeking independent living was a credo of the mental health movement. One of his cousins out in Wisconsin lived in a group home near a McDonald's, where he worked 4 days a week. As admirable as Helen's hiring policy on the mentally challenged was, this sounded like the same kind of program intervention.

He decided to push ahead. "I stand corrected, Helen. But hiring people with disabilities is a good service innovation, not a special kind of leadership. What's that got to do with what Mr. Morrissey thinks is a new approach to management?"

"You're right Nick. Just hiring a disabled person for a job isn't exactly new. I never said it was."

She paused and looked over at the African drum and Irish lyre lying in the corner across from her desk. "In fact, I couldn't agree with you more. If a leader of an agency does one service innovation here and one management technique there, it's just new variations on an old, old theme, even if it's good work. When you see that, it's usually because an agency learned that some foundation will fund it, not that the leadership truly wants it.

"I learned that about 8 years ago, when this agency was growing faster and faster and I was spinning faster still. It all would have crashed in on me, except a lot of people around here saved me from myself. Without them, I wouldn't be here. And I doubt the agency would be either."

"Who are 'they'? Can I meet them?"

"Sure, Nick. You already met two."

Critical Thinking

Go back to Nick's visit to Allison's agency. What is different about Helen's agency? Specifically, what is different about the physical condition of each place and the people and their initial interactions together?

14

CASTING A LURE

Helen Jacques checked her watch. "If you don't mind, I have to ask Gloria to contact the executive team about our budgetary meeting at 3:00."

The executive director reached for the phone. "Gloria? Please let the Fab Five know we're still on for 3. Thanks!"

Hanging up the receiver, she smiled at Nick Costello. "My guess is you'll want to be at that one.

"But let's start at the beginning. If anything's special about this place, I guess it began about 8 years ago. I was at a leadership workshop that one of those foundations provides for burned-out executives every 6 months or so. There were about 20 of us in the room. To tell you the truth, I don't remember what the exact topic was. Might have been 'benchmarking for optimal outcomes,' or maybe it was something on 'quality indicators of service.' Whatever it was, the subject faded because the morning's icebreaker affected me so much I barely paid attention. You know how icebreakers work, don't you?"

"Actually, I don't."

Nick's freelancing status had rarely led to invitations to attend foundation retreats.

"At those events, facilitators start the morning off with some exercise to warm the group up—you know, 'break the ice.' They're usually nice-enough activities, helping relax you and get you open to the day's tasks ahead.

"I'd arrived at the retreat completely exhausted. My senior staff made me attend. I'd just come off the third grant proposal cycle of all-night meetings and weekend rewrites and was more than a little frazzled."

She looked over at Nick and grinned. "Folks around here told me my brain was more tightly coiled than my dreads!"

The reference to her dreadlocks startled Nick again, throwing him off just for a moment. Another underlining entered his notebook.

"Anyway, I'm sitting at the retreat, munching on my buttered bran muffin and sipping the strongest coffee this side of Puerto Rico, when this friendly-looking White guy in a three-piece suit stands up and welcomes us to the day. I'm sitting there half-listening, blah-de-blah, 'the agenda for the day is' . . . blah-de-blah-de-blah. I'm a lot more interested in my muffin than I am in him, obviously.

"Then he tells us to get into threesomes. I join Pete Morrissey and Jorge Pacheco, who are sitting next to me. The facilitator gives us three instructions:

"First, who was the most important teacher or mentor in our lives? It could be a real teacher or anybody else, in or out of school.

"Second, what was his or her full name? He stressed that point twice, reminding us to say their full names.

"Finally, what lessons did they impart that we carried with us still?

"That seemed easy enough. Pete spoke first. He mentioned his grandfather, a retired watchmaker. When Pete was 7 years old, he had had childhood asthma that kept him home one summer. His grandfather was in a wheelchair by that time and was living with his family. During the day when nobody else was home, the old man would talk to Pete about the lessons of his life in a way that kept Pete's spirits up. He'd talk about the art of fishing as he taught the little boy how to string his fishing pole and make lures for catching fish. Whenever he'd lose his patience, his grandfather would help Pete take a longer view, helping the frustrated 7-year-old notice what he'd already accomplished and how much fun lay ahead once he was over the asthma.

"When Pete finished, Jorge gently reminded him he'd left out his full name. As Pete said his name—'my grandpa's name was William Morrissey Jr.'—his eyes filled with tears. Then my eyes filled with tears, and I didn't know why!"

She caught her breath, overcome with emotion, the memory as real as if recalled from yesterday.

"Jorge went next. His mentor had been a favorite aunt, *Tia Blanca,* Blanca Pacheco-Garcia. Jorge had lost his mother when he was 5, and from that time on his aunt had always been there for him, no matter what. He had been a wild teenager back in San Juan, getting into fights and almost getting arrested. At first Jorge spoke quickly. 'I'd come home with a cut over my eye, and she'd always bandage it, no questions asked. But then she'd kiss my forehead and hold me close. *Mi pobre jefecito,* she'd say, *my poor little chief.* The same words, each time. She was the one person I never felt judged by. At the same time, I knew she thought I was a lot better than I thought I was.' Then Jorge began to fumble as he went on, too, searching for the right words. 'When I started to move away from the streets, somehow it was my *Tia Blanca* who was guiding me. Because of her, once I started, I never looked back.' I was amazed, Nick. His face was as flushed as Pete's.

"I was last. Mine was the only actual teacher, Mrs. Olive Peterson. She was my seventh-grade teacher, the first Black teacher I ever had. It was 1969, I was 13 going on 20, and if you'll recall, those were pretty intense times in America—racially, the Vietnam War, everything. When I walked into her classroom, I thought I'd died and gone to heaven."

Her face flowed with the memories. "Boy, was I mistaken! Mrs. Olive Peterson taught math, and she was hard! I mean *hard!* This lady was an equal-opportunity taskmaster and a disciplinarian to boot! Nobody fooled around in her class, not the jocks, not the antiwar folks, not the potheads, and certainly not Helen Jacques. That woman scared me to death from day one!"

"She doesn't sound like that wise grandfather or the caring aunt, though."

Nick couldn't imagine why she'd chosen such a difficult teacher.

"But she was a lot like them, really!"

Helen quickly went on. "I struggled in that class so much I finally had to go see her after school. I went to her room, my knees knocking the whole way. Looking in, I saw her behind her big mahogany desk grading papers, a big red pencil moving a mile a minute. I had almost turned around to flee when she spotted me. 'Come in, Miss Jacques,' she said. She always called us by our formal names.

"She worked with me for 45 minutes, going over all my algebraic mistakes clearly. She spoke about the concepts in math, not just the equations. Mrs. Peterson said it was hard to grasp them for people like me who were more comfortable with writing and history, but with effort she believed I could do far better than the D on my first report card. She'd be happy to work with me anytime I wanted to come by.

"I did come by, probably every other week for the rest of the term. By Christmas I had a B-minus for the semester. I was more proud of that grade than I was of anything else, even if it did keep me off the high honor roll. By the end of the school year, it was all the way up to a solid B."

She paused again, emotion catching in her throat. "The last day of school, I went to her room again to say goodbye and to thank her. There she sat, still at her desk, grading away. But when I went over to her and said I wanted to thank her, she stood up and hugged me. It was a quick hug, the only one she ever gave me, even when I graduated. Then she said something that has stayed with me all my life. 'No, Helen Jacques, it is I who should be thanking you.' It was the only time she called me Helen, too."

"What did she mean, she should be thanking you?" Nick was curious.

"That took me a couple of years after the retreat to really figure out, Nick, but I'll come back to that later. Promise."

She went on, her mind drawn back to the retreat. "What was amazing was everybody in the room reported stories like ours. Here we were, a group of 20 executives whose combined agencies' budgets must have been over $300 million, and half the people in the room have their eyes filled with tears when they reported to the group.

"But as I listened, I started to notice something. All of the important mentors and teachers were little people! Nobody remotely famous. Nobody with any real power. A watchmaker. A carpenter. A mom who found time to run a Girl Scout troop and a Boy Scout troop for her 2 children and 40 other kids as well. Nobody outside their small circle of influence had ever heard of them. But they each had left a legacy that lived on for years and years that was priceless.

"The facilitator helped us see that almost all of our mentors and teachers shared a few things in common. First, they were people who gave a consistent message about what they valued, day in and day out. They didn't change what they believed to suit the times or to follow trends. They were guided by their inner compass, not outer circumstance.

"Second, they believed in us, even when we didn't. Jorge and I weren't the only people who spoke lovingly about a relative or teacher who gave a message of support and belief in what we could accomplish that at first we rejected. It was only later that we realized they were holding us to a standard that we hadn't realized we had within us. But they had. It was only later that we could appreciate their insight.

"Third, many helped us understand that achieving excellence was worth it *because* it was hard, not easy. Because Mrs. Peterson didn't lower either her standards or her expectations about my work, I grew in confidence about both. I was thrilled with my solid B because it showed how far I'd grown and what hard work could do to overcome my limitations. I had "A's" elsewhere that also gave me confidence, sure, in subjects that were a lot easier for me. But Mrs. Peterson's real lessons taught me that people don't want the bar lowered, Nick. They want the support it takes to reach it.

"Finally, they all had a vision about what mattered that showed up in the little things they did, not the big things they said. Like they say, talk is cheap, especially in a field with people who say they're committed to helping others. These mentors lived their vision through concrete expressions of the little things that gave value to their own lives, whether it was a cool washcloth pressed against a troubled teenager's head or a patient grandpa helping a little boy learn to make a fishing lure, again and again."

Helen stood up and walked over to the water cooler behind Nick's chair. Wordlessly, she passed him a cup and then took one for herself. "I kept thinking about that icebreaker the rest of that day. Pete's grandpa. Jorge's *tia*. Mrs. Peterson. Ordinary people. Little people. I looked around the room. Nobody I was sitting with would ever describe themselves as 'ordinary.' These were men and women who had built large agencies, had plaques on their walls, and were on a first-name basis with major politicians and dignitaries. I was becoming one of them. There was real power and accomplishment in the room.

"But after we retired, would anybody's eyes tear up when people spoke our names 5 years later? Or even 6 months? I sat there in the workshop thinking about me and my work back in the Bronx. We were definitely growing; we were twice as big as when we'd started. I had plaques on the wall, too. Unfortunately, the last time I'd caused anybody to cry had been 2 days earlier, when I'd yelled at my associate director so harshly that she'd gone running from the room. What kind of legacy was that?

"The other real lightning bolt of the day came towards the end of the workshop. Working in small groups on some plan or another, the facilitator asked us to use our mentor's or teacher's message in the way we approached each other in the group. As Pete started to counsel his grandfather's patience, it hit me: Our agencies are full of those so-called little people! Earlier in the day, people had listed cooks, carpenters, homemakers, a part-time secretary. Guess who worked for me? *They did!*

"I realized I had to figure out a way to tap into that greatness. But I didn't have a clue as to how. I was stymied because I was smart enough and experienced enough to know you don't just walk in and change the way you operate. People who've been working with you in a certain way for years will think you're nuts and won't change an inch. Anything drastic would be perceived as some management fad to be tolerated."

"So what did you do?"

Helen laughed. "Well, inspired by the day, I held onto William Morrissey Jr.'s patience and Mrs. Peterson's steadfast commitment to excellence. I would make my own lure and cast it out there, just a little bit at a time, and see if anyone responded. I figured I could work with that."

Her eyes lit up as she looked toward the door. "Then, of course, I got lucky."

"Lucky? How so?"

"Oliver Trumbull walked through my door. Just as he is now."

She motioned toward the door.

Nick turned as the door opened. The agency's resident gardener was standing there, a bouquet of zinnias and Black-eyed Susans in his hand.

Personal Reflection Exercise

Helen told Nick about her most important teacher, someone supportive and very, very demanding. Other mentors mentioned included a caring aunt and a grandpa in a wheelchair dispensing fishing lessons. Take a moment to recall your most important mentor or teacher, someone whose relationship still matters to you and how you live your life.

Personal reflection: Who was your most important teacher or mentor? (Include his or her full name.)

_____

_____

_____

What "lessons" did he or she provide that mattered so much to you?

_____

_____

_____

How are the values in those lessons a concrete part of your life today? (Remember to be concrete!)

_____

_____

_____

Why did Mrs. Peterson thank Helen when she had been the one who did the extra tutoring?

_____

_____

_____

15

MR. TRUMBULL'S MOTTO

Oliver Trumbull came in and sat down at the small table across from Nick Costello. Helen Jacques took the bouquet, breathed deeply, and shared the scent with Nick. The flowers' sweetness filled him with pleasure. The executive director pulled out a blue vase, poured in some water from the cooler, and placed the arrangement in the center of the table. A reporter's suspicion suddenly gripped him. Was Helen setting him up?

She spoke first after briefly filling in the gardener. "Of course, I'd promised people I'd report on the retreat at our all-staff meeting a couple of days later. It was a full agenda with our expansion plans and new grant possibilities, so I didn't want to waste a lot of time on it. But during my executive report, I mentioned the icebreaker. Talked about how I was sure this agency had that same kind of untapped wisdom. Said I hoped to work with people on locating their talents, too."

"Took all of 5 minutes, as I recall," Oliver reported.

"Didn't cast that first lure too far, did I, Mr. Trumbull?"

"It was far enough for me."

He looked squarely at Nick. "I was here working security then, best job I'd had. I heard Helen at that meeting, and I thought I caught something in her voice like she meant it. Plus, the lady looked exhausted. The circles under her eyes had circles! Figured I had nothing to lose to seek her out."

Helen leaned into the table toward the reporter for emphasis. "Nick, you're here to see what makes this agency special to Pete Morrissey, so you're about to find out what we've created here. Since I knew you were curious about why our glass is always full, I wanted you to meet the source of that life lesson."

She pointed to a flip chart stuck into a far corner of the room. "We've printed all the life lessons on that flip chart for you. I'll give them to you later. But I asked Mr. Trumbull to join us at the beginning of your day. After all, without Oliver Trumbull we wouldn't have started at all!"

The older gentleman sat back, removing his cap. A crop of bushy white hair popped into view. He rubbed the top of his head as he began to speak, pushing his hair slightly backward. Nick expected him to be nervous, but nothing in his voice suggested he was.

"Yes, I'm the 'glass is always full' man around here. But to understand my motto, you've got to know some of my story. Any motto that works for a person doesn't arrive overnight. Least not for me.

"Won't bore you with the whole thing. Came out of the Vietnam War, bitter. Two years in the heat and mud while my two children were growing up left me with an edge. Got worse when I couldn't get a house under the GI Bill. Nobody'd sell to us Black folks. All that anger led to no good. Started hanging with the wrong crowd, real wrong. Ended up driving for two guys who promised me easy money from a mom and pop store over on the Lower East Side. They didn't tell me about the guns. Eight armed robberies later, we get caught, and I'm in prison. When I got out 15 years later, I was still brooding. Had lost my family, didn't have a dime to my name. First lucky break I got was Miss Jacques's agency agreed to hire me as a security guard. I thought that was kinda funny, but my parole officer said I'd better take it, so I did."

"Mr. Trumbull, I appreciate your story, but I'll be honest. I still have no idea where this is headed."

The older gentleman had obviously gotten his life together, as had Gloria Samuels, the receptionist, but they weren't the first success stories the reporter had met, either. Where was the leadership lesson that affected this agency?

Oliver smiled over at him. "For what it's worth, I didn't know where I was headed either, Mr. Costello. After a while, though, some good news. I got reunited with my son and daughter. By now they had their own families. I was a grandfather! They didn't live far from me, and as time went on I got to see those grandkids more and more.

"Problem was, I was still brooding, still measuring me and my life all the time. I'd be sitting there with my youngest grandson playing checkers, but inside I'd be thinking how easy it was to go from half-full to half-empty in a minute. One day the glass would be half-empty, and I'd be my miserable self and then some. The next day it was half-full, and I was happy as a pig in a poke. Up one day, down the next.

"But what's 'half-empty' really about? It's the past and what didn't happen. How it's making your life a mess and nothing can change 'cause the deck's stacked against you. All that energy, spilling into that glass, measuring what might have been.

"And 'half-full'? It's the future and 'what could be' and 'if only this happens, then things'll be great' and 'if I get that raise, I can buy me' . . . more wasted energy, hoping about what hasn't arrived yet."

Oliver pushed at his hair again, a wry smile stealing across his face. "So one morning, I'm sitting there mulling over how's the day gonna be. Half-empty? Half-full? All of a sudden, I feel a tug on my knee. It's my 4-year-old grandson, Rodney, looking up at me, a huge smile on his beautiful little face. 'Look, Papi! Look what I just did! I poured me a full glass of water all by myself!' He was as proud of his little self as if he'd hit a home run at Yankee Stadium.

"But the glass wasn't full, not even close. Most of it was on the floor. But to my Rodney it was. Then it hit me! While I was mulling over my half a glass, I was missing out on the life right in front of me. For every minute spent on gauging how the problems of the past weighed me down or how the imaginary hopes of the future could buoy me up, I wasn't fully living with what was present. At that very moment, I had a sweet little boy who loved his Papi enough to tell me what he just did—turning on the water faucet, filling the glass, turning off the faucet, climbing down from the chair, and running to me to tell me all about it. Spilling most of the water along the way.

"That little boy's smile changed me forever. I got it: Any energy spent distracted on 'half-full' or 'half-empty' robbed me of what was in front of me, right here today. *It was up to me to choose fullness or only half.* Hugging that little boy close to my chest, I decided to choose to look at life with the glass always full. Some of what's in there is water to drink. Some's air to breathe. Coming from my cupboard, some's going to be dust to clean. Still makes it full, day in, day out. Like my grandson and his full cup of water, it was a choice I was going to make every day, all by myself.

"Don't get me wrong, Mr. Costello. Seeing my life each day as full doesn't take away pain when it happens. That day with Rodney was so much fun! I took him to the park, played catch, wrestled with him on the living room floor before he went home to his folks. The next day when I got up, I was as stiff as a board. My joints ached, my back was sore, and my big toe with the bunion was throbbing!

"First thing I did? I went right back to half-empty! *You foolish old man, look what you did to yourself. A man your age shouldn't have. . . .* Then I caught myself. Here I was again, the very next day, dwelling on the past to make misery in the present. I'd had the best day in a month of Sundays, so what's the problem? *Look at your world differently, Trumbull. See it full!* Of course I ached; I was supposed to at 67 years of age. So take a tub. Swallow a couple of aspirin. Put a hot compress on the bunion and change your shoes to those comfy sneakers.

"I ached the whole day and the next day, too. Didn't matter. When the glass is full, aches are part of life. I still had to deal with them, hobbling around. But the day before didn't mean I had to look at today as a loss or that if the pain went away the next day, all would be peaches and cream. I chose to make that day wonderful. *I had what I needed to care for me, and I had the presence of mind to focus on that.* All the half-empty glasses from my past and the half-full ones of my hoped-for future were gone. The present was good enough for me."

Nick was impressed. He himself spent way too much time thinking about all the lost opportunities for a full-time reporter's position: He'd gone to the wrong college; he'd made a mistake in turning down that opening up at that Delaware newspaper 6 years ago. And, he mused to himself, thinking about the future was his specialty. Half his anxiety about this gig was energy spent on wondering what might happen if he wrote the perfect article. How many times had he said lately "if only" and attached the phrase to his editor's name?

Nick stopped himself and asked a question to get back on track. "I think I'm starting to get it. But how did all this relate to your agency, Helen?"

"At first, not at all. After I made my little speech about the wisdom and resources inside us all, I just went back to work; . . . another grant, another deadline, more bad hair days."

She grinned at Oliver. "Then later in the week, Oliver Trumbull walked into my office, a bouquet of flowers in his hand from his garden. He asked if he could talk with me.

"I said sure; I had 20 minutes. Turned into 2 hours."

"I was honest with her. I told her I appreciated how she'd taken a chance on me 5 years earlier. That I respected how hard she and others around here worked for the children and the others who needed help. Then I took a breath and let her know she looked way too tired for a young woman her age. That I saw her looking so intense, even angry, whenever there was a writing project to do or when word came down that those city and state auditors were paying a visit.

"I told her my story with Rodney and how I saw her as just like my old self, way too often."

"Actually, what he said was I was too lovely a lady to look so unhappy all the time. That if I didn't watch out, half-empty would shrivel my heart up."

"Like it did me. Or almost did."

"The more I listened, the more I got what he was saying. Every grant was an exercise in misery among the staff, people yelling at each other, being short-tempered, and me leading the pack. Mr. Trumbull just listened to my excuse for why such work had to be intense. Then he asked me, 'Did you all ever miss a deadline?' Well, no, we hadn't. 'So why the craziness?' he said. Said it as calmly as we're talking right now.

"It was then that I got it. All that intensity and wasted energy came from framing agency work as half-empty or half-full, living on the edge of both. Half-empty: We won't get the grant; the auditors will find us in default. Half-full wasn't much better. The rush that my senior staff and I got from a completed grant or successful audit had more to do with the momentary expectation that things would be smooth sailing after that than with a job well done. Feeling like maybe things are going to be perfect ever after doesn't prepare you for the humdrum of the next day, does it? It just brings back half-empty that much sooner.

"I knew Mr. Trumbull was on to something, and I wanted to embrace it."

Helen shook her dreads and stared at the floor for a second, a look of chagrin on her face that surprised the reporter. "So here Mr. Trumbull sat, flowers in his hand and wisdom from his lips. Exactly what I'd been seeking after the retreat had shown up in my office, not 2 days later.

"I was elated! I would follow his example and approach the agency and my work with a full glass, too. All that freed-up energy would do me and this agency a world of good!"

"Excuse me for my bluntness"—Nick had to ask—"but why the funny look on your face?"

"You mean that wistful, preoccupied look I just got? That's because of what happened next."

"What happened?"

Nick imagined she gave Oliver a raise.

"Oh, after we finished up and I thanked him, I sat down and wrote 'the glass is always full' on a big notepad. No more walking miserably through the jagged slopes of the past. No more wasted time in la-la land, hoping about the future. All that new energy, devoted to the present, fully in front of me."

"And?" The reporter was getting impatient again.

"That newfound energy lasted about 15 minutes. About as long as it took until I walked out that door, to be exact.

"Which is where you need to go, if you want to learn what this place is really about."

She saw Nick's momentary consternation. "Don't worry. You'll find out what happened to me that day soon enough. Others will let you know."

Oliver stood up to leave. "I hope I was helpful, Mr. Costello. If you have any other questions, you can find me over at the playground, where the 3-year-olds go in the morning." He put his hat back on and waved as he headed out the door.

"My clinical program director, Marjorie Jessup, wants to see you next. But before I take you over there, let me show you the life lessons that flow from Mr. Trumbull's gift. They pretty much will guide you to what lies ahead. I know they guide us."

The executive director stood up and walked toward the flip chart. For the first time, Nick was looking forward to what came next.

Critical Thinking

Nonprofessionals seem to play important roles in this agency. What roles did they play in the first agency Nick visited? Both are run by caring people. Why the difference?

Personal Reflection Exercise

Helen reports that Oliver's story is the foundation to the agency's success in developing a new leadership model. Which lesson seems most important?

1. His grandson's happiness in pouring a "full" glass.

2. The internal struggle to make each day "full" regardless of events.

3. A full day may include pain as well as pleasure.

Could it be "all of the above"?

_____
_____
_____

16

THE SECOND GOLDEN RULE

Helen Jacques walked over to the flip chart and removed the blank cover page. Six expressions were grouped beneath Oliver Trumbull's insight. "I could explain each of these lessons, Nick, but it will be better for you to see what others have to say. Check out whether or not they're being used. Actions speak louder than words, right?"

Nick Costello wrote them down quickly. He now understood the first lesson that framed the rest. The others, he soon realized, would require as much explanation.

The Glass Is Always Full

1. Practice the Second Golden Rule If You Want to Live the First

2. Clean As You Go

3. Carry Your Vision in Your Pocket

4. Politeness Doesn't Cost a Cent

5. Take the Cover Off the Book

6. Build a Community and They Will Come…Again

"I'll walk you over to the next building, where Marjorie is. Give me a chance to stretch my legs."

The executive director walked into the corridor and beckoned Nick to follow.

"Say, any chance I could have a cup of coffee?"

Nick realized he could use a little jolt of caffeine to keep him sharp.

"We don't have any here, but the bodega around the corner does. I hear it'll knock your socks off! Happy to take you there first."

The reporter backed off, surprised. "No, that's OK. Just thought it was the elixir of choice in your line of work."

"Used to be. Not anymore. You'll see why."

It was already midmorning, and the brightly lit corridor connecting the two buildings was bustling with people. Young women with toddlers in strollers walked past, shyly saying a brief hello to the director as they headed toward the day care room. A custodian, dressed in neat khakis that matched Oliver's, had his tool kit out, repairing a light switch. Two staff members—one a young Asian-American woman wearing bib overalls and carrying a huge tray of paint supplies, the other a somewhat older, thin African American man with a short, pointed goatee and long arms loaded down with a box of children's books—in unison cheerily boomed, "Good morning, Helen!" as they hurried past the executive director.

"Activities staff and day care, back from operations with new supplies," Helen explained.

The executive director pushed a thick door open and turned right again. "Marjorie Jessup runs our clinical programs. Oversees supervisors from child welfare, homeless services, the mental health program. I've worked with her longer than anyone else. One busy lady."

She pointed in the direction of a tall, solidly built White woman with brown hair who was finishing a conversation with a young, Latina caseworker. A serious expression on her face, the younger woman nodded, opened a light green door, and headed into a small, dark room off to the side.

For a moment Nick could swear he smelled incense.

The clinical director walked toward them. "Nick, I want you to meet Marjorie Jessup, our very white knight of the South Bronx, female version. She's been up here working longer than me."

Nick immediately blanched. Why was this Black woman introducing her clinical director in such an off-putting way? Was this an updated version of a subtle racial power trip he didn't quite understand?

The two women stood next to each other, warmly smiling. Marjorie poked her tanned arm next to Helen's. "Hey, watch out, Helen! It's summer! This is the time of year I catch up with you. Before August's out, I'll match you mocha for mocha!"

Helen laughed and then quickly turned to go. "I'll leave you two. Marjorie can explain how she manages clinical work the South Bronx Multi-Services way."

She looked at her clinical director. "Since Carrie just went inside the Quiet Room, I guess we're on life lesson number one."

The reporter was perplexed. Just when he'd been impressed, things started getting weird again. *Quiet Room?* Had they time-traveled back to kindergarten? What had the young caseworker done, thrown a temper tantrum?

"Did the caseworker do something wrong? Why is she in that Quiet Room? And what is a Quiet Room, anyway?"

Nick and the clinical director were seated in her narrow office. The room would have seemed more cramped than it did, but the well-trimmed hanging plants at the front and back of the office gave the space a surprising sense of height.

"Who? Carrie Alvarez? 'Wrong?'"

The clinical director looked confused and then started to chuckle. "Oh no, Mr. Costello, just the opposite!"

The director took a carrot stick from a plastic cup that she handed to the reporter. Nick took a stalk and began to munch as she went on to explain. "Carrie works in therapeutic foster care. That's really rough work, believe me. The most damaged kids from the most damaged families in child welfare. You know those kids who make the front pages of the newspapers? The tragic deaths that create the investigations and politicians' calls for reform?

"A lot of those kids who died have siblings. They're the children we get in therapeutic foster care."

She paused for only a second. "It's bad enough reading about them in the newspaper, but eventually people put the paper down and go about their business. Carrie doesn't get to do that. Those kids are her business. In 15 minutes she'll be working with two boys, 6 and 8. When the city gave them to us, they still had cigarette burns on their backsides. The younger one's left hand is scarred from scalding water. The older one limps because his left leg was fractured 3 years ago. Wasn't set for 2 weeks. He still won't tell anybody what happened."

Nick couldn't help but shudder. "That's horrible. It must be gruesome work."

"Lot of people think it is, Nick. Those kids have had gruesome lives, for sure. But we prefer to think of it as God's work. Carrie does."

"I still don't understand that room."

"I'll get there, Nick, I promise. But you can't understand the Quiet Room without knowing the life lesson first."

She took another carrot stick. "I'm pretty sure Helen and Oliver Trumbull explained the 'glass is always full' to you."

The clinical director grinned again. "She usually leaves it to me to tell what happened next."

"I thought it might be you."

Actually, Nick felt clueless at the moment, but he figured agreement would move things along.

"Right after her big breakthrough, Helen Jacques decided to come to my office to tell me what happened. Unfortunately, at that very minute I was on my way to see her. Wanted her to know our director for homeless services had resigned that morning. Seems she couldn't stand the pressure from the top that she said kept pounding down on her. 'Every time the city's contract officer visits it's like the agency's preparing for the Grand Inquisitor!' she told me. All that crazed intensity over a bimonthly review wasn't worth it to her anymore.

"When I told Ms. Jacques exactly what the director said, she exploded. At me. Loudly. Right out there in that corridor. I was already frazzled, coming off those grant proposals, suddenly with a new position to fill and all that coverage to handle. Helen and I go way back together. So I responded in kind, just as loud.

"We're standing there, going toe to toe, when we look around and see Gloria Samuels at her desk. She's looking at us with shock, then upset. Her voice was trembling, but the lady spoke right up. 'You two, just stop that. Stop that yelling!' In two seconds we both realized we'd made a mistake, airing our business in front of others. We shut right up.

"But Gloria kept speaking, almost choking the words out of herself. 'You're both nice people. You don't have to be like that, do you? The Good Book says to love one another. Why can't you be nice to each other?' Then tears started to roll down her cheeks.

"Helen walked into her office and sat down at her desk and started to cry. I mean, she was weeping. She sat there for maybe 10 minutes, head bowed, sobbing into her arms.

"By now I was crying, too. I loved this woman. She drove me crazy half the time, but I figured that goes with the turf. After all, I was no picnic myself. But I hated to see her so upset!"

"What next?"

Nick was amazed at Marjorie's openness.

"Finally, she stopped crying. Through her tears she told me why she had walked over to see me. 'I was coming to tell you how Mr. Trumbull had given me this revelation that was going to change my life! A real revelation! *I could choose to be full, not half-empty!*' She started dabbing her eyes about then with a Kleenex. 'Some commitment I kept! Lost it in 10 minutes!' Then she started to cry again."

Another carrot stick disappeared. Nick took another as well. "After a while, Helen explained how Oliver had opened her to a whole new way of thinking, how a person could choose how to see and act on the world. But then our fight had thrown her off completely. 'How could I lose it so easily with you, someone I care about? Maybe I'm not nice! Marjorie, am I not a nice person? Are you?' she asked.

"I tried to comfort her. 'Of course, we're nice, Helen. Gloria wouldn't have said it if she didn't mean it. She's always said her minister father taught her right from wrong. She tries to live the gospel every day. So do you. Me, too. We're the regular Golden Rule Girls.' I thought I got to her, because she suddenly became quiet, her whole body still.

"All of a sudden, she jumped out of her seat. 'That's it, Marjorie! Gloria Samuels was trying to tell us something. What's the Golden Rule? *Do unto others as you would have them do unto you.* That's why we do this work, to help others the way we want to be helped.

"'The problem's not that rule; it's that we don't practice what we preach with ourselves! With you and me!' She stood up and wrote on that flip chart she always has in her office. *Do unto yourself what you seek to do unto others.*

"'How can we be good to others if we're not good to ourselves?' she asked. 'How can I see that the glass is always full if I'm running on empty? I can't create fullness in an agency if I can't feel it in myself.'

"I got it, Mr. Costello. In the back of my mind it had always bothered me that we would bend over backwards for a client but not for our own selves. I suddenly realized it wasn't OK to fight abuse of a child and accept it from each other."

She paused for emphasis. "Or to give it."

"That's a pretty powerful insight, Ms. Jessup. But having another life lesson on a flip chart doesn't make it any more likely it will be followed. That 'full glass' tipped over as soon as Ms. Jacques left her office."

"Sure did. Tipped over a lot as we went along. Still does, Mr. Costello, for everyone around here. That's part of being human."

The last carrot disappeared. "That's what the Quiet Room is all about."

Nick was intrigued. "So tell me."

"Like just about everything else, Nick, we didn't start with the Quiet Room. We ended with it. We've had it for 2 years now. Eight years ago we were a little more basic.

"Helen realized that we couldn't be whole in this work if we weren't whole with ourselves. She started by going out and thanking Gloria Samuels for her courage and her insight. Told her that without her honesty, we would never see what we had to do to be nice people. She thanked Gloria's father, too.

"Helen knew she wanted to be whole. She knew she needed to take care of herself for that to happen. But she also recognized that a person as driven as she'd been couldn't look to herself for answers."

Marjorie laughed again. "God knows I wasn't much help!

"She had to look for wisdom elsewhere. So she and I went back to Oliver Trumbull. Helen knew he'd been an angry man most of his life, but somehow he'd overcome that to live fully and contented in his world. We went out to see him on the playground, where he was on duty. The answer was so obvious we'd been walking past it every day.

"'I garden, ladies. Right here. Every day, rain or shine. Even in the snow, I can work on my mulch pile out back, even for a minute. It's that minute that counts,' he replied.

"Of course, it wasn't the gardening that was the difference, he said. 'I garden to take care of me, make sure I can stay full,' he went on. We pushed him on that. Personally, I knew I hated to garden, and what were we to do, turn the South Bronx into a berry patch? He just laughed. 'All I knew was I had to find what kept me from looking at "full" every morning. Wanting to be whole doesn't make you whole,' he said. 'You gotta find a way to make that happen. Find something on the outside to do that helps you feel complete on the inside. Then you gotta hang on to it the rest of your life.'

"Of course, Helen and I were disappointed. We wanted there to be a magic bullet of some kind or maybe another cute phrase that would get us through the day. No such luck.

"'Damn!' she said. 'Do unto yourself' means we're have to *do* something!' Then we laughed."

"Then what?"

The reporter was interested. He wouldn't mind living each day on something other than half-empty himself.

"Took two more years to figure out how to make it part of the agency. We started with ourselves. I joined a gym. Helen joined Weight Watchers. I exercised more each day; she ate less."

"And then?"

Nick's impatience was back.

"What else? We quit! Three months later, my muscles stopped being taut, and Helen got her belly back, plus an inch. Of course, we were denying what had happened.

"There was too much work, all those deadlines, yatta yatta. Someplace else, some easy line of work, dieting and exercise might work, but not here. She and I were real good together, the dynamic duo of denial. Fortunately for us, in an agency like this, living in denial wasn't really possible."

"Why not? I know lots of people who join and quit gyms every 6 months."

Nick was one of them.

"Mr. Oliver Trumbull. We'd pass that man every day, working in his garden, either before his shift or after. Winter, summer, spring, or fall, the man was *there!* And while we each started to slip, he rarely did. Always had a thoughtful comment, a smile of genuine pleasure. His glass stayed full, while ours was tipping over one day to the next.

"Do you know what it's like every day to walk past a genuinely contented human being who makes one-quarter your salary? To be around a person who's been in prison 15 years who is still far more able to enjoy the world than you are?

"Finally, one day Helen went nuts again. We were in her office. She had just bitten into these delicious, extra large bran muffins with gobs of gooey cream cheese when Helen stained her new suit. She stood up and started to yell, then caught herself. There was Oliver Trumbull. Standing in her doorway, back with those beautiful flowers he brings to every unit once a week.

"'Oliver Trumbull, I can't stand it!' she said. 'Why can you change but we can't? Your glass is still full, and my $300 suit just got a big stain on it and I'm miserable! And Miss Jessup and I are as fat as ever! Why is it so hard?'

"He just looked at us. Put the plants in the blue vase that she still uses, I think. 'Helen, you think taking care of yourself is some experiment to make you better. I fuss with my flowers each and every day because *they're part of my life.* If you're really serious about that Second Golden Rule you told me about, you're gonna have to stop half-steppin'. If that second rule's golden, it's not some add-on. It's gotta *be* you, too.'

"That was it. From that time forward, Helen and I changed. We changed. The *agency* changed. Little by little, one step at a time. Ms. Jacques was always a brilliant administrator; she knew you don't just throw out the old and put in the new and expect to see people sign on. But from that day on, she was *committed as a daily act of faith* to changing herself and the life of the agency to emphasize the self-care and self-worth of each person who crossed our doorstep, client *and* staff.

"First she invited a speaker from some drug company, Pfizer's, to come in and speak about the wellness/fitness program they gave employees at lunch hour. People who left the building to walk or exercise got an extra 10-minute grace period. The company found they made up the time in saved sick days. Well, if they could do it, we could too.

"Then the local public school dietitian came over and spoke about meals. Helen asked the public health nurse to check staff for hypertension and blood pressure. Not all at once but gradually, people got to see that their own health mattered, not just their clients'. If homeless families need a regular checkup, so did our home health aides. Turned out many of them were in worse shape than our clients. Nobody had ever noticed before.

"Helen walked what she talked. That woman loved her coffee; she drank tons of it! She replaced her coffee pot with a water cooler, then made sure the others in the agency stayed filled. A woman famous for the 10-minute lunch break, she left the office at 12:30 each day, walking at least 20 minutes. Like Mr. Trumbull, she didn't preach her gospel. She lived it. And more and more of us joined her.

"You know what happened? She and I lost weight—lots of us did—and kept most of it off. *Most of it, not all of it.* Hey, we're still full-figured girls, but it's about being firm, not skinny! That made a lot of us ladies happy around here, believe me. But that was just the most obvious thing, not the most important."

She paused and thought for a second before speaking. "The most important change was in how we saw things.

"No, that's not right, exactly."

Nyack College
Wilson Library

She paused again. "We felt good enough about ourselves to consider how we thought about things. We became more able to choose how we looked at the world in front of us."

Nick was surprised by Marjorie's genuine intensity. "Nick, I know that's a long way to put it, but that's my way. For the first time in my adult life, I could walk around here and see that the glass was always full. The clinical work was still hard, the kids still in pain, the schools struggling to help kids read. But my struggle, that inner struggle fed by anxiety and anger, was gone. I come here every day, still finding my caseload too big and too many children with trauma, and my glass is still full."

The tears that rimmed Marjorie's eyes made Nick realize how sincere she was.

"So the Quiet Room is some part of that?"

"It's the other option to the Exercise Room we have in the basement. Remember, I said that these kids in therapeutic foster care have experienced real trauma when they get here. It's in their eyes and on their bodies. The more we took care of ourselves each day, the more we realized that taking care of these kids doesn't begin and end with a 50-minute session. Left unattended, that wrenching pain enters a professional's body, too. Comes back later as an ulcer, hypertension, maybe a chronic back problem.

"The Quiet Room's part of our answer. We don't wait for people to get sick or let them deal with it in the normal ways the rest of us do. A walk around the block may not be enough. We ask them to choose what works for them, before or after the sessions, when we've clinically agreed the clients have severe trauma. We turned an extra broom closet into a space for meditation. It's small, but staff painted it and fixed it up nicely. There's a little boombox for folks who prefer music. Whatever helps them find a space to keep them centered before and after their session. A small exercise room in the basement, with a couple of bikes and weights, does the same thing for people who prefer that."

"Don't outsiders think it's a little, you know, weird? What do funders think?"

"At first they thought we were as flaky as you probably do. A lot of new staff get spooked at first, too. All those seminars I mentioned before, we still have them on a regular basis. Lot of people walking after lunch or down in the weight room. That stuff's normal, now.

"As for the funders, George Applethorp, our chief operations officer, was ready with some data after a year. 'Based on a comparison of sick days of our clinical staff working in therapeutic foster care over the past 4 years, which would you prefer?' he asked. 'An average illness rate of 9 days a year per worker or last year's 4? And,' he went on to point out, 'that data didn't count the lost hours after a session sitting at a desk making believe you're working when you can't.' George can be very persuasive with a spreadsheet in front of him. It wasn't Helen's goal, but over the last 5 years, practicing both Golden Rules turned out to save us money, too."

Nick was trying not to be moved by what he'd heard. His girlfriend, Meredith, had been after him to join a gym and change his diet for the last 2 years. Having reached his late 30s, his waistline had begun to grow, and high blood pressure ran in his family. He kept promising to deal with it but never quite got around to it. His excuses sounded a lot like the ones he'd heard repeated today. He promised himself that he would talk with his girlfriend that evening.

But he had to try and stay objective here as well. Taking care of yourself each day so you can approach your work in a centered way sounded wonderful, but it was all still a little vague in its broader application. An agency has a lot to get done, too. After all, it was in business to serve clients, not make staff feel better.

"This has been great, Ms. Jessup. I admit I've learned things that I could do in my own life, too. But an agency or school can't run on just good intentions . . . even full ones!"

He hoped she appreciated his humor and was pleased to see her grin in response. "How do you guarantee that things get done on time . . . and done well? Like I've learned elsewhere, units of service are units of service, right?"

"They sure are, Mr. Costello. We've got to have systems that get the job done—get it done well—if we're going to keep our funding. That's why it's time for you to go to our cooking class. You need to meet *Doña* Carmen Santiago-Ostrada. *La reina de nuestra cocina.* The queen of our kitchen."

She laughed again as she ushered him out the door. "Emphasis on the queen!"

— Critical Thinking —

How can self-care of a professional affect a larger system of an agency? Why do Helen Jacques and others link them? Does this interfere with the real work of the agency? If not, why not?

Personal Reflection Exercise

Take a minute to review how you handle stress at work. What do you build into your day to lessen traumas that may happen? What do you do at the end of a demanding work cycle?

1. Take a 15-minute walk.

2. Find time to emotionally debrief.

3. Take "quiet time" to spiritually and/or emotionally heal.

4. Do something physical to "let off steam."

When is the last time you did these activities with any consistency?

_____

_____

_____

What changes can you commit to as the work goes forward?

_____

_____

_____

Can you share these ideas with someone above you?

_____

_____

_____

17

CLEAN AS YOU GO

"She's more than our cook, Mr. Costello, as valuable as that is."

Marjorie Jessup and Nick Costello were walking toward the adjoining building. A few younger staff members walked by, pausing to speak with the clinical director. As she consulted with them, Nick looked into a well-lit classroom and saw elderly people engrossed in what looked like a heated conversation being led by a very old, bald man wearing a beret. Every time he spoke, he used a tapered cane of blond wood to tap on the floor for emphasis.

"*Doña* Carmen has helped us with far more than with her wonderful cooking. Remember Helen's icebreaker about mentors? After that—and especially after Oliver Trumbull changed her life—she reminded all of us to be on the lookout for the 'richness in the room,' as she put it. She said something back then that really stuck with me. 'If you hear that somebody's got common sense, don't believe it's common at all,' she told us. 'More often, common sense is brilliance without status or power.' The more I thought about it, the more sense that made, don't you think?"

Nick was too busy writing to know what he thought, but he made sure he wrote the phrase down correctly.

"Common sense and doing things simply are pretty much the same things. It's often being able to see what's in front of you and learn its lessons. What *Doña* Carmen taught us is as basic as it gets. What wasn't so basic was to apply it across the agency. You'll see what I mean."

The clinical director ushered him down another narrow corridor. She continued speaking as they walked. "One day, George Applethorp and I are leading an orientation session for new staff. He goes over the policies and procedures, while I review the steps for getting case files done in a timely way. He's great at this. Very systematic. I'm not as organized, but I've learned the hard way that if caseworkers don't stay on top of paperwork or if teachers don't update lesson plans, they're in deep trouble. George and I were a pretty good team, we thought. We'd use each other's examples to reinforce our own. 'Just like Ms. Jessup said about case recording's being up-to-date, our security codes in case of fire are reviewed monthly'—that kind of thing.

"I knew it was a mostly boring but necessary review so that from the beginning staff understood that we're serious about how things get done around here. So we're doing our dog-and-pony show on systems when one of our new caseworkers, Louisa Fuentes, gets a funny look on her face. Without meaning to, she blurts out, 'This sounds so like my godmother talking, only a little more boring.' She suddenly realized what she said and got so embarrassed she talked some more. 'I'm sorry! You're not that boring! . . . I mean, . . . it's just she's a cook, and cooking can be fun. Besides, she works for you!'

"So that's how this agency really got to know *Doña* Carmen. She had been hired a year earlier to oversee our meals programs for the elderly and for day care. At least that's what she originally was hired to do. Since that orientation session, her work's expanded. She's part of orientation, too. Plus she teaches a kids' class in cooking. Today's are second graders who are here from our day camp."

Marjorie gave the reporter a wry look as they walked into the kitchen area. "Of course, the rest of her students range in age from 25 to 50!"

Nick walked into a gleaming kitchen. Its industrial size, complete with three stoves and two sinks, was initially intimidating. His own tiny kitchenette served as space for a microwave and a toaster, with fewer used pans than *Doña* Carmen had stoves. He couldn't imagine what she did here.

He also couldn't believe the students standing around the immaculate counter space. There were six 8-year-olds, two young adults in their 20s (whom he'd noticed earlier in the child welfare unit), and a nattily dressed Latino gentleman in his late 40s who was removing his jacket and tie. *Doña* Carmen, on the other hand, was all of 4 ft, 10 in. tall. She was intently looking over the array of groceries in front of her. The kitchen's queen spotted the clinical director and reporter and waved them closer as she continued to speak.

"OK, *mis hijos,* let's see if Donald and Francine brought all our baking supplies. Do you remember the first rule about shopping?"

"Don't settle for second best!"

Six young voices sang out in unison. The two shoppers looked slightly embarrassed. The older gentleman simply sat there, the slightest of smiles creasing his face.

"That's right, only the best, *la mejor que hay.* If you and I don't deserve the best, who does?"

"Nobody!" They sang out again.

The kitchen's *jefe* asked the two shoppers to empty the remaining bag. Marjorie leaned over to the reporter. "Our two new child welfare workers flunked this part of orientation last Wednesday. When they brought back the wrong kind of butter for Carmen's muffin recipe, she told them they'd have to go back again this week. 'Children, second best is for that silly camp game, Horseshoes,' she tells anyone who stints on quality. 'We don't play Horseshoes in the South Bronx. People make mistakes only once in this kitchen.'"

The clinical director excused herself to head back to her office after briefly introducing Nick to the kitchen class and its petite teacher. The reporter found himself shyly sitting between an 8-year-old named Jaime Calderon and the 45-year-old Head Start director by the name of Gregory Ochoa. The Head Start director leaned over from his stool to introduce himself, handing Nick an extra apron in the process. "I've got some tough decisions to make later at that 3:00 meeting, so I dropped in for a systems refresher. Today this'll help me more than my usual lunch walk."

Nick nodded in response. He was catching on to the way things worked around here.

A woman close to 60 with a wiry, no-nonsense frame in constant movement, *Doña* Carmen rapped a wooden spoon on the countertop as she glared at her two oldest students. *"Atención, mis hijos!* My children, when we cook, we pay attention to what we do. Tasteless bread shows up on your table from a mistake you make in your recipe! There is no time to make mistakes today!"

She turned toward the young child welfare workers. "Donald and Francine, you did *perfectamente* today. This unsalted, whipped butter is *perfecto* for our cornbread! *Bien hecho!* Well done!"

The two new workers' embarrassed pride at their shopping success gave their young faces a warm, open glow.

"Because they have done so well, they have the honor to help us prepare for later."

Prepare for later? Nick was momentarily confused. The two new hires stood up and walked over to the stoves, where the older woman had pointed. They turned the knobs at the back of each, adjusting them carefully to the correct temperature. "In cooking, sometimes we must do first what will only be needed later. In 20 minutes, your wonderful recipes will be in your pans. Can anybody bake your beautiful cornbread with an unlit stove?"

The students quickly paired into couples, young and old mixed together as much as possible. Each couple had a small, rectangular baking pan in front of it. They were making cornbread for dinner. (Lunch, Nick learned later, was already completed and being prepared by other staff for serving in the dining area.) Little Jaime showed Nick what to do next. *"Doña* Carmen tells us we supposed to do things one at a time. Do you know what 'one thing at a time' means?"

The little boy looked at Nick with all the gravity an 8-year-old can muster. "It means you do one thing before you do the next thing."

Nick smiled and said he was pretty sure he got it but that he'd follow Jaime's lead. The little boy thought that was a very good idea. "First we put butter in the baking pan. It's gotta touch all the bottom. Especially the corners. But not too much! This is the fun part."

The little chef leaned over and took a dollop of butter onto a small, rubber baking spatula. He held it up for his teacher to see.

Doña Carmen nodded, and the boy proceeded with gusto to coat the pan's bottom.

The dry ingredients were next. Nick and Jaime joined the other teams in mixing the stone-ground cornmeal, unbleached flour, and baking powder in a bowl. This took longer than Nick had thought it would, as each couple was reminded that its measurements had to be done with *solamente perfección*—only perfection would suffice. The red lines on the glass measuring cups were there for a reason, the kitchen *maestra* reminded her pupils. "Those red lines are there to help us be who we want to be, *mis hijos*. A perfect cornbread enriches the belly and the baker!"

Each couple repeated the process with the wet ingredients, from corn kernels to low-fat sour cream, in a separate bowl. *Doña* Carmen moved from couple to couple, gently suggesting how to stroke the batter to one pair and firmly reminding another to measure just a bit more carefully. Mixing both bowls' ingredients together, the students soon had their pans full with the smooth yellow mixture, ready to bake. After they placed the mixture in the ovens, Jaime immediately ran back to his stool. He hurriedly waved for Nick to follow.

The kitchen director stood in front of the stoves, hand on hips. "OK, *mis hijos,* tell me!"

"Clean as you go!" sang all but one voice in the room.

"*Exactamente!*" *Doña* Carmen sang in return. "Clean as you go! You do not wait for the end to clean up what is before you. Your cornbread will bake just as well while you clean. If we do not clean now, you won't be able to eat your delicious food when it is time. Your hands will be too wet and soapy! Clean as you go, and your kitchen will always be spotless.

"When a spotless kitchen awaits its cook, wonderful meals will always be prepared. So, *ándale, mis hijos!* Get going! Let us have your wonderful kitchen ready to greet your perfect cornbread!"

The cleaning began with as much spirit as the bread making. Nick laughed as he found himself neatly wiping down the counter twice, making certain to sweep up every bit of spilled flour.

Gregory spoke to him again. "I drop in here two or three times a year, Mr. Costello. As Head Start director, I've learned I'm great at getting parents involved, starting new programs, making our kids feel safe and secure. But I've yet to meet a system that I liked. I hate paperwork! Hate keeping records, you name it."

He, too, swept his counter space a second time.

"Just because I know it's important doesn't mean I can do it well. I'm always finding a reason why it isn't, at least in the moment. Then come audit time, I would be half-crazed trying to catch up. When that happens, I ask *Doña* Carmen if I can visit. I get reacquainted with why systems matter."

"But as a director, aren't you supposed to handle systems anyway? They're a major part of your job."

"Sure they are. But Ms. Jacques knows that most adults in this field learn by doing things, you know, experientially. She tells every senior staff member to use some concrete activity to help us stay centered and on top of our jobs. For me, that glass isn't staying full if my systems are a mess.

"Other people don't have systems as their 'tipping' issue. They're great at keeping things in order but have a hard time looking at new things in a fresh way. George Applethorp will tell you he gets rigid at times. He found a way to loosen up by reading stories to little kids in my program. Once a month or so he'll drop in and 'get a taste of their magic,' as he puts it. He needs to find a way to keep him open to change. Me, I need 'clean as you go.'"

"But your jobs don't have time for all this. I would think your auditors would go nuts finding you over here cooking."

"We told Helen the same thing. 'They'll eat us alive,' we told her. She was as calm about that as she could be. 'Look,' she said. 'Right now we waste more time stewing in our own juices and call it "working late." Let's try a different way.' After about 2 months, we got it. Me in my messy systems juice, needing extra hours to catch up. George in his rigidity, trying to fit his square pegs into all the round holes that show up on his desk. It's amazing how much time we waste like that. At all the other jobs

I've had, when we'd waste time by running around with paperwork in our hand, looking frantic, sleep deprivation on our faces, we'd call that 'going the extra mile' and 'being professional.' We were actually proud of being exhausted half the time. Like fatigue made you a better professional.

"For me, instead of going the extra mile by killing myself, I work hard inside myself to clean as I go. Then when a real crisis shows up and working overtime makes sense, I can handle that more easily, too. When I work late, it's for a genuine reason, not because of my overdue mess."

"What about your line staff?"

"This place takes some adjustment from other work people have done, so we get people adjusted to our routines here. Every 3 months we have orientation for new hires. They start here in the kitchen, then learn about other systems. We find we have to repeat ourselves on the job a lot less now. They learn to walk each day, start taking care of themselves. Just throwing everything at them would be the same as what you see happen with all those folks who join the gyms in January, those 'New Year's resolution' people. They all work out like crazy at first, at the gym every day, in exercise classes, hitting the free weights, running the treadmills. Then they pull a muscle from all that new, strenuous activity and call it quits. We're committed to people staying in our South Bronx gym for the long haul, not just a month. So we layer it in, a little at a time. It helps them arrive at their own way of taking care of themselves to do this work. Otherwise, we're just imposing our way of thinking onto them. In the long run, that can't work. It takes awhile for things to sink in, to get it right."

A big grin ran across the Head Start director's face as he looked behind him. "Just like a cornbread recipe!"

Jaime was standing there, two huge potholder gloves running up his arms. A beautiful cornbread, its top a crusty, golden brown, lay on top of them. "Mr. Nick, *Doña* Carmen said you were the best cleaner-upper today, so you get to have the first piece. Here it is. Here's our perfect cornbread!"

Personal Reflection Exercise

Gauge your response to improving your performance on the job. Do you consider it important enough to make it part of your day? When did you last take time to strengthen a professional deficit, whether recordkeeping systems work or interpersonal communication?

_____

_____

Do you build in time during your week to "clean as you go"? How much time is added to your day/week for crisis management—that is, for cleaning up "messes" that didn't really have to happen in the first place?

_____

_____

Choose a neglected area of your work that could be improved through a little preventive "cleanup" before it becomes a bigger problem.

_____

_____

Now choose a concrete way to improve your "cleaning habits." (This might include getting suggestions from someone who is quite skilled in the area in which you are not. Maybe you could "barter" your own skill set in an area in which he or she needs professional improvement!)

18

CARRY YOUR VISION IN YOUR POCKET

Nick Costello and Gregory Ochoa were walking down to the local bodega for a sandwich. Accompanying them was Frankie Lee Chan, an Asian American who served as chief custodian for the agency. A short, compact man with a thick, muscular frame, he strode along next to them easily, even though his left leg had a slight limp. As they walked along, he occasionally leaned over and picked up a stray piece of paper that dotted the curb.

Nick grinned. "What's this, Mr. Chan, another variation of 'clean as you go'?"

The three men laughed.

"I never thought of that, Mr. Costello, but I guess it is; I guess it is."

They neared the small store on the corner and went inside. Its shelves were stuffed with Goya products, single rolls of toilet paper, and enough chilled beer and soda for Nick's hometown in Wisconsin. Following his companions' lead, Nick ordered a ham and Swiss cheese sandwich with lettuce and mustard on wheat bread.

Frankie spoke quietly as the friendly Latino counterman began to make the sandwiches. "Sure, Helen wanted me to speak with you. I am honored that she did. I guess it's because of this."

He pulled a small key chain from inside his pocket and held it up for the reporter to see. On it was a gleaming brass shell casing from what had once been a very large bullet.

"Four years ago we were in an all-staff meeting. No, it was a retreat. Two days. We were doing the staff's part of the agency strategic plan. First, we had reviewed the mission that the executive team and the consultant had put together. You've seen it around here: 'fully dedicated to helping support, build upon, and celebrate the strengths and capacities of the people of this South Bronx neighborhood.' Short and sweet. Everybody was pretty happy with it."

Nick had indeed seen the statement on the walls of the agency.

"Anyway, now we're in small groups. We're with our units—you know, the people we work with. Each unit's to come up with our own vision for how we're supposed to implement that mission. It was supposed to be tangible, something concrete enough so people saw what we meant right away. That was the easy part. The hard part was the vision had to also say something about each of us, how we wanted to see ourselves in that vision, 'so when you leave here, people remember in a clear way what your contribution was,' Ms. Jacques said. She came over and sat in our group. Each exec went into a group. She was in ours."

They got their sandwiches and headed out the door, Nick happily carrying a large container of coffee. He planned to drink it with the remains of his cornbread.

"The guys were having the hardest time figuring out what this vision thing was supposed to mean. Patricio, our night supervisor, kept asking, 'How you make a vision concrete and put me in it, too? How you make a vision concrete and put me in it, too?' We weren't getting anywhere.

"Then I realized I was carrying my vision. In my pocket. I took the shell casing out. It was an M16 casing, the kind we used in 'Nam. I told the guys, 'Here's my vision.' Helen just looked at me. 'OK, Frankie,' she said. 'You gotta tell us what you mean.' So I did.

"In 1967, I had just graduated form high school, Seward Park over in Brooklyn. My family's immigrants from China; we're proud to be in America, so I enlist. Didn't want to go to college; school was never my thing. So signing up to fight for my country made my whole family proud.

"I trained in communications, radio operator. Enjoyed that. Being in Vietnam was another story. I don't want to talk about it, but let's just say a few guys in my unit didn't want anything to do with me. 'Only good gook is a dead gook,' that kinda thing. But our first sergeant was Henry James Smith; we called him 'Smithie.' Tough-as-nails White guy from Alabama, he was all-army and all-tough, too. Wouldn't let guys divide our unit. Only had to stick up for me once. 'Anybody rides Chan rides me. We got an enemy in this jungle trying to take us out day and night. If you think you're gonna do it from the inside, you better see me first.' He said it a lot rougher than that, but I didn't want to swear in front of Ms. Jacques."

Frankie paused as he recollected the memory from deep inside himself. "About a month later, we're trapped in a dogfight outside of Da Nang. They've got us pinned down from some pillbox on the side of a ridge we didn't even notice 'til it was too late. Guys are getting hit on both sides of me. Tell you the truth, I thought I was a dead man.

"Smithie yells over for me head to my right, where some bushes are. 'Chan, get cover and call in reinforcements!' he yelled. I told him that was crazy; he'd be too exposed if the unit lost any more men. He gave me that look of his and yelled again. 'I can handle 'em! This unit needs you to do your job! I can sweep 'em clean for you! That's my job!'"

The custodian paused again, clearing the thickness from his throat.

"Those were the last words I ever heard Smithie speak. After I call in for support, the area was ours by dusk. Before they flew him and the other guys we lost outta there, I went over to where Smithie was. His M16 was still in his hand."

He held the key chain up for Nick to see. "Took this shell casing that was lying there, next to him.

"Every day, when I get out my keys to start my daily rounds, that casing reminds me of Smithie and what he said. His final sweep, the final job he did, saved my life. When I do my job, I figure I can try to do it as well as he did for me. Not so important, maybe, but just as good. When I sweep, even if it's just dirt or paper in the gutter, I'm making things better for people, too. Maybe even a little safer. That M16 casing helps me remember how one guy can make a difference, too. Even me."

"Frankie made it clear for us, even Patricio," Gregory added. "A vision's supposed to be a concrete example of how you see yourself carrying out the agency's mission. But it had to be more than that. A vision's got to be usable. Frankie got us thinking. What goes into your pockets or purse? Stuff you're going to *use*. Keys to your home or office. Pocket change for a meter. A little piece of pink paper with a phone number you're calling later that day. They're all tools of one kind or another."

"Helen helped me see I wasn't just carrying Smithie's memory. It was a tool I used to remind me of how I wanted me and my guys to work here. We keep this place as spotless as we can because people deserve a nice place to visit. You can feel good walking around this agency, even if you have all sorts of other troubles. A clean place makes people know they're respected, maybe. Safe, too."

The head custodian stuffed the key chain back into his pocket.

"Frankie's whole unit got key chains like his after that, too. A new guy gets one, too, as well as a little bit of the story. When they see guys working in a way that makes the story real, the key chain becomes real to them, too. You always know it's working when once in a while you spot a new guy polishing that shell."

"Does every unit use a shell casing?"

The reporter couldn't imagine how a bullet could be incorporated into Head Start or child welfare services.

"No, of course not. We all had to come up with our own tool that made our vision alive. Too many people in social services and education walk around with visions that are more lofty than real. You know, 'committed to and honoring excellence,' that kind of vague statement that sounds beautiful and is so broad you couldn't fit it in a Hummer, let alone your pocket. For us in Head Start, it's a small, laminated card from a page of the book *Goodnight Moon*, the one where the grandma bunny is reading to the baby bunny. Poetry, magic, and safety, told in a few words and a picture. Just what we want Head Start to provide our kids. We're all trying to be like that grandma. The child welfare unit has a shiny penny. Nobody thinks about pennies anymore. Nobody thinks about kids in foster care very much either. But every dollar starts with a penny. A shiny penny may be small, but its shine tells you it's not neglected. It's got worth, too. That shiny penny helps people remember every day how they want to work with their kids."

"What's Helen's?"

"What do you think? Took her 3 months, but she finally found it at a flea market in upstate New York. Two tiny green glass goblets, each filled to the brim!"

"Why two?"

"One's for her; the other's for you and me. Whoever she's with."

Nick sipped his coffee and took a final bite of his cornbread. It was as delicious as *Doña* Carmen had predicted. The reporter wondered what vision he could carry in his own pocket. He and Meredith had a lot to talk about this evening.

Critical Thinking

In what ways is Frankie Lee Chan's vision different from an agency mission? What makes it so powerful? How can one be used to help the other?

Personal Reflection Exercise

Jot down your agency or school's mission (as best as you can remember it).

_____

_____

Now take some time to reflect about how your vision can concretely bring that mission to life. What do you do to capture the value of your work in ways that make that broader mission come alive?

_____

_____

Finally, what would "fit in your pocket"? Think about this and talk about it with others so you can construct a small, real item that is as meaningful as the work you do and can be a daily, gentle reminder of your work's value.

_____

_____

19

POLITENESS DOESN'T COST A CENT

Helen Jacques greeted Nick Costello as he finished the last of his lunch. Returning from a brisk walk after her own lunch, she was pleased to learn his visit to the agency was going well. "Gloria Samuels is taking her walk after lunch. I asked her to take you over to our drug program. It's four blocks away. You can use the hike to learn a little bit more about her contribution. I had to prod her to tell you what she's added to this agency. Gloria doesn't like to talk about it because she's afraid it will embarrass me. I've told her I'm not embarrassed—I'm thankful—but it still bothers her. Gloria Samuels is a very proper lady."

The receptionist was waiting by the front door. She had traded her black flats for pink and white sneakers with socks to match. After reminding Nick that the 3:00 meeting would be held back in the small conference room outside her office, Helen left them and headed back to work.

They started down the hill toward the subway station from which Nick had debarked earlier that morning. When he asked her about her contribution to the agency, Gloria looked away. "Miss Jacques wants me to say, but I didn't do anything special. You know . . ."

She paused, searching for the right word in her slow, careful manner. "It was right after that time she and Miss Jessup . . . had . . . words . . . and I spoke to them. They were always nice ladies, Mr. Costello. Always nice. . . . Anyway, she and Miss Jessup went back into her office and stayed there awhile. Later she came out to my desk and thanked me for what I said."

She paused, a distant look crossing her face. "'All I did,' I said, 'was tell you that you were nice. That the Good Book tells nice people to love one another, like my father taught me.'

"'Oh no,' she said, 'you taught Marjorie and me more than that. You made us look at ourselves. We're not enough like your father. We don't practice what we preach, like he did. You do. You're patient and polite to everybody. Because of you, we're going to try.'

"I was so surprised by what she said I don't know what came over me! I looked at her and replied, 'Miss Jacques, it can be easy! Just remember: With patience, politeness doesn't cost a cent.'

"Well, she looked at me in such a strange way I thought I'd said something wrong. I started to get so nervous, but she hugged me close and just said, 'Thank you! Thank you, Gloria!'"

A smile crept across the receptionist's face. "At the next all-staff meeting she told everybody what I said and how much it meant to her. That it could help our agency. That was very nice of her."

By now they were standing in front of a small office building on the main avenue, its windows covered with pots of ivy. "She told me to tell you that you could best understand what I gave the agency by coming over here."

The receptionist proudly opened the door for Nick and motioned for him to enter. "This is our HIV/AIDS prevention program for drug users."

Drug users? With HIV and AIDS? Nick was taken aback. How did politeness fit inside a program like this?

There to greet them was a thirtyish African American man of medium build and height wearing a light blue, short-sleeved dress shirt with a paisley tie. Two pens, one a Bic and the other a more expensive-looking fountain pen, were clipped over his front shirt pocket. His manner was as forceful as his handshake.

"Welcome, Ms. Samuels! You, too, sir!"

Gloria briefly slowed things down through her careful introductions and her polite but insistent withdrawal. She had 20 more minutes of walking to do, she explained, if she were to be as sharp as she wanted to be for her afternoon's tasks.

The program director's name was Alfred Cousins. "Call me Cous'," he warmly requested upon meeting the reporter. He gave Nick a brief tour of the office: two counseling rooms, an open-space area in the front for meetings and meals, a small kitchen area, a staff space with three cubicles, and his own office. As the counseling rooms were occupied and the young staff and three other neighborhood people were busy preparing what looked like a late lunch, the program director and Nick met in his cramped office toward the back of the store.

"We eat a community lunch around 2:00 here. Junkies don't get up early, so we found it better to serve a meal a little later in the day. The three people helping our staff pulled their early shift today. Other folks will get here in about a half-hour.

"This program started about three-and-a-half years ago. Having been in recovery for 5 years and from the neighborhood awhile back, I was hired by Ms. Jacques to be assistant program director."

He looked closely at Nick to judge his reaction. The reporter nodded, seeking more explanation. Cousins was happy to oblige.

"Marge Jessup's assistant director was in charge then, Shondelle Williams. Both Ms. Jacques and Ms. Jessup sat us down and went over how they wanted the program to work. I'd been in drug programs one way or another for years, but this one, they said, had to run differently. There were a few parts to this program since it was supposed to be about prevention. First, there was an outreach and counseling program. That's where the Centers for Disease Control funding came from. People would get $20 to come in for an interview.

"We were set up to interview people on how healthy they were or not. Some of it related to sexual practices, too—you know, safe sex. That was the point of the funding, to study what was going on in poor communities. That interview included the usual postinterview services, like information and referral, if people wanted that. Counseling was available, too, if people were open to it."

"Sounds like standard stuff so far."

Nick was waiting for Gloria's etiquette lesson to show up somewhere.

"Tell you the truth, on the face of things, it was so much the usual drug outreach program that I thought it would be duller than dirt. If I hadn't needed a job, I would've been out of there in 2 months, I thought.

"But those two ladies had different ideas, man, let me tell you. They told us the program's got four rules: no drugs, no drinking, no judgment. Talked about how 'politeness doesn't cost a cent' was a key to winning people to this program. We put that saying up on the wall first.

"Then there was one final rule. Everybody who showed up was invited to pitch in and help out with lunch.

"*Lunch?* I thought they were crazy. Those two ladies were crazy like a fox. Asked me to think for a minute. 'What would preparing, serving, and cleaning up after lunch look like between staff and a bunch of addicts?'

"I thought for a while and started to get it. The first two rules gotta be there. You don't live in la-la land with addicts. Limits are limits, or they walk all over you. Trust me; I've been there. But after his craving and trying to score, what's an addict deal with the most, inside himself? Shame. Let's face it: People think addicts are the lowest of the low, the scum of the Earth. Addicts do, too.

"Wherever they show up, people are watching them like hawks. Mistrust every move they make. Look at 'em more like a bunch of ferrets than human beings. Addicts get so used to feeling like scum they beat you to the punch and play the fool before you have a chance to tell 'em so."

He scratched his bearded chin for a second before continuing. "Helen understood that. 'Look,' she said, 'in a lot of ways an addict is just an extreme version of every client we've got when they first walk through our doors—more needy, more demanding, trying to "get over" more. If we're really supposed to meet clients where they're at, we've got to make this office a space where everybody can show up together and treat each other with respect, no matter how people present themselves.

"'Those first two rules stay. We're not stupid. But maybe if we politely break bread together, we'll start to deliver a message that'll get folks to come back here, even when money's not part of the picture.'

"I got it. 'So,' I said, 'we're polite with people who aren't expecting it. This way we'll let them know we're not judging them.'

"'Hey, what's politeness?' she replied. 'A code of behavior that lets us know that we're all the same, at least some of the time. It may not be equality before the law, but politeness sure makes us equal at the dinner table.' The lady blew me away."

"Easier said than done, don't you think?"

Nick was curious to see how such a lofty idea could work in practice. This storefront wasn't the late Reverend Samuels's Episcopal church, and its participants weren't from his choir.

"Are you kidding? First couple of months nobody'd do more than give an interview, score their $20, and split. I admit my patience for this project was starting to run thin. Finally, a couple of guys stuck around for some roast beef sandwiches. Pretty soon, we had about six more. Guys couldn't believe it. 'We just gotta help out? No prob!' was the attitude."

The site director pointed to the walls. Nick saw a list of neatly lettered rules on poster board. "Got them to draft their own rules for the place. Pretty much followed the ones we had already, plus a few more. Interesting, don't you think? Say grace at every meal. Everyone pitches in. Call people by their names. No 'dissing' . . . you know, no disrespect inside these walls. If kids are here, no swearing. Guys started to bring their kids in, once in a while, for a meal, too.

"The kids helped us with their parents. The addicts didn't want their children to become like them. So after lunch, we'd read stories from the anti-drug comic books we got from the federal program. Had the parents read one cartoon panel apiece so nobody got embarrassed about how well they read.

"Might have been the first time the guys shared something other than a needle in a long, long time. And you know what? Giving their kids that anti-drug message—guess who else heard it?"

His laugh was like a happy bark. "They did!"

By now Nick thought he knew how to listen for the leadership principles embedded in South Bronx Multi-Services practices, but so far he wasn't hearing them. "So, how's this good work tie in to the special way things operate up here? Sounds like a great program for clients, but what's that got to do with how the staff work together?"

"Oh, that's easy. Shondelle and I and our staff were putting a lot of energy into getting our clients on board. Working with addicts is like climbing the same hill a lot of times. . . . You know that Buddhist saying, 'fall down seven times, get up eight'? He musta used that first while working with junkies. All that resistance and denial can wear you out.

"Plus, we're trying Ms. Jacques's new way of involving people, which made us anxious. Who knew if the program would catch on? Wanting to mix 'rights and responsibilities' with a hot lunch sounds good in a grant, but could it really happen? We sure didn't know. Let's face it: By now patience was at a premium.

"So one day, Shondelle and I are in this office, discussing how things are going. She's a very detailed lady; me—I'm the more spontaneous type. When things were going good, we were great together. But when we weren't? That was a horse of another color, and it wasn't pretty!

"That particular afternoon was one of those not-so-good-days. I was in a hurry; Shondelle was slowing me down. Of course, she was thinking I was sloppy while she was getting things in order. Like I said, we were going at it.

"All of a sudden, there's a knock on the door. It's Richie, one of the roast beef guys. Hands us a piece of paper and leaves right away. I mean, he runs out of there!"

"What was on it?" Nick asked.

"The ground rules from the wall. Guess what Richie had added?"

For once Nick knew. "Politeness doesn't cost a cent."

Cousins was impressed. "Exactly. You see, we staff were using up our good energy on politeness for everybody *but* us. After all that hard work being empathic and respectful, we didn't have much left to communicate the same respect to each other. It reminded me of the family I grew up in. My folks were sweet as sugar to the neighbors. Inside our walls, forget it! World War III, minus the nukes.

"Like my parents, Shondelle and I had spent our last dime of respect on the outside world, not ourselves. But who were we kidding? As Richie said later, 'Hey, hearing you guys bark at each other once or twice a week made me feel that all that politeness was just a new version of getting over. I liked being here, but I figured that "respect and reciprocity" crap was just another con. Until you changed.'"

"How'd you change?"

"Hey, Mr. Costello, you've already heard the other stories. There's no magic to having that full glass. No magic to 'politeness doesn't cost a cent' either. If you want it, it's yours for free. But you gotta be willing to work on yourself, developing that patience, to make it happen.

"Shondelle and I started taking those after-lunch walks together. Before that we thought it was kinda cute. Me and my background—I saw it as worse than cute, to tell you the truth. Ms. Jacques said we had to stick with it for at least 2 months for it to matter, so we did."

He barked his laugh again. "We both started losing weight about the time we gained a new perspective."

"And what was that?"

"In every part of my life, politeness *didn't* have to cost a cent. I just had to care about myself enough every day by taking that walk, working on who I wanted to be to keep my own glass full, for me to be free enough to keep it that way."

For the first time, Cousins looked completely serious, his voice almost somber. "It's no joke, Mr. Costello, really. If I can't love myself for free, *if I can't be patient and polite to me,* how can politeness be free?"

He put his hand on the reporter's shoulder for emphasis. "Politeness doesn't cost a cent, Nick, only if we know our own worth is gold."

He walked Nick to the door. "Treasure's everywhere, all around us, even in a program full of addicts. It's the prospecting, especially on ourselves, that's so hard."

Personal Reflection Exercise

Almost everyone knows how to be polite. What causes your politeness to disappear? Is it really because others are impolite first? Or are you easily irritated in your response?

_____

_____

Are staff members where you work treated with the same type of respect that they have been taught to give clients?

_____

Reflect on staff-to-staff relations. How do the relationships between staff members compare to those between staff members and clients? How are they the same? How are they different? Why?

_____

20

TWO TRUTHS

Nick Costello hurried back to the main office. He wanted to see what Helen Jacques was up to right before the meeting. It never hurt to see how a person truly sets her agenda. He found the executive director in the meeting room reviewing some spreadsheets.

She looked up and waved him over to sit next to her. "Hope your day's been more interesting than these spreadsheets. Reviewing work schedules can be a pain in the butt. There's only so many contingencies we can plan for."

"What do you mean, 'contingencies'?"

"Marjorie gets her people to draw up quarterly work schedules for their staff. We try to build in where we'll need per diems or where we'll be short-staffed and need more coverage. Can't always predict for sure, but a little forecasting helps. Every agency like ours has turnover. Young people go back to school; people have illness in their family; folks find out this work doesn't suit them."

"Hey, I thought you wouldn't have that last problem."

"Are you kidding? First, our salaries are still a lot less than we'd like. We can't pay more than the city allocates or the foundations offer. Lot of folks think they'll love the work but then find out they don't love it enough for the pay they get. Happens in education, hospitals, social services. You gotta be happy doing this 'cause nobody's gonna get rich. Twenty percent of new hires find that out in a year or so and are gone. Others have to hold two jobs to make ends meet and find it's too much for them.

"Then there are those who don't agree with our way of doing things. Some people do this work where they think 'help' is all about making others get better, not themselves. You know: 'It's OK for poor folks to have to struggle, not me.' Professionals who look only at others' troubles and not their own don't work out here."

"You expect a lot from people, don't you?"

"Why not? If you don't have great expectations for somebody, what do you get? It becomes real easy to settle for second best."

She folded up the spreadsheets and put them in a manila folder. "Truth is, though, if anything makes us unique, it's not that we have great expectations for clients. It's that we've got them for ourselves."

Nick paused in his note taking. "Doesn't that make you elitist?"

"Being great isn't about being better than somebody else. It's about being able to see and feel greatness that's right in front of you, *that's in you.* You think that's easy? Trying to feel the fullness of the world when people are in pain is the hardest thing I've ever had to do in my life. Like Mr. Trumbull said, the only way he could feel good about himself when his body ached all over *was to work at just that, every day.* A lot of days are full of aches and pains, Nick. That doesn't mean we have to see them as less full."

She pulled out another folder and checked her watch. It was five minutes before three o'clock. "Even one as difficult as this is about to be."

She looked at Nick with a sad but steady gaze on her face. "We're about to lay people off."

The rest of the executive team was there promptly, Marjorie Jessup rushing in at 3:02. Nick met them: Shondelle Williams, now in charge of administration, including human resources; George Applethorp, the chief fiscal officer; and Delia, head of development. Helen returned to reviewing the purpose of the meeting and what the agency hoped to get out of it. South Bronx Multi-Services, like Allison Smith's agency, was facing a shortfall of almost $200,000 in revenue. Whatever efficiencies it couldn't achieve would lead to layoffs. By the end of the meeting, the team had to decide what to do. Having been through a meeting like this only a few days ago, Nick sat back and grimly watched for what would happen next.

The executive director surprised him again. Given Helen's reported preference for efficient, no-nonsense meetings, Nick expected problem solving to start right away. Instead she opened with a question. "So, for check-in, how is everybody? How you feeling today?"

She looked at each person around the table. "I'll start. I was feeling kind of low, given we're in a financial hole again." She looked briefly at Nick. "Having Mr. Trumbull in to tell Nick his story helped a bit, but what finally made the difference was walking past the playground and seeing all those kids jumping up and down. Little Susie Haynes was in the sandbox, and she stood up and showed me her beautiful mud pies. Hey, they were the same mud pies I made in a sandbox like that, a long time ago! Lot's happened in 40 years, good and bad, but little girls are still making the same ol' mud pies! So I'm OK now."

"I was not pleased with those numbers I showed you last week, and I was still thinking about them this morning."

George, a large, dark-skinned African American man with a crisp white shirt, blue bow tie, and matching suspenders, was speaking. He looked at the group as he went on, a twinkle in his eyes. "I am known not to like that."

The group laughed, aware of a man who profoundly disliked being agitated by the unforeseen. "But I called the city a third time this week at 9:01 and got my good friend Rafael Campion our contract officer, on the phone for a chat on those vacant lines from last quarter."

He removed a gold pen from his pocket. "I still don't like what the numbers tell me, but I'm fine."

Delia, a tall, thin Asian-American in her mid-30s with short, spiked black hair and three tiny hoop earrings in each ear, went next. "I wish I could say I was OK, but I'm not. Any time we talk layoffs I have a knot in my stomach all week. I walked and I meditated, but it's still there. This is the part of the job I truly hate."

"Is there anything you'd like from us?" Helen asked.

"No, Helen, it's OK. This time is better than the last time, which was better than the first. I'm still growing into this position. Affecting other people's lives like this isn't easy."

"That's so true," Helen replied. "If it ever gets easy, it's time for us to leave. But you know me and my sayings, Angie. Today's about 'two truths.' The first truth is that with this shortfall we have to lay off someone who needs this job. That truth's painful. The second truth is that we'll be in a place together as a team to do those layoffs with as much foresight and integrity as we can. If we can keep that truth present, then we can respect ourselves. One truth doesn't cancel out the other."

"But sometimes it's so hard to hold two truths!" Delia responded. "I feel like I can barely hold one!"

Marjorie spoke up. "The reason you're here, Delia is because you do try. The hardest part of this job for me isn't laying people off—that's the second hardest. It's making sure I show up to handle as many truths that appear each day as well."

The young fundraiser smiled as she acknowledged her older peer, thanking her. Nick saw her sit back in her chair and relax slightly as Marjorie continued the check-in. "I'm OK now. Took 15 minutes before this meeting in the Quiet Room. Put on a little Thelonious Monk's piano music and let him take me where he does. When I hear things that will be eternal, it gives me the perspective I need for today. I know that two of my people have to go. I also know Shondelle and her people will do what they can in reemployment, too. It'll hurt, and it will be all right later on. My Mr. Monk always helps me remember that change and dissonance are forever. When I can hold on to that, I'm fine."

Helen briefly turned to the reporter. "We don't start important meetings with the work. We start by making sure people are OK to do the work. If our heads are somewhere else, how good will the work be? These 15 minutes on a personal check-in speed up our meetings by half."

Her words were an accurate prophecy. George reviewed the projected shortfalls. The drop-in homelessness over the summer combined with the decreased population in child welfare due to improved reporting and services over the last 4 years had led to budget reductions across the city. However, as the executive team had forecast some of these trends at its annual January retreat, it would be able to use savings and agreed-upon staff line transfers from vacancies to shore up over half the deficit. Shondelle's HR people had been working with an operations team of staff and supervisors on how to better handle shift transfers and coverage within the various programs, the arena that had caused the most headaches and greatest staff turnover in the past. With better systems and more accurate reporting from one shift to another, the team could transfer personnel to other duties without more expense.

Finally, the program director reviewed who would have to be let go. Marjorie then led the executive team on an intense programmatic review, assessing programmatic needs, staffing patterns involving mandated caseload sizes, and possible logistical problems before deciding who would go.

Nick looked at the group carefully as the discussion unfolded. People tried not to but occasionally interrupted each other. Their words were sharp, precise. The focus remained on the problems, spelling out various scenarios with one type of staffing pattern and then another. At 4:40, the decisions were made: Three personnel—one caseworker in child welfare and two in homeless, one from its operations unit and the other the most recently hired social services staff member—would go. After Marjorie and her supervisors met with the staff, Shondelle would help set up supports for employment searches. Then they spoke about the three effected personnel.

"I think Haley will be OK."

Marjorie was speaking about the child welfare worker. "She still lives at home with her parents and has talked about going back to school. She was aware this might happen, given what we've all read about the downsizing of child welfare. Fewer kids in the system, fewer workers. This'll sting, but when she gets a good reference, it will help.

"I wish I could say the same about the others. Our homeless director tells me that Francisco loves his job; he's grown a lot. And Melanie needed this job to pay off her school loans."

Marjorie looked very upset, her mouth drawn. "Shondelle, you've got your work cut out for you. They're going to be hurting."

The head of administration sighed inwardly, nodding her head. She quickly made notes on the legal pad in front of her.

The executives sat quietly for a minute, sadness in the room. Helen quietly brought them back. "It never gets easy, does it?" she said to no one in particular. Everyone at the table silently nodded in agreement. "Anything anybody wants or needs to say?"

George twiddled his gold pen in his hands, and Delia looked vacantly at the folders in front of her. The executive director spoke again. "We all did good work today, people. No one said good was easy."

She paused again. "Thank you for being good, too."

The reporter stayed after for just a minute. The executive director was still a little distracted from the rough decision making of the last hour and a half, but she looked at him agreeably. "You guys didn't pull any punches there, did you? That had to be hard."

"'Hard'? Sure it is, but it beats the alternative. We used to avoid these discussions until the last minute, never planned for what happened every year, making believe this never occurs, even though it always does. Then, when it did, we'd scream at each other and make some decision, usually much worse. There'd be so much anger and hurt we wouldn't speak for days, and then we'd go on like nothing happened. We didn't call that hard. We called it 'goes with the turf.' A lot like AstroTurf, that stuff on football fields. A much rougher game than this.

"As for today, right now we all hurt. And we'll be OK, too."

She almost smiled, but not quite. "Two truths."

Nick stood up to go. "I learned a lot today, Helen, thanks."

He checked his watch. He knew he had to return again, for he had a few unanswered questions—what was the story, for example, with all that racial bantering? He wanted to see how the layoffs went, too. "Is it OK to come back tomorrow?"

"You can come back tomorrow or any day, Nick, but I can't take a lot of time the rest of this week. Feel free to come, but I can't meet until either next Tuesday or Wednesday, whichever you prefer."

Nick thought for a second and realized next week would be fine. It was 5:00 when he headed out the door for the subway; he checked his watch. He and Meredith were meeting at 7 for dinner at the bistro they liked. But he had other plans. The farmers' market at the park near his home stayed open in summer until 6. If he hurried, he could buy some fresh mozzarella, tomatoes, and basil for an appetizer and then get two of those little organic Cornish hens his girlfriend loved. It would be fun to cook at home tonight.

Critical Thinking

How does using "two truths" help agency professionals respond more effectively to their job? Couldn't "two truths" complicate their work instead?

Personal Reflection Exercise

Helen commented that "a full life doesn't mean it's easy." Reflect on what that means in terms of your work. What are its "truths"?

_____

_____

How do people develop their capacity to "hold two truths"? What was the experience of Delia in doing so? What can you expect if you are to develop this capacity?

_____

_____

Where can you spot the lessons from _Doña_ Carmen in the work of these executives?

_____

Where might you and your team apply similar lessons related to financial planning?

_____

_____

21

TAKE THE COVER OFF THE BOOK

The flowers looked wonderful, even if the gardener was nowhere to be seen. Nick Costello had arrived a little later for his appointment with Helen Jacques the next Tuesday at 10. She had had an early-morning meeting downtown. An early riser, Nick had used the extra time to jog on the running path alongside the Hudson River. At the moment, the muscles in his calves ached.

Gloria Samuels again greeted him, as formal and polite as before. "Good morning, sir. How can I help you?"

She asked him to wait as she called inside. "Ms. Jacques called to say she will be here any second. Would you like a glass of water while you wait?"

Nick accepted the cup proffered him and sat down. Next to him were 3- or 4-year-old twin girls dressed in matching red and white shorts and tops. They hopped up and down on their chairs, jostling their mother, a young Latina whose belly looked so large she might give birth within the hour. She smiled sweetly at the reporter as she shooed her girls to sit down.

Nick learned that the young mother and her family were here for relocation services. They were about to move in to a new apartment and were meeting with a homeless staff member to make sure the housing transition went smoothly. "It was a hard 5 months here, but it was worth it."

She patted her bulging middle. "We got our home just in time!"

"Why so hard?"

The young woman seemed embarrassed for a second, shyly looking away. "Oh, you know, when I got here, I didn't want nothing but to get an apartment and get out of here. Things had been hard before, you know."

Nick noticed she wasn't wearing a wedding ring and realized she was raising her children alone. "But they expect a lot out of you in this place. I was in so many programs; at times I felt like I was back in school."

Her face flushed with pride. "Actually, I was! Got my GED here. I was always good in school, before Maria and Maritza came along. Once I got started, only took me 3 months."

Nick wanted to know a bit more. Laws for homeless residents didn't mandate shelter residents to go to school—or to any program for that matter. "Having twin girls and another on the way, I can see why you felt you had enough to do just surviving here. So what motivated you to enroll in that program so quickly?"

"Wasn't any one thing. Saw people at dinner talking about their classes in a nice way, almost like it was fun sometimes. Some people who worked here had once been in the program. Could you believe that? Anyway, at dinner one night, they announced a graduation. I thought it was for the Head Start kids, but it was the moms! That did it for me. Showed up the next day."

A smiling young White woman with short black hair, angular black glasses that nicely accentuated her high cheekbones, and a silver metal cane with a matching brace encircling her shortened left leg stood before them. "Sorry to interrupt. Ana, you and my two cuties ready for me?"

The little girls had jumped up to hug the staff member around her waist.

They were walking back inside the inner offices as Helen arrived. "Nick, sorry I'm late."

She checked her watch. "You wait for funders whether you want to or not."

"I appreciate you taking a little more time."

Back in her office, there was a new vase of flowers on her desk. This week they were sunflowers and daisies, whose splash of color matched the bright orange suit Helen had worn for her earlier meeting. "I'll be honest. Things do work differently around here. The more I looked at my notes, I could see it's all in the little things. Never expected to find leadership principles in the little things.

"Except for the intent of keeping that glass full. That's big, real big. Having an intention to show up seeing the world full each day reframes everything else you do in a major way. I think that's what Pete Morrissey's so impressed about. But I don't think he quite has a handle on it, either. Your programs are the same programs as everybody else's. If a person doesn't know what he or she's looking for, all those little sayings about 'politeness doesn't cost a cent' and 'clean as you go' sound like so much window dressing. I think that's why Morrissey wanted me up here as much as anything else. To see if you're for real."

"Pete's a strategic guy, but I don't think he's quite that scheming. He and I have had a lot of talks over the last few years. He's built an amazing program, three times bigger than this place. But when he hit $50 million, Pete realized just being big wasn't necessarily the most important thing. I think that 'most important mentor' icebreaker got to him, too."

"As good as your leadership model is, I've got one or two more questions. One's about the community around here. The other . . ."

Nick was stalling, uncomfortable with what he was about to say. "The other's about race. Everyone seems to get along on the surface, but then you bring something up right to their face, talk about their Whiteness or how Black you are."

Nick felt the perspiration break out under his arms. "It looks like racial one-upmanship to me. What's going on?"

"'One-upmanship'?"

For the first time, Helen laughed long and hard. "Hey, Nick, I'll give you credit. For a White guy, you've got guts."

Then she laughed again, only to stop and apologize when she saw the stricken look on the reporter's face. "No, I'm sorry. That's not fair. Let me back up. Way back!

"This may take awhile, so bear with me. You know what's the most frequent question between two people—one White, one Black, or any other mix, for that matter—when they're disagreeing about something?"

Nick knew a rhetorical question when he heard one. Helen went on. "Simple. It's 'Is she saying that to me because I'm a . . . ?' Or 'Are we arguing because he's a . . . ?' It may sound pretentious, Nick, but I'm convinced that more bad work happens in organizations across America because somebody is asking *that question* rather than getting the work done.

"Soon as that question shows its ugly head, standards drop, blood pressures go up, and nobody wins. And I mean nobody, Black or White, Latino, Asian American, Native American. For that matter, men and women, gays and straights, differing abilities, too. All of us."

Helen's intensity barely lessened as she took a sip of water. "Any time spent worrying about the answer to that question is time wasted. Damn, it's lives wasted, too.

"A long time ago, I was talking about that question and the mess it makes with a good friend of mine. She used to work for the phone company. Started as a messenger right out of high school, ended up the first Latina executive in the place. She had no patience for that kind of nonsense. 'When I started moving up the ladder at the company,' she said, 'there were all sorts of White men who put up roadblocks every step of the way. But you know what? There were some who helped me, a lot. It was up to me to figure out who was setting standards for me to achieve and who used them as a weapon. If I'd spent time on that other question, I'd still be answering phones!'

"But my friend Betha was a special lady. She didn't let those things throw her like it does most people. It got me to thinking: How can we help people get rid of that damned question so they can focus on the work they've got to do? What did we have to do inside this agency to get those elephants out of the room so people can rise to the top, like Betha?

"About a month later, I was at some meeting on staffing when Marjorie responded to a question about a new hire. 'Hey, don't judge a book by its cover! That guy's better than you think.' She was referring to a White guy in casework who seemed way too shy to do this work. She'd found him deeply engaged with his clients, making up for his shy manner by always going the extra mile. He's head of the social services unit today. Clients love him.

"Anyway, Margie gave me the answer to why that elephant's always in a racially mixed room. *We do judge the book by its cover!* When we don't deal openly with race or some other possible 'ism,' it goes something like this. People are there at the table, working away at some complicated project. Everybody's doing their best, but they're sitting on eggshells, too. Folks aren't just working on the project, as hard as that might be. *They're making sure we're all 'OK' because we're all so different. Isn't it wonderful how we can get along . . . ?*

"Everything's just fine until . . . two people disagree! Then that ol' elephant walks out of the corner, plops his big butt in the middle of the table, and everyone runs for cover . . . 'Oh, I can't disagree with him; he'll think I'm a . . . ' 'Oh, she's upset because she's a . . . I better not go there.' Then back to la-la-la, while all the time the project just became less than it ought to be. Than it's got to be."

Nick saw how impassioned she was about the topic. "If you care so much about these racial dynamics, why do you make jokes all the time? When I've heard you mention race, it's like you're making light of it."

"'Making light of it'? Not really, Nick. I just take the cover off the book. We hate to admit it, but we judge people all the time, especially about race. We judge that book cover in a nano-second."

"But what's the big deal? In my background reading for this story, I read material on assessment that you guys make with clients in schools, agencies, hospitals. That's pretty fundamental to what you do. Are you saying people here aren't supposed to analyze these issues?"

"Just the opposite. But it starts with taking the cover off, getting clear who we are, showing us what's different and what isn't. If we don't start there, that question never goes away. People who work in this agency have to be open about racial differences. That's how we get past them."

"I still don't get it. If you have people noticing racial and ethnic differences, aren't you just fanning the flames?"

Helen looked at him quietly for a few seconds before speaking. "You asked the perfect question, Nick. In fact, your wording makes clear how you feel about difference."

Nick's underarm perspiration grew heavier. "Wait a second! Asking a question doesn't make me a racist!"

His stomach tightened as he looked at Helen.

"Hey, Nick, slow down."

Helen smiled warmly at him. "You just found the elephant lurking over in that corner and invited him to sit down next to us.

I didn't say you were racist. I said that I could tell by your question how you felt about *difference*."

"No offense, Helen, but between the lurking elephants and the hidden questions, you're losing me."

Helen laughed again. "Hang in there, Nick; I'll get there. Let me ask you a question. It may take awhile to answer, so think for a minute if you have to. Think back to when you were a little boy, maybe 4 or 5, maybe a little older."

Nick thought about his small hometown in rural Wisconsin, 6,000 inhabitants, all of them White. "Tell me: What was your first experience with difference? Take a second. When was the first time you realized there were differences in the world, whatever they might be?"

Nick took a minute before the memory flooded back to him. It was in kindergarten. He was the only left-handed student in the class. Two other boys, Donnie Payne and Melvin Packer, had laughed at him when he'd held his crayon. They later became his best friends, but that day he'd gone home crying.

Helen leaned over the table toward Nick to emphasize her point. "Hold that memory while I take another detour. I studied 'race and difference' with a brilliant lady up in Boston. Her research found that almost everybody's first remembered experience with difference as a child is negative. Then adults compound the problem by interpreting their explanation in abstract ways that a 5-year-old's thinking can't handle. So the imprint's set to see any new difference as a threat."

Nick looked at her, suddenly relieved. "You mean we grow up feeling about difference the way we did as a child?"

"You bet, emphasis on *feeling*. That Boston College professor made the distinction clearer. *For most of us, when race shows up, it's different, with 'different' and 'problem' meaning the same thing.* Later on in life, we *think* we're fine because by now we're well-meaning people out to save the world. Unfortunately, as soon as the group becomes socially mixed we still *feel* anxious. *That old childhood anxiety leads us as adults to feel any social difference as a negative, even when we don't think that way about a group.*"

Her index finger pounded the table for emphasis. "Left uncovered, people say the right things while acting stupid. Our past trips us up, even while we try to do the right thing in the present."

Nick paused in his note taking, reflecting on what she was saying. "So my 'fanning the flames' question showed up as judging difference as a threat. I heard you speaking about racial difference and putting me down when all you were doing was commenting on my behavior."

He jotted some more notes into his pad. "Ouch."

"Hey, no 'ouch,' Nick. You think somebody in America hops over this in the time it takes to download a few songs from iTunes? I don't think so."

"So what do you do up here? People don't begin at your agency that much different than me, do they?"

"Nobody does, regardless of race or any other social issue. Taking the cover off the book is just another way of telling people it's important to be who you are, to stake a claim to it. In this way, nobody gets to be who you're perceived to be around here for very long. Then, when we do struggle around difference, it's simply a difference of opinion."

"Easier said than done."

Nick remembered too many arguments in his own family and among his friends to be sold too quickly.

"That's why you see Marjorie and me fooling with each other so much, comparing suntans. We're modeling for newer staff that what a lot of folks think is a big deal doesn't have to be. We tell them that the elephant leaves the room as soon as they can get 'comfortable with discomfort.' If they take the cover off with each other, live through that childhood anxiety keeping 'em asking the wrong questions, they can get down to the real work."

She smiled. "I'm happy to say young people in their 20s get this a lot easier than old folks like you."

They both laughed.

Helen poured another cup of water and handed it to the reporter. "Like I said, it's not easy. The first few times you own who's really in the room, you and everybody else reacts nervously. Later, after you relax, new people don't. When you name a difference out loud, people first get nervous. That's where you dig in and keep going."

"But why? There's gotta be an easier way."

"Like I said last week, who said greatness was easy? It's hard! This is as hard as it gets. Like the man said, the only way to get past it is through it, Nick. Be honest with me. You ever work in a place where that question wasn't in the room? *Where people just argued about the work?*"

Nick couldn't think of one. "So 'taking the cover off the book' is the great equalizer?"

Helen rolled her eyes, a wry look across her face. "I wish. Are you kidding? All we're doing with the cover off is getting to difference where it *feels good.* At least neutral. If the elephant's out of the room or maybe down to the size of a mouse, we've got enough space to work on what *is* different. Get to the stuff where the answers take work. The backbreaking kind."

"Like what?"

She used her fingers to make an imaginary list, ticking issues off one by one, pausing between each so the reporter could write them down correctly.

"Who gets promoted, a White worker who writes her reports well or a Black worker who's always late with hers but whom the clients feel comfortable to open up to?

"How do you support a great Latino super who can't pass his qualifying exams for his boiler's license?

"How do you get White people to understand what's racially going on in America when they only realize they're White *after* a person of color walks in the room?

"How do you handle the tensions between Africans from Nigeria working in security for $9.50 an hour who resent a homeless African American family getting subsidized housing?"

Nick paused from his rapid note taking, shaking his wrist to get the knot out of it. "Sounds like you've got a lot more questions than answers, Helen."

"Nick, when you came here last week, I said I didn't think we were that special. Truth is, I think we do some special things, but like you said this morning, they're mostly little ones. Taking the cover off the book, getting folks 'comfortable with discomfort'—those are more little things. You want to deal with race in America, we're talking about a pretty thick book. The book ain't about giving easy answers; it's about asking tough questions."

Nick paused again. "Yes, it is. I guess with the cover off, you and your team at least get to turn the pages."

It was the executive director's turn to pause. She leaned forward, her smile back. "Hey, not bad for a White guy from Wisconsin, Nick, not bad! A middle-aged Black woman like me is impressed."

Nick couldn't help himself. "Helen, you haven't seen anything. Wait 'til you see me dance!"

Critical Thinking

What does "getting comfortable with discomfort" mean? How can a person develop this "ability"?

Personal Reflection Activities

Reflect on your workplace. What are its "elephants"?

_____

How do you respond to these issues when they are raised? Is there a willingness to discuss these issues among staff members? Have there been meaningful trainings that provided people with tools on how to respond more effectively? Describe some of these tools.

_____

_____

What would make it possible for people to disagree and to understand the disagreement as being based just on the substance of the issue and not on other, underlying social factors?

_____

_____

22

BUILD YOUR COMMUNITY
AND THEY WILL COME . . . AGAIN

Helen Jacques was laughing as she stood up and motioned for Nick Costello to follow her. "I know you want to talk some more, so walk with me."

"I have just one other question. Why the thick iron gates running up the windows? You seem so inviting to the community, but those gates make you look like a fortress."

Helen looked at the reporter. "Nick, we may fight poverty, but we don't stop it. You can have the nicest family in the world, but if a cousin's on drugs, he'll rob you blind anyway. Just because we love this community doesn't mean we're stupid. Three blocks away somebody's shooting up as we speak. Those gates are for them, not our neighbors."

"Do your neighbors know the difference?"

"Fair question. I don't think you ever really know. But what I've placed my bets on is that if we build our own community, the rest of the community will come—and then come again, too."

She walked toward the agency's front door. "Come on. Maybe you can see what I mean. I'm heading over to the neighborhood elementary school. There's a parents' meeting with the principal that I want to drop in on."

"A parents' meeting with the principal in July? That's a first. Did they invite you for support? I hear principals and parents don't always get along."

At his family's yearly Christmas reunion in Wisconsin, Nick's older sister always gave her annual report on the school wars she took part in while her children were growing up in California. He didn't expect much difference in New York.

"Actually, the principal reminded me of the meeting. They're seeing what needs to be done to get more active parent participation in each class. Seems they want more class reps in the lower grades.

"Would have been different a few years ago. Our parents' organization helped oust the last principal. Reading scores had stayed at the bottom for 5 years running, and they'd had enough. That principal refused to even see them, let alone admit there was a problem. We had a lot of organizing to do before he opened his door. By then it was too late."

She turned a corner by the bodega where Nick had gotten his ham and cheese sandwich last week. "Our parents had organized enough support where they demanded that he go. He fought for a while, but the handwriting was on the wall when our local city councilmember backed us. We wished it hadn't come to that, but kids were being passed on to the fourth and fifth grade who couldn't read. Parents were too angry. How would you feel if you knew your kid was being tracked into a minimum-wage job for life?"

"So the new principal's afraid of your parents?"

"Just the opposite. They don't always agree, but the disagreements are mostly over how to use resources, not whether people are committed to improving learning. Makes a big difference."

Just then they heard voices behind them calling to Helen. She and Nick turned around to see two women, one a gray-haired Latina in a flowered dress with a radiant smile on her face and the other a tall, striking African American with long dreads and gold hoop earrings the size of bracelets. After a brief hug with Helen and a quick introduction to the reporter, they immediately joined the conversation.

Maria Fernandez and Andrea Marshall had both been parent leaders for more than 4 years, the former as the grandmother of a fourth grader and a fifth grader and the latter with children in the sixth and first grades. Knowing of his sister's first tentative steps inside his nieces' school years ago, Nick asked them how they had worked up the courage to get rid of their children's principal.

The older woman paused for a second before speaking. "You ask good questions, don't you? We've talked about that before, you know. When it was over, when that principal was gone, we couldn't believe what we'd done."

She looked at Helen and then her younger counterpart.

"Poor people like us have it in us to be brave, but a lot of times it gets beaten out of you, you know what I mean? Bad jobs, bosses who yell at you, landlords who won't return your calls. When I first went into child welfare before the reforms to get my grandchildren out of foster care and into my home, some people treated me like dirt. After a while, there's a part of you that feels like dirt, too."

Andrea silently nodded in agreement, her eyes cast downward. "You can't find your courage if you don't respect yourself."

"Where'd you two find respect?"

"I didn't at first."

It was Andrea's turn to talk as they walked along. "Wasn't looking for courage. Wasn't looking for respect, either."

She laughed grimly. "I was looking for cover. You know, shelter. Given what I'd been through, the basics would have been good enough.

"The very first day I arrive here at the agency, it's raining cats and dogs. My little boy is soaked, my baby is crying, and all my stuff is falling out on the ground. It may have been the worst day of my life. Anyway, the only thing worse than the weather is my mood. I don't want people talking to me, looking at me, going near me! Then this nice lady walks over and hands me a towel—two towels, actually. She speaks to me in a polite voice and asks me to be seated.

"Of course, at the time I don't hear her being nice; I'm too angry for that. But later on, it registered. Took awhile, but I could see I was getting respect even when I wasn't able to give it back. Had a big impact on me."

Helen interjected. "When people first arrive here from homeless services, they're pretty beaten down. We figured our welcome should show them that they matter. We know they can't hear it right away, but after a while good people can if they find out the message is for real. It just has to show up consistently in lots of little interactions between staff and clients for people to believe it. After all, politeness doesn't cost a cent, does it?"

Helen and the two other women smiled. Gloria Samuels's words had reached quite a few people.

"Where else does it show up?"

"It showed up with those towels. Then it showed up in the 'Welcome Bag' every new resident family gets. The bag's standard stuff for any family shelter: toothpaste and brushes, soap, diapers if you need 'em. What was special was the ribbon."

The young mother had a look of amazement on her face. "The bag came with a pretty purple ribbon! That was the one thing that registered that day. I remember thinking, 'Ribbon? What's this pretty ribbon doing on my bag?' Figured it had to be a mistake. Felt good to find out it wasn't."

"Ms. Jacques mentions all those 'little interactions.'"

The grandmother in the group chuckled.

"They're built into everything! But not just 'respect' by being nice. Sometimes *respeto* is making you do things you didn't know you could do. Or wanted to do. But they make you do 'em anyway."

By now Nick recognized a familiar echo. "What do you mean, 'do things you didn't know you could do'? How is that respect?"

"That's simple. Staff were always polite around here, but that didn't mean they were easy. When I started in kinship foster care, I wasn't ready. I'd raised my own children, and now because of *las drogas* I had to do it again? I wanted to die. *Por dios,* what I really wanted was to be taken care of, too!

"My caseworker, Miss Priscilla Fellin, was always polite and kind, but every time we met, there were things she had to do *and* things I had to do. She'd call it our contract. Said this made us partners. Like Andrea was saying, at first I didn't pay any attention. I was too needy for that. But after a while, I saw that to be here meant it was a two-way street. My worker had her things to do, and I had mine. If I fell down on the job, we worked out what happened. I still had that job to do. Maybe she did more than me, but what I did mattered. We couldn't get things squared away for my grandchildren if I wasn't doing my part, too.

"And guess what? I started to realize by doing my job I was more confident about seeing Miss Fellin do her job, too. Since I was feeling good about me and not so dependent on her, I could see what we both had to do together. Just as she was holding me accountable, I felt easier to do that to her."

The older woman paused to catch her breath as the school came into view. "How can I find the courage to talk to a professional about their job if I don't have the courage to do my own? If I back down on my responsibility, I'll back down on theirs, too."

"As time went on inside the agency, we'd all hear about these client groups—you know, residents' councils, child advocates' meetings, the drug program, that kind of thing."

The younger woman glanced at the executive director as they walked on. "Nobody'd pressure us to join, but you'd hear about what they were doing, and after a while they sounded interesting. I was feeling better about myself. Since it felt like people were working with me as a partner and not a problem, the agency started to be interesting. I felt like I belonged enough where it mattered. Where *I mattered.*

"Ms. Jacques and her people got us involved inside the agency community by letting us know it was here in lots of ways. You know, announcements at dinner that come from other residents and not just staff. Invited to celebrations for kids graduating Head Start or their parents with GEDs. Having speakers in who were experts where staff and clients could come. Not talking down to us. All that subtle stuff builds up to mean something after a while."

"Andrea and me joined the parents' group at the same time. We'd already done things inside the agency before we got involved outside. First time they ask me to read a flyer at a parents' meeting, I was shaking like a leaf! But I did it. Andrea, too. Little by little we could take on more. But by then we were ready.

"I was already living in the neighborhood. Andrea was working with housing relocation staff to do the same. We both liked being here. We felt like we had a base of support we hadn't had before. When the agency you're part of feels like a community, you want to be a part of that community. We're neighbors now—me, Andrea, South Bronx Multi-Services, other parents who live here. It means something when you can count on your neighbors, you know?"

They stood resting for a moment before the school. "You know, Mr. Costello, once you feel like a real member of a community, you like that feeling. You want it elsewhere, too. It's sorta like that genie in a bottle. Once it's out, you can't put it back."

"That principal from a few years back learned that the hard way. If he'd been willing to meet us halfway, he'd still be here. But he treated us like ignorant peons. Broke appointments. Didn't do what we'd all agreed to do, then said it was our problem.

"We found our courage then, Mr. Costello. But we had our self-respect before that. We'd experienced what it felt like to be partners, to work on a team. Look, being on a team doesn't mean we're all equal and do the same things. I write in Spanish; my writing in English isn't so good. Andrea's going to community college; it's only her first year. There's things the staff do better than us. But we matter, too. We know what our kids need. We know how to get them to listen, at least some of the time. So we deserve a voice at the table, too."

Maria looked at the school right before they entered. "Now we're at a bigger table. But we couldn't be here if we hadn't learned how to first sit down at one back at the agency. More and more of us live in the neighborhood. Staff members do, too. Some are involved in the schools. Some with the local community board. Others in their churches. We all do different things, but that's OK. We figure if a little of the way this agency operates shows up elsewhere, we're doing some good things. Making the community stronger, one day at a time. One place at a time."

"Like this one."

Helen opened the door and waved at the woman striding toward the group. "And here's our principal now, Delores Brown."

The principal smiled at the group in front of her as she held the school's inner doors open. "Welcome! I appreciate you taking the time to meet during the summer break. Maybe now we can figure out how to increase parents' involvement!"

Nick copied his final notes for the day. He couldn't help but notice Delores had greeted them happily. And she'd been very, very polite.

The group went inside, joining six others at a long cafeteria table. They had work to do.

Nick turned to the three women he'd walked with and thanked them for their time. He shook Helen's hand for the last time, gripping it firmly. The reporter promised to be in touch. It was time for him to go. Nick had his work to do, too.

Personal Reflection Exercise

The parents referred to "the little things" that helped them feel respected. What were they?

_____

_____

_____

They spoke about gaining respect even though staff placed demands on them and that the demands helped them become stronger. What did they mean?

_____

_____

_____

They suggested "community" happens over time as people feel and give support to each other. What does support "look like" in concrete form? Is the "building of community" a linear process, or does it happen in some other way? What are some of the concrete activities to "building community" that you could recommend to your agency or school?

_____

_____

_____

_____

23

THE CROSSROADS

"So you think we're at a crossroads?"

It was Pete Morrissey calling Nick Costello on his cell phone.

Nick's feature had just appeared as a two-part series. While brief mention was made of the Human Service Alliance and its future agenda, the article had focused on the type of leadership choices that lay ahead for human service executives and public school educators. The series revealed a lot of hardworking, dedicated, and caring people. It also made clear that hard work by good people wasn't enough. If an alliance was to bear fruit, it concluded, its own leadership house would first have to be in better order.

The crossroads were clearly marked. One road had the well-worn contours of crisis management, personal exhaustion of staff, and diminished expectations of both clients and the professions in which those good people toiled. That road held little promise for renewal. The other was a model of leadership that framed its work on great expectations, grounding those expectations in people who recognized that their own self-worth and that of the communities in which they worked were as inseparable as they were in need of great care.

Interestingly enough, the reporter provided evidence that this new approach was hardly easy, that those who practiced it were the first to admit what a challenge it was each day to frame their efforts in a positive and open manner. Helen Jacques had been quoted more than once on how hard it was to practice this leadership model. She and others also had made it clear that the effort was worth it. The executive director and a smiling Oliver Trumbull were pictured in front of the agency's garden. Peeking from behind them both was Gloria Samuels.

"Mr. Morrissey, I think you know you're at a crossroads, too. Isn't that why you sent me up to the South Bronx in the first place?"

"Hey, Nick, you must be a good reporter. You never stop with the questions!"

The executive paused. "Got a call from Jorge Pacheco today. He wasn't pleased with what you wrote. "A few of my colleagues aren't.""

"I didn't write this to make people happy. And you still didn't answer my question, did you?"

Pete paused but only for a second. His voice was serious. "I wasn't aware I was doing that, Nick, but I probably wanted you up there, somebody to see if what I saw in that agency was as good as I thought it, was. It's hard to think you've got to do things differently than you have for 25 years."

"I think Helen would tell you that's half the battle. If you start each day with a commitment to look at the world differently than you did before—take it all in fully—the rest can happen. The hard part's staying open to that."

Nick heard a sigh at the other end of the phone. "'Every day' is a lotta days. But Helen already told me it gets easier over time. So that's my hope."

Pete changed the subject. "So what's next for you?"

"That article got a good response, so I'm taking my own risk, Mr. Morrissey. I'm writing a book. I'm a little nervous about it but excited, too. I talked to my girlfriend, and she said to go for it, too, so I am. What have I got to lose? After all, no matter what happens, the glass is always full, right?"

Learning Guide: Reflective Questions for Discussion and Classroom Integration

Based on Austin, Brody, and Packard's (2008) approach, we have divided the guide into three distinct sections: (a) Developing Practice Wisdom, (b) Professional Development of New Agency Leaders, and (c) Community Building: Joining Personal Development to Agency Improvement.

Developing Practice Wisdom

The two agencies you have just read about have equally committed people who work hard and never give up. Were you to get a job interview at either place, you'd be impressed with the staff's commitment and dedication. These case studies are not about one group of good people and one group of bad; each agency is run by well-meaning, nice folks. Yet, were you offered a job by both, you would have a very different experience based on the one you chose. It's important to reflect on what causes such differences in response to practice, whether in working with a client, in attending to agency operations, or in handling diversity.

The following questions have been drawn directly from these two stories and are meant to stimulate and develop your own practice wisdom. Included as well are specific challenges to take up that may bridge your classroom readings/discussions and your field/work experience.

- Each agency's leaders care about their clients. So why is one agency's lobby so shabby? Does it really matter as long as staff members work hard? Is the problem one of financial resources?
  o For the reader's professional development (RPD): Take an inventory of the agencies' lobbies in which students have field placement or in which students work. Is there any correlation between the look of the lobby and other issues related to practice and program results?
  o The primary leaders in each agency approach their work with a very different focus. What is the primary focus of Allison Smith? What is that of Helen Jacques? How does each woman's particular focus translate into how she approaches her day related to (a) herself, (b) how she works with others on staff, and (c) her commitments to practice?
  o RPD: Every human service agency has a written message that is uplifting. Examine the mission statement of your agency. In what ways does the focus of the leaders' work concretely correspond to that mission?
  o Create a list of concrete examples from those related to Allison or Helen.
- Both agencies' senior teams are committed to creating a progressive, multicultural work environment. Yet in only one are people comfortable with racial, ethnic, and other social

differences. Why? What is the root cause of tension in Allison's agency? Is it a matter of blatant racism? Or are there other dynamics at play that foster racial tension?

- o Why do Helen and others talk about "the elephants in the room" even though some people may be initially uncomfortable?
- o Is this ongoing discussion enough to end the problems related to racial and other social tensions inside an agency?
- o Why does "self-care" matter on an issue like this?
- o RPD: After reflection, openly discuss with your field instructor or supervisor how his or her agency approaches diversity. If possible, discuss topics that include "elephants in the room," levels of personal and team discomfort with these issues, and ways in which the agency "walks the talk" on diversity.

- Every good manager works at improving systems. There clearly are smart people at each agency. Why does one agency's systems seem to always be breaking down while the other has a much smoother operation? Is it related simply to money?
- o In what ways does Allison and her team's approach to client crises affect other systems, including operations?
- o What are the reasons Helen and her staff are on top of systems improvement? Are they financially better off?
- o RPD: After this discussion, approach your field agency's operations and program directors to examine in what ways they understand and support each other's very different tasks and responsibilities.

- Are operations staff (information technology, human resources, maintenance) perceived by others in your agency as valuable? If so, how is that appreciation concretely expressed?
- o Outline concrete steps that can be taken to improve relationships between operations and program staff.

_____

_____

_____

Professional Development of New Agency Leaders

As Helen Jacques made clear, she did not become an effective leader overnight. Whether you are new to the profession or challenging yourself to take the next step up in your own professional development, what are some of the key lessons from her story? List three that you believe can help you:

1. _____
2. _____
3. _____

What can you learn from a formerly incarcerated person like Oliver Trumbull?

1. _____
2. _____
3. _____

It is clear that Gloria Samuels has a mental health condition. What can you learn from Gloria that can improve you as a manager and a leader?

1. _____
2. _____
3. _____

The following reflective rating scale on your professional development is for your own use. As you reflect, stay open to the issues at hand:

- How often do you practice self-care each day? How often do you practice it each week?
- Are you "comfortable with the discomfort" that social issues raise?
- Are you reflective or reactive about how you do your job?
- Do you thrive in crisis and get bothered by the "care and tending" to procedures and systems?

PROFESSIONAL DEVELOPMENT SELF-ASSESSMENT

Area of Professional Development	I Am Highly Effective in This PD Area (1)/ I Need to Commit to Working on This (5)				
Self-care	1	2	3	4	5
Practicing patience and politeness	1	2	3	4	5
Being reflective, not reactive to client crises	1	2	3	4	5
Engage in systems improvement	1	2	3	4	5
Live my vision in concrete ways	1	2	3	4	5
Being comfortable with discussions of diversity at work	1	2	3	4	5

Identify one area with a score of 3 or higher. Commit to working on this area of professional development over the next week. Track your concrete shifts. Make a new commitment, and chart steps forward, where it was difficult to make changes, and the concrete steps you will take the following week. Review weekly, measuring actual increments.

Community Building: Joining Personal Development to Agency Improvement

As we saw in Helen Jacques's agency, community building takes hold inside an organization when the ongoing improvement of the agency supports a similar ongoing improvement of the people who work within it. Identify examples in Helen's agency's story as to where this happens. Is it always planned? How does the growth of a person affect the growth of the agency? How does the improvement of the agency seem to improve the lives of staff?

- How does Oliver Trumbull's gardening affect community building . . . and Oliver himself?
- What is the importance of Gloria Samuels bringing Nick Costello a glass of water? Is it just an issue of politeness?
- *Doña* Carmen is very strict in her kitchen. Why are people not afraid of her?
- Frankie Lee Chan's vision stems from the distant past. How does it stay relevant to today?
- Is the Quiet Room really possible for workers? Won't this focus make them less productive? Could this be coddling workers?
- In what ways does the story of Helen Jacques and Marjorie Jessup's failure to keep their commitments inspire their staff with their model of leadership? Isn't "failure" the sign of a weak leader?
  o How can their story be translated to empower clients?

ACTION STEPS FOR LASTING TRANSFORMATION

Action Steps Taken	When	With Whom	The Result	Next Steps
Improving the look and feel of the workplace				
Practicing politeness with clients				
Practicing politeness with staff				
Improving a system or procedure				
Your 'vision as a tool'				
Developing balance in work & life				

Remember: There are no "right" steps here in the development of both your own leadership and a community inside your agency or school. The secret is to begin . . . and to do so again the very next day!

PART III

A Leadership Model of Personal and Organizational Transformation

STARTING BEFORE THE BEGINNING

The two agencies described in this book are not real, but their work is. We have been witness to agency and school life in which remarkable people do great things . . . and in which other, equally fine individuals attempt good work only to undermine its value. The crossroads at which those who have chosen to work in public and nonprofit fields now stand is equally real. We live in a time, in the emergence of this globalized 21st century, where there is little reason for Americans to embrace service and educational interventions whose daily encounters between clients and staff diminish them both. There is also every reason to expect growing support when those encounters accumulate in ways that lead those same people to imagine a world more full of possibility than it was before.

What follows is the model of personal and organizational transformation that has guided the writing of this book. As Fabricant and Fisher (2002) did in developing their community-building model, we have developed our model from the concrete, real experiences of people who have dedicated their lives to the lives of others. Some, like Barbara Byrd-Bennett, former chief executive officer of the Cleveland Municipal School District, and Nicholas Scoppetta, former head of the New York City Administration for Children's Services, are national leaders in their fields. Others, like Gilbert Guzman, the late head of facilities management at an American Red Cross homeless shelter, built an equally lasting legacy within a smaller but no-less-valuable world.

We will also make note of some of the invaluable management and leadership literature that has helped us shape those experiences into a broader framework for others to use. As the stories in Parts 1 and 2 make clear, *our model is built through a number of simple, little things to do, constructed through an animating framework of daily commitment to how we each wish to be.*

Most leadership models begin with an outline of a paradigm and then explain its parts, helping connect them chapter by chapter. You will find that here, but not in the next chapter. As rich as we believe our paradigm to be, its usefulness as a tool of transformation must begin at an earlier point. If the goal of one's work is transformation—organizational and personal—we must begin with you.

24

IF THE WORK IS SACRED,
THEN SO ARE YOU

Sacred is defined as "worthy of esteem and reverence, often because of age and experience" (Berube, 1999, p. 973). What greater work is deserving of such esteem than caring for the ill, providing for the destitute, teaching the young, and providing safety for those at risk, whether neglected children or ignored elders?

There are many reasons why some people hold such work in far less than reverence. Some of those reasons can be partly explained in terms of social policy and shifting definitions of *deserving* and *undeserving* (Jansson, 2001; Trattner, 1999). Likewise, political and economic decisions on what is worthy of investment play a significant part in popular societal measures of value (Krugman, 2002; Phillips, 2003).

We briefly mention these broader contextual issues because they cannot be ignored by those seeking to transform our schools, child welfare agencies, mental health programs, and homeless services (Fabricant & Fisher, 2002). However, as our two stories make clear, these larger debates will be influenced, for good or ill, by the willingness of those who engage in this sacred work to toil each day in ways that, like any sacred act, inspire those touched by its presence. For that to happen, one must frame his or her work as Helen Jacques, Oliver Trumbull, and Marjorie Jessup do. And, as their daily struggles to remain open to genuine engagement in their day-to-day tasks make clear, such openness cannot happen if you do not see yourself as sacred, too.

The greatest challenge we have confronted as teachers, as consultants, and in our own lives has never been the lack of knowledge and understanding needed to improve ourselves. It has been the stubborn, perplexing, deep-seated unwillingness to personally change, even when confronted with overwhelming external evidence and internal desire to do so. Examples abound in every part of our lives and with those with whom we work. We each belong to a gym; Steve's is in Greenwich Village, and Willie's is in Harlem. Each January and again in May, the gym floors fill with new and eager members who set about pumping iron, running treadmills, and stretching calves. Having watched with alarm as they joined the 66.7% of adult Americans who are overweight (Centers for Disease Control and Prevention [CDC], 2009) and desperate to slim down, they are immediately noticeable for their intense efforts . . . and their disappearance 1 month later. Only 30% of all health club members continue going to the gym after 2 months, even when they spend upwards of a thousand dollars on a yearlong membership; less than half of that 30% rejoin the gym the following year. Why do so many people who clearly wish to change how they look and feel find themselves unable to do so?

It is no different in most organizational trainings. When we began our consulting work, our trainings—whether on leadership, team building, systems improvement, or cultural competency—uniformly received excellent ratings. We were thrilled, especially because participants rated our work so highly on its usefulness and applicability to their jobs. The thrill soon faded when we learned that our lessons almost never appeared back at the workplace after more than a week or two. *How could it be that people who learned from and found useful our new techniques on communications and building a winning team would not continue to use what made their own work more effective and easier to do?*

Where in your lives and where in your work does the commitment to being and doing manifest in ways that support both?

Frankly, our arrival at this distinction has come as a result of great personal and professional angst. As consultants, we find it so very rewarding to hear from an audience approving and knowing applause. People come up to us and share how much they are moved by our trainings and talks, and after years of doing this work as professors and consultants, we hear from many people who tell us how much our teachings have meant to their lives. And then there is a kind of gnawing knowing that talk is cheap.

Are we as committed to "being" and "doing," too? This question confronted us all over again in the spring of 2008. For the past 4 years, we have been on a roller coaster of sorts, bumping up against our internal rascals. For Willie, the struggle is saying no to every request for speaking, training, and facilitation. Steve's challenge shows up around the work—what do people want, what is the budget, and how can we get bigger?

For our partner Liz, the tumult is about the products. If a training session starts at 9 a.m., she is up at 4 a.m., unable to rest, going over in her head all of the logistics required to produce an exceptional event. This happens notwithstanding the fact that our trainings are met with rave reviews. And Ed holds the reins on the fiscal aspects of the business; hunkered down with paper and pen, he checks the figures once, twice, and then again, missing every opportunity to share his years of wisdom garnered from experiencing life from many corners of the world.

Our response to this external validation for our work and the internal strife/disbelief has been to emphasize the "imaginings" rather than focus on what is, as Oliver Trumbull did so well. "What is" is that we are consultants and professors with rewarding opportunities to make a difference in the lives of many people. People who are engaged in this work with us have begged us to stay the course and to honor its sacredness. For brief moments, we have been able to hold the sacred and revere the spaces where beleaguered workers arrive at the beginning of a 10-session training and leave as renewed individuals filled with passion for their work. Yet, not unlike Allison Smith, what has been all too constant for us is the mental anguish of "what we have and who we are is not enough."

Our first exposure to "being" as an organizational/leadership concept came in 1999 when one of us attended a 4-day session where people examined how their thoughts and verbal communications related to what showed up as reality in their lives. Tolle (2008) drew attention to our inability to remain in the present. In the forward section of the participant manual for our signature 10-session training is a reminder to participants: "Be here now." This is good advice; however, do not ask either of us how to do it easily!

So much energy in organizations, families, and relationships is spent in the past or in the future. It is so very difficult to be present right here, right now. *Being is not doing. It is neither embracing nor carrying.* It is becoming one with what is being carried or embraced. The implication of this is that, for each of us, "I am my vision."

We were "doing" meditation and physical exercise. It was practice. We were like a basketball team that has wonderful practice sessions and loses every game. Therefore, when our minds brought forward concern for the next contract, startup for a new training, an invitation to speak, or getting out a budget, all too often there was too little practice of mindfulness to enable us to recognize the illusions that had taken over the present (Zukav, 2006). "Being" requires a capacity to stay present, a real presence, right now. Have you ever noticed that the person you are speaking with really is not paying attention? He or she is not present, and you can no longer feel his or her presence.

Notwithstanding a library filled with books urging mindfulness, hope, and living in the present, powerful mental activity continuously took us over, and we wrestled in both conversations and alone in search of the magic that would make all of this go away.

There is no magic out there. Remember the people who show up at the gym every January wanting to drop 10 or 20 pounds. The end result is accomplished by a change in which the goal and the necessary steps to bring the goal into being become a part of the life like eating and sleeping.

A spirituality and healing weekend course provided the opportunity for an interesting exchange as to how trapped we can be by our own thoughts; "mindlessness" rules far more often than mindfulness. Two participants were working on an exercise to uncover their mental models and noticed that how they thought about a specific task in their life was affected by their thoughts. The participants were stuck and called Willie over for a consult. When he arrived, the following conversation took place. It illustrates how the mind plays tricks on us:

Participant 1:   "I need to clean my house."

Willie Tolliver: "How long have you been saying this to yourself?"

P1:   "Two years."

WT: "Is your house clean?"

P1:   "No."

WT: "So, how long will you keep this practice that has not resulted in the outcome that you want?"

P1:   "What do I do?"

The participant's statement, "I need to clean," was enough to assuage the mind. She could say it and then simply move on to the next thing that she needed to do. The net result? She ended up with a long list of things to do but none of the cleaning actually done.

Making a statement does not make the thing that we want come into existence. Action is required, and the energy needed to bring about the action is accessed by a number of steps.

Otto Scharmer's (2007) *Theory U* has been very helpful to us in our journey. The "U process" helps take people away from judgment, cynicism, and fear and provides them with new tools to open themselves up to transformation. This process conceptualizes human beings in relationship together as a social field, and as is true for a field—an expanse of land, that is—visible and invisible elements are critical to just how productive a social field is. A productive field requires the visible and invisible elements to work together and interact, both letting go of the past and working to create a new future . . . or not.

A potato farmer knows just how many years are needed to prepare a field to grow potatoes. He grows other crops in the field to prepare it for the prized potato crop. He knows that he cannot cheat on the formula.

What is the formula to prepare a social field of human beings for a high yield at harvest?

In the illustration from the spirituality and healing workshop, something at the invisible level is affecting the desired product—a clean house. When the invisible is finally in alignment with the visible, the desired outcome is produced. A farmer has to take care of the field. The same is true for a social field. Long conversations are required in which we make inquiries to understand each other and we harvest our conversations in order to have a record of our journey together and learn about the invisible elements of our group as a social field.

This work has brought us to the knowledge that our own struggle to commit to "being"—to trust ourselves—has emerged as our hardest work. We really are enough, and the accolades come to affirm that this is so. Our mistake has been to order our actions for the accolades. "Could we really be that good?" "People like us, and they want more of us."

Our struggles and challenges held us captive to an unending need for external validation, and this need kept us locked into saying yes to almost every request, diverting us farther and farther away from our purpose for being.

We began our journey as a group of friends out to make a difference in the lives of people who work with children. Now we know that the acknowledgments have little or nothing to do with our purpose for being. This knowledge frees us to pursue our real purpose and to make choices freely that further the realization of our reasons for being. Through such mindfulness, of course, the "doing" becomes richer still; "if the work is sacred, then so are you" slowly comes to be experienced.

The most difficult task in reframing how we live and work in our lives is not to see the glass as always full. *It is to believe that we are worth the struggle it will take each and every day to remain open to interpreting the world as rich in possibility and promise.* Oliver Trumbull realized he spent so much time living inside his head and measuring the past (half-empty) or hoping about the future (half-full) that he could not fully see what was right in front of him. That insight led him to have a wonderful day with his grandson . . . the "fullest" day of his life. Like the newest member of a gym, he thought that "first workout" with his grandchild was wonderful. The true challenge only took place the next day, when everything ached. *Then the challenge was to internally make the effort to value the day on its terms, pain and all.*

Oliver met that challenge by giving into it. By recognizing how hard it was to remain open, he placed himself within the sacred arc of his life's purpose by beginning each day with a pledge to care for himself—not for narcissistic pleasure but to reclaim his worth. For him, the small act of gardening reconnected him to the world in ways that gave balance and perspective to what lay ahead. Only then could he keep seeing the glass as full.

The person who gave us the title to this book was the late Gilbert Guzman. Guzman, who worked as the facilities coordinator for an American Red Cross homeless shelter, was a wise man who lived a profoundly simple life. Never bothered by the upsets around him, he focused on the tasks of the day so that care packages for clients and maintenance supplies were always on hand. Preferring gardening to long conversation, he let his acts of generosity speak for what was of value to him. He kept an immaculate and beautiful home and was rarely upset by others' intensity or frustrations, offering support through his quiet presence. When asked how he stayed so calm and unflustered, he smiled and spoke of "taking it a day at a time." When pressed as to what that meant, he thought for a while before responding. "I start each day thankful I'm here," he said. "I make sure I don't measure one thing too much against the other. You do that, and after a while the glass is always full."

Gilbert Guzman never made more than $35,000 a year, yet he died a far more fulfilled man than so many of the people with whom we work who make at least triple his salary. What made him special was his commitment to fullness on life's terms, to being satisfied regardless of what appeared at his door, whether at his home or at his office. What made his story extraordinary was his awareness that such a vow could be sustained only by his daily, personal effort to gain perspective before that door opened up.

Sacred acts usually imply ritual if they are to be sustained. As writers as recent as Thomas Moore (2002) and as ancient as Buddha and Moses emphasize, it is not possible to sustain belief, whether religious or secular, in universal transcendence without acknowledging its presence through some consistent act of consecration. In more formal religions, these acts are witnessed in churches, synagogues, mosques, and temples each day. In spiritual practices, they are found in such physical activities as yoga and meditation. If you seek personal and organizational transformation, you must find your own consecrated acts that bear witness to your value and your sacred work as well. Otherwise, transformation cannot occur, no matter how desperately you seek it.

At the end of this chapter, we lay out the tasks and activities you can use in creating your own sacred promise to your worth and your work. The tasks speak to the two domains neglected most by those who work with others: the physical and the spiritual. Graduate and postgraduate work, whether in business, education, or social work, overwhelmingly emphasizes intellectual development. Most trainings focus on learning new, results-based approaches to the organizational difficulties of managerial and professional life. We take such work as important—and present— in your development.

We also know that this exclusive emphasis on intellectual growth and managerial skill is insufficient to take on the more profound tasks of personal and organizational transformation (Bolman & Deal, 2001; Senge, 2006; Senge, Kleiner, Roberts, Ross, & Smith, 1994). We began to be aware of these limitations through our own consulting work, as trainees returned from their midday lunches happy with the morning lessons . . . and too sleepy to focus much longer. Taking a risk borne of our own personal experience, we introduced a silent 10-minute meditation into each training session. Trainee consternation at something so foreign to the training's results' focus gave way to one of our most eagerly awaited portions of the day, as trainees found themselves reenergized and capable of effort that previously was thought impossible. By spending a few minutes on restoring themselves, they restored their vigor to do the work ahead. Transformation will require no less.

What we mean by "starting before the beginning" is as subtle as it is simple. We are asking you to start the process of your transformation with an internal commitment—*a sacred promise to your own worth*—as the anchor from which your Personal Mastery will grow and develop. It is the Second Golden Rule for all of those who work inside human services, education, and health care: *Do unto yourself as you seek to do unto others.*

Only if you make this promise can you stay the course of what is required thereafter. *Such a promise is a pledge to stay grounded in an activity that, in a short while, you simply will not want to do.* Helen Jacques and Marjorie Jessup were excited to follow Oliver Trumbull's example, seeing its value throughout their lives . . . and then they were back to their old ways in a month. Like those of us who join and avoid gyms or attend trainings only to ignore the skills they teach, Helen and Marjorie initially failed to distinguish initial desire from genuine commitment. These two women could commit to the struggle for daily Personal Mastery only after they had grounded their lives in actions that each day acknowledged both the difficulty of their effort and the supreme value in their attempt.

It will be no less challenging for anyone who seeks to live seeing the glass as always full, for life does not show up brimming with only good news.

The great paradox underlining the Personal Mastery demonstrated by Oliver and Helen is that you need this sacred promise to yourself *because* you will fail—when irritation makes you fly off the handle at a close colleague, when the urge for that oversized bran muffin gets too great in the middle of your diet regimen, when you start judging yourself and others against imagined markers of accomplishment that exist more in your head than in an audit. Working to *rethink how we think*—perhaps the key outcome to Personal Mastery (Senge, Kleiner, Roberts, Ross, & Smith, 1994)—wouldn't be needed if we lived our lives only where we excelled, where we confronted challenges with ease and accomplishment in time.

But we do not. As Loehr and Schwartz (2003) wrote about people's difficulty in taking on the challenge of deep personal change:

> More often, [people's] self-deception is unconscious and provides short term relief while prompting long-term costs. At the most basic level, we deceive ourselves in order to protect our self-esteem—our image of who we are and wish to be. To keep at bay the truths that we find most painful and unacceptable—most notably the places in our lives where our behavior conflicts with our deepest values—we use a range of strategies. Drugs and alcohol can temporarily blot out uncomfortable feelings and provide the illusion of well being. *So in a similar way, do overeating, casual sex, and even seemingly harmless addictions such as workaholism and service to others.* "Every form of addiction is bad," wrote Jung, "no matter whether the narcotic be alcohol or morphine or idealism" [italics added]. (pp. 150–151)

It is only by recognizing and embracing this daily challenge to our erected self-esteem as a welcome part of our growth that we can embark on personal and organizational transformation. That it won't be easy doesn't make it any less compelling.

As adults working in service of and for others, we are so programmed to be averse to our own struggles that our strategies to avoid them become normal, everyday habits that undermine our pledge to ourselves. In the workplace, these strategies often play out based on how much formal power and authority we may or may not have. The most common strategic response from front-line staff to our challenges is personalistic fatalism (e.g., "I'm just that way," "I've tried to change, but I just can't," or "I've been this way for years, so get used to it!"). If we buttress these failures by holding on to what we do well, our internal measurement against success or failure will keep us permanently and worriedly focused on spillage from the glass. Fullness becomes an impossibility.

Those with some semblance of organizational power as executives or middle managers join the same personal fatalism with decision making that all too often wards off having to examine those mistakes and shortcomings at all. Rewarding those who ignore or cover up their mistakes, such managers and executives rationalize the inevitable organizational dysfunctions as the failures of either those who work beneath them or systems requiring adjustment. Seeing mistakes as only external in nature forces us to constantly and with frustration focus on how hard we are working to keep pouring water into the glass. Here, fullness is an illusion.

When these two strategies meet head-on inside an agency, a school, or a health facility, an organizational culture of reactive defensiveness on all sides results. Allison Smith's irritability and brusque demands joined with Gilsea Carrera's insecurity and defensiveness to create a toxic atmosphere again and again. The resulting impasse led to executive frustration and supervisee fear, with little or no change in the foreseeable future, even though both were motivated to do good work. Such an impasse can be broken only by making a pledge to see those moments of frustration and fear, of irritability and anger, as life's opportunities to grow more fully. As Oliver Trumbull said, it won't lessen the aches, but it will make them far more bearable.

By recognizing the limitations that life will bring forth to and from us each day, our sacred, daily commitment to our own worth frames each day as new and full as it is, *even when we fail.*

Because this is so difficult to master, that internal vow must simultaneously be joined with daily physical acts that connect you to those domains of your life that you are most likely to ignore at work—your spiritual and physical well-being. This is why Oliver gardened. Gardening, *joined with his internal commitment to see the world fully,* gave him the perspective—the Personal Mastery— to then go about his day open and able to take in and appreciate what it had to offer, whether aches and pains or the smile on his grandson's face.

The last section of this chapter covers the specific types of meditation and/or contemplation that anyone can easily do. (Subsequent chapters explain other kinds of exercises as well.) It is your choice to use our suggestions or to find others that are more meaningful to you. What is not a choice is whether or not to choose an exercise and frame it within your pledge to you and your sacred work. Likewise, you must commit to your physical well-being. Allison Smith, the hardworking and well-meaning executive in our first agency, placed her well-being at the bottom of her own commitments, rationalizing daily the extra doughnuts and bad coffee as all she could do to create energy, given how busy she was at the office. Such rationalization, *framed around a model of personal worth sacrificed for others,* exacted a great toll on her well-being . . . and her true effectiveness on the job.

A brief review of diet and wellness programs shows they each have unique properties. They also share three fundamental elements: drinking water, consistent exercise, and portion control over your food. The secret, of course, is that each of these habits builds off the others. The more we drink water, the less hungry we feel; the more we exercise, the less out of control we feel; the more we eat well, the better perspective we have on whether we are hungry for food or hungry to be fulfilled.

We have learned that you cannot ask people to do too much and expect the habits of a lifetime to be overcome—especially the habit of expecting immediate results from great effort. (That's why people join and quit so many health clubs.) Helen Jacques added walking to her agency staff's routine, just a mere half-hour a day. She provided water coolers in accessible areas for everyone. Whatever menus the agency had offered good food, period. And Helen modeled how she hoped to be. Our approach models what we have focused on in our trainings regarding all acts toward transformation. As part of your sacred pledge to begin your personal and organizational transformation, we ask you to do the following as part of your commitment to keeping the glass full:

1. *Add in; don't add on:* Whatever you do physically must be added in to your day, not on to it. Already-overstretched

people are likely to drop any new activities they take on. Add in walking each day to and from work or during a lunch break. By being part of your day, the new activity stands a chance of succeeding where other exciting and laudable add-ons do not.

2. *Practice consistency, not constancy:* Unlike the gym-rats-for a-month, commit to consistent efforts that show up over time, not an immense effort that fades with time. The most effective form of permanent weight loss has been found in those who walked every day, 365 days a year, rather than those who joined gyms and sweated through intense aerobic classes (CDC, 2009). By joining your commitment to your worth with a daily dose of physical activity, you increase the value of each, making you that much more prepared to meet life on its terms, not just your own.

3. *You don't have to do a lot, and you must do a little if transformation is to occur:* For the rest of this transformative paradigm to succeed, all you have to do is a little bit each day. And, if you don't commit to that, no lasting change will occur at all.

One final note here: Keeping the glass always full requires a commitment to oneself and to various daily practices that over time build the internal balance and perspective required to live fully and well in the world. To that end, there are countless practices, from the deeply religious to the clear-cut and mechanical, that can be found in every bookstore and across the Internet. In fact, googling any of the activities we describe at the end of each of the following chapters will locate hundreds—and at times thousands—of possible ways to develop personal inner balance and culturally aware, engaged leadership habits. It would be presumptuous of us to suggest that what we recommend at the end of each chapter is definitive to your particular needs.

With that understood, the recommendations we do offer have worked for us and the people with whom we work. You need not commit to more than a half-hour of additional activity a day, 7 days a week, for these activities to take root so that your leadership transformation can be sustained. In fact, once your transformation is maintained with regularity, far more time will be freed up in your day as energy is located and wasted time and anxiety are replaced with consistent engagement in the world around you, whether at home or in the office.

In short, no one practice is "the answer." Taken together, however, these practices help weave a more powerful and more reasoned way to live and act on improving your approach to leading—and living—in the world of which we are all a part.

We lay out our model in the next chapters. As you will see, it is framed within your personal commitment to your worth. As you can expect, it is filled with little things to do. By having committed to the daily struggle of how you deserve to be, the little things will become easier and easier to perform. After all, transformation, once truly begun, can't be stopped!

Commitment to Being

Meditation Exercises

Meditation is a technique millions use to help focus and calm the mind. Although meditation is often associated with religion, the practice of meditation does not have to be religious. The techniques used are designed to help people gain insight and to assess or manage the issues, whether very large (in the spiritual realm) or very small (do I want to buy that doughnut every morning?), of their lives. Meditation exercises may help people as busy as human service executives, principals, and managers reduce stress and recenter or refocus themselves in the midst of a tornado of to-do lists, concerns, and worries. Equally important, such exercises can be done alone and in the middle of your workday, before or after work, or before retiring for the night.

We will look at three times in the day when meditation may be most easily used: before breakfast, right before a demanding meeting or project deadline, and before going to sleep. Each serves a different purpose in realigning yourself to be in balance through the remainder of the day.

Before breakfast:

When you are in a good mood, the day ahead seems smooth; potential problems seem easily resolved, and pressing issues are not so difficult. This is an example of how much the attitude you adopt as you start the day has to do with how well your day actually turns out to be. If people wake up thinking how terrible the day is going to be or how large the mountain of paperwork is on their desk, they will be upset more easily by small events that occur over the course of the day. If people wake up with enthusiasm and happiness, they are less vulnerable to being upset by minor disappointments or setbacks. In short, they are less likely to feel stressed.

A meditation exercise helps you start the day in a strong and positive frame of mind. It can be done while still lying in bed after the alarm has gone off or between the time the snooze button was hit and the time the alarm goes off again. The steps for this exercise are as follows:

1. With your eyes closed, take a few deep breaths in through the nose and out through the mouth. With each breath, imagine your body getting stronger and healthier until it is radiating with powerful energy.

2. Imagine yourself standing in a beautiful place just after sunrise, such as the beach by the ocean or the top of a mountain. Feel the sun shining warmly and the breeze blowing all around you. Listen for the sounds that you would hear in this place as life all around you is waking up to another day.

3. Imagine yourself stretching your arms out to embrace the new day, claiming it as your adventure. Then imagine yourself speaking in an unusually deep, clear, and powerful voice as you state your intentions for the day despite any obstacles. For example, "No matter what happens today, I will maintain my sense of humor" or "No matter what this day may bring, I will not forget what is truly important in my life."

Take a moment to feel the effect of those words, and then begin your daily adventure!

(Continued)

(Continued)

Right before a demanding project or important meeting:

As anxiety builds before important meetings or activities, it can be helpful to do a meditation exercise that relieves stress rather than allows it to get worse as time ticks by. Getting stressed out will not help that meeting go better or the report be clearer, and it is often harmful. Therefore, people are encouraged to try a meditation exercise such as the following:

1. Close your eyes and take a few deep breaths, in through the nose and out through the mouth.

2. Imagine yourself at the top of 10 stairs that lead down to a door. Imagine yourself taking one step down toward the door. As you do, your body feels more heavy and relaxed, sinking gently into whatever chair you may be sitting in. With each step that you take toward the door, your body continues to feel heavier and more relaxed.

3. As you reach the door, you open it and step out into the most beautiful, relaxing scene that you can imagine. Perhaps you find yourself by a waterfall, in a cool forest, or in the best vacation spot that you have ever seen.

4. Spend a few moments soaking in the sights, sounds, textures, smells, and even tastes that you associate with this place.

5. Before coming back from this place, take something with you to give you strength and a reminder of this relaxing break from the worries of the day.

6. Come back through the door and climb back up those steps, feeling more refreshed and stronger with every step that you take.

7. Take a deep breath and open your eyes.

Prior to sleep:

Of course, not everything in the day goes perfectly. Our rascals— those people who challenge us the most in our lives or that issue that we never seem to get on top of—can and will show up to cause us strain and worry. They are often the very people or issues we think of before going to bed, thus triggering the stress we wish to avoid, which is the exact opposite of what the body requires in order to wind down and go to sleep. A meditation exercise can help people shift their attention from their racing thoughts to their hardworking body's need for sleep. The following meditation exercise may be done with soft music, nature sounds (e.g., a light wind), or a relaxation tape playing in the background.

Each step of this exercise can be done while lying in bed. The steps are as follows:

1. Close your eyes and take three deep, cleansing breaths. Focus on inhaling clean air and exhaling stale air.

2. Continuing to breathe deeply, spend a few moments focusing your attention on your toes. You will have fully focused your attention on this part of your body when you can mentally visualize the position of each toe. This in itself can be quite relaxing as attention shifts from the mind to the body. Imagine your toes are warm, limp, and relaxed.

3. Now focus your attention on your ankles. Imagine any knots or tension in your ankles loosening and unraveling, falling away as you continue to breathe in fresh, cleansing air.

4. Continue to spread this blanket of warmth and relaxation up over your knees, thighs, pelvis, stomach, and chest.

5. When you reach your shoulders, imagine massaging fingers working out the tension in your shoulders, upper arms, forearms, hands, and fingertips. Let those massaging fingers continue to massage up your neck, jaw, and cheeks until you feel completely relaxed from your cheeks all the way down to your toes.

6. Now imagine a cool facecloth over your forehead, soothing away any doubts, worries, or concerns that you may have.

7. Feeling relaxed from head to toe, continue to take deep breaths and remember that you can achieve this state of relaxation whenever you want to.

From Inner Balance to
Outer Energy: Diet and Exercise

There are more diet and exercise books sold in the United States each year than in any other country, yet as a people Americans have some of the worst levels of obesity in the world. Having read many of these books, as well as many Web pages on the subject, we found the simple and direct material offered by the Centers for Disease Control and Prevention's preventive health program (see http://www.cdc.gov/nccdphp/dnpa/) is straightforward in its simplicity and thoroughness.

Exercise

Regular physical activity is an important part of your commitment to yourself. Through effective weight control, you are creating more balance in your life as well. Physical exertion helps control your weight by using excess calories that otherwise would be stored as fat. Exercise also helps prevent many diseases and improve your overall health. Finally, exercise releases endorphins, those hormones that signal pleasure and relax the body . . . just what a busy executive needs to keep balance throughout the day.

Your weight is determined by the number of calories you eat each day minus what your body uses. Everything you eat contains calories, and everything you do uses calories, including sleeping, breathing, and digesting food. Any physical activity in addition to what you normally do will burn those extra calories.

Balancing the number of calories you expend through exercise and physical activity with the calories you eat will help you achieve your desired weight. The key to successful weight control and improved overall health is making physical activity a part of your daily routine. Like so many practices in this book, it is the consistency of modest effort (in this case, physical) that is needed for long-term effectiveness in maintaining a centered and reflective approach to your day.

What Are the Health Benefits of Exercise?

Research consistently shows that regular exercise, combined with sensible eating, is the most efficient and healthful way to control your weight.

In addition to helping control your weight, research shows that regular physical activity can reduce your risk for several diseases and conditions and improve your overall quality of life. Regular exercise can help prevent:

- **Heart disease and stroke.** Daily physical activity can help prevent heart disease and stroke by strengthening your heart muscle, lowering your blood pressure, raising your HDL ("good") and lowering your LDL ("bad") cholesterol, improving blood flow, and increasing your heart's working capacity.
- **High blood pressure.** Regular exercise reduces blood pressure in people with high blood pressure (hypertension).
- **Diabetes.** By reducing body fat, physical activity can help prevent and control Type 2 diabetes.
- **Back pain.** By increasing muscle strength and endurance and improving flexibility and posture, regular exercise can prevent back pain.
- **Osteoporosis.** Regular weight-bearing exercise promotes bone formation and may prevent many forms of bone loss associated with aging.

Regular physical activity can also improve mood and the way you feel about yourself. Exercise is likely to reduce depression and anxiety and help you better manage stress. Notice how many benefits related to your mental as well as physical well-being grow from your regular physical activity!

With so many evident benefits from exercise, it is always a question why we all don't do it more often. Recognizing this dilemma, it is important to keep our methodology's principles in place with exercise, too!

What Type of Exercise Is Best?

No matter what type of physical activity you perform—sports, planned exercise, household chores, yard work, or work-related tasks—all are beneficial. Choose those that are easiest to integrate into your day.

Over the past few years, ads for health clubs and exercise machines have targeted simplified exercise routines for weight reduction and maintenance. Some of these ads sell the belief that one machine will work your entire body and give you the results you need. However, many of these machines may be good for only one type of conditioning, such as cardiovascular; these machines also have limitations to the type of exercise you can do, and they are not good for everyone. To determine the best type of exercise program for you, talk to your doctor and a certified athletic trainer.

Furthermore, choose activities that will not force you to go far outside your daily routine: Don't join the fancy gym across town when the smaller one is two blocks away; choose to walk around the streets by your office after lunch each day rather than imagine you'll make it to the scenic park for a weekend jog that's 10 miles away. The hardest muscle to develop related to exercise is the mental resilience to act each and every day on behalf of your body and well-being.

How Much Exercise Should You Do?

Studies show that even the most inactive people can gain significant health benefits if they accumulate just 30 minutes or more of physical activity per day.

For the greatest overall health benefits, experts suggest doing 30 minutes of moderate-intensity aerobic exercise three or more times per week plus some form of anaerobic exercise, such as muscle strengthening activity or stretching, twice a week.

If you have been inactive for a while, you may want to start with such less strenuous activities as walking or swimming at a comfortable pace. Beginning at a slow pace will allow you to become physically fit without straining your body. Once you are in better shape, you can gradually do more strenuous activity. If you are seriously overweight or have not exercised in more than a year, start with 15 minutes of mild walking, and 2 months later, you'll be up to 30 minutes. If you start with too ambitious an approach, on the other hand, in 2 months you won't be exercising at all.

Aerobic exercise, or any activity involving large muscles done for an extended period of time, can promote weight loss, but it also provides cardiovascular benefits, improving and strengthening the heart and lungs. Examples of aerobic exercise include walking, biking, jogging, swimming, aerobic classes, and cross-country skiing.

Anaerobic exercise usually refers to resistance training and is done primarily for increased muscle mass. Weight training is a form of anaerobic exercise.

Moderate-Intensity Activities
That May Fit Better Into Your Day

Moderate-intensity activities include some of the things you may already be doing during a day or a week, such as gardening and housework. These activities can be done in short spurts—10 minutes here, 8 minutes there. Alone, each action does not have a great effect on your health, but *regularly accumulating 30 minutes of activity over the course of the day* can result in substantial health benefits. Please note that it's got to be a regular 30-minute daily activity, not a 3-hour weekend gardening adventure, that makes the difference.

To become more active throughout your day, take advantage of any chance to get up and move around. Here are some examples:

- Take a walk around the block.
- Rake leaves.
- Play actively with the kids.
- Walk up the stairs instead of taking the elevator.

- Mow the lawn or clean the floor.
- Take an activity break—get up and stretch or walk around.
- Park your car a little farther away from your destination and walk the extra distance.
- Get off the bus or subway a stop or two earlier than your actual destination.

The point is not to make physical activity an unwelcome chore but to make the most of the opportunities you have to be active.

25

THE TRANSFORMATIVE MODEL

As our two stories make clear, the most difficult tasks you face are less of what you do than of how you perceive yourself and what you do. What distinguishes Allison Smith from Helen Jacques over the course of the day are relatively few actions. Each woman holds the same meetings, writes the same grants, and tries to improve the same lives. What leads to such profoundly different outcomes has to do with the way each mentally frames herself and her interpretation of what the day holds. It is this difference—the difference between their mental maps (Senge, 2006)—that shapes the contours of their day.

What is a mental map? As Senge (2006) wrote, it is perhaps easiest to think about it as *how people go about thinking*. It's not just thoughts but the way we order and give meaning to those thoughts that helps define a mental map. For adults, long experienced in the ways of the world and confronted often with more thoughts and demands than one can address in a crisis-ridden day, examining one's own way of "how we go about thinking" is understandably a supreme challenge.

A mental map covers not only familiar terrain but also those areas different people may leave out or overemphasize when looking at the same territory. Why this matters so much can perhaps be best understood through the following example.

Put yourself in the place of a supervisor new to her job who has been invited by her executive to the country for a staff retreat. The executive is excited for her staff to make the trip because a new and scenic route has just been opened that she hopes will relax her staff so they arrive revitalized and ready to begin the retreat in a powerful and focused manner.

Now imagine, like that new supervisor, you are to take that trip from the city to Mountainside Resort for the first time. Once you get the directions, on the trip you focus only on them: Take the State Thruway, take Exit 18 to Small City, take County Road 44 to Route 209, turn left, and travel 6 miles. You arrive, slightly stressed but pleased to be there without a glitch. When your host asks you how the trip was, your mind frames the question in terms of the directions, not the scenic beauty along the route, the cute shops in Small City, or the lovely views of the mountains. The beauty and distinctiveness of the trip are not a part of how you think about answering the question; *how you frame the material you sift in your mind to answer the question* is based on a mental map emphasizing only markers and directions. *That the host is asking about the trip in terms of the route's beauty no more enters your mind than the markers and directions enter your host's.* Her question and your answer—"Fine," and you mean it: You saw all the markers, made all the turns, and reached your destination— are based on very different maps as to what matters in terms of enjoyment. Neither of you is aware of what the other is talking about. When the retreat begins and you and some of your colleagues are slow to get started, your executive host is frustrated: For the life of her she cannot understand why you're still frazzled. You, in turn, grow upset: You can't believe she's being so task oriented after such a stressful trip!

Even though the highway was designed along a very scenic route that the executive host had wished to share with her new staff, your thoughts overemphasized clear road signs and the destination itself *because the mental map inside your mind looked for and found very different things along the way.* Scenic beauty, the opportunity to see the new route as more relaxing and pleasurable while objectively present, was not seized upon because you never framed "beauty" in your mind as part of what the journey was about. The executive's desire for a new way of looking at things along the scenic route couldn't happen because the new staff's inner maps looked at the same trip in distinctly different ways from her own. The purpose of the retreat was undermined before it began. Cast across a longer route of executive reform inside agencies and schools, it is easy to understand why so many go awry—not because of the quality of the initiatives but because so many actors mentally interpret the work in such different ways from the start.

Allison Smith has the same mental map that she had when she entered the field: Work hard for people you care about, learn as you go, and deal with the messes that occur along the way. Her emphasis is on the markers along the way, whether compliance data or audits. That more rather than less mess has entered this hardworking woman's life propels her to work harder, drink more coffee, and live with increasing frustration regarding the people who work beside her. Lacking awareness of the rigidity in her mental map, she keeps trying to do good work from a half-empty glass.

Helen Jacques's mental map, on the other hand, has changed profoundly from when she first began her career. Because she recognizes the difficulty in "how you go about thinking," her *transformation begins with her commitment to herself each day so that she can acknowledge and embrace that challenge,* as developed in the previous chapter. From that commitment she incorporates daily physical and spiritual practices that allow her to keep the glass full by being able to work fully with whatever appears during the day, *especially those challenges that cause her the most struggle and difficulty.* For her to continue a process of organizational and personal transformation, she—and you—must adopt what Parker Palmer (1999) identified as the outermost extent of your community—the person or issue with which you are least comfortable and have the poorest alignment. It is within that arena of tension and conflict that your greatest growth and learning will occur.

By first grounding herself in her worth through her own physical and spiritual well-being, Helen would be prepared for the difficulties of a road trip to a mountainside resort. She would know she would otherwise miss the scenic beauty as well as some of the roadside markers.

Facing the reality of that daily struggle to remain open to how you think and act is a key to your and your organization's transformation. It is not another variation of how to live with less. It will, of course, at times cause discomfort. Who likes to address what he or she does worst? How can you stand to keep looking at where your mistakes occur, where you stand not in alignment with a colleague but in unending, seemingly normative friction? This is why the day begins with a commitment to your worth, consecrated daily through physical and spiritual activity. Joining new, daily behaviors to powerful and affirming thoughts then frames what "shows up" over the day—what life will require of you that day—and allows you to move forward positively with openness to fully engage in whatever may occur.

Only by recognizing that you must ground yourself fully in daily physical acts that become part of your ritual of self-renewal—spending time in a mediation room after seeing a stressful client, going for that walk after lunch, your morning of contemplation and meditation—can you be prepared to *confront and appreciate* the conflicts and dilemmas that will be part of your work with the poor, those at risk, and the isolated.

Another way to understand what transformation requires is to look at the difference between what the occasional "weekend warrior" must do and what a serious athlete must do in order to perform at the highest levels of his or her sport. For the occasional pickup basketball player or twice-a-week tennis player, there is probably a little stretching before the game at hand, 10 minutes of practice (whether shooting hoops or hitting serves), and then beginning to play. Afterward, a hot shower and a little salve for the aching joints probably follows a postgame lunch or round of drinks, complete with a review of missed and made shots. Perhaps commitments are made for another game later that week, as well as declarations for personal improvement. Each performance is more or less the same as the last.

For the serious athlete, *the last part of his or her performance is the competition itself.* What precedes his or her entry into the game are two preceding activities that have gone on long before an actual game is played: conditioning and training. Interestingly enough, coaches find that the greater the level of athletic competition (where inherent natural talent of the players is uniformly high), the more important conditioning and training become. Conditioning, like transformative commitment discussed above, is year-round. It is focused on how a great athlete prepares his or her body and mind for eventual performance. It is a daily commitment to addressing one's entire physical self so that later training and game-day performance will go well. It may require particular emphasis on a previously identified deficit (speed, arm strength, agility), but the overall focus is framed on preparing to perform, not performance. For us, conditioning is the equivalent of our daily commitment to ourselves to be prepared to address the challenges that lie ahead.

Training is where athletes practice what they have prepared for, specifically performing as if they were in an actual competition. In many ways, it operates as the physical embodiment of what Senge et al. (1999) suggested people do in order to expand their mental maps—change how they go about thinking. As the real game is only simulated during training, games stop at decisive moments where players are instructed on how to alter and improve their approach to a particular aspect of their performance: a better pivot from which to throw the ball to first base, for example, a slight turn to the left when rushing the net to return a tennis volley, or the practice of the pick-and-roll as players drive to the basket.

True greatness on the playing field most often occurs among those athletes who commit to mastering their mistakes, again and again, before the real game begins. So it is for transformation in one's personal and organizational life. Your daily personal commitment to your worth, consecrated in physical and spiritual preparation, is your conditioning.

Your training is committing to adjust your own mental map each day to stay open inside yourself so that you can fully embrace what will arrive, whether clients in distress, workers who don't perform, or a grant that has, in fact, been funded. Having practiced your own pivot, you too can make the play. And unlike the gifted athlete, who at best performs only a fraction of the year, you are playing every day of the week.

What you see in Figure 25.1 is an image of our transformative model. Encircling the entire figure is your daily commitment to your worth, consecrated through physical and spiritual activity. *This sacred commitment in turn influences the mental map that encompasses but does not encase the "little things" that permeate and give shape to the worthiness of your day.* These things are what you and all employees in an agency or a school must do, for better or for worse: Communicate with others, improve systems, carry forth a vision, handle diversity, and build community. The competencies these tasks require are no different than they have been for decades. Both Allison Smith and Helen Jacques must do them all. They—and you—are in the "game" that public and nonprofit services and schools demand of their leaders and teams every day. Those tasks have been decided by the playing field you have entered. What has not been decided are the choices of fullness you will or will not make.

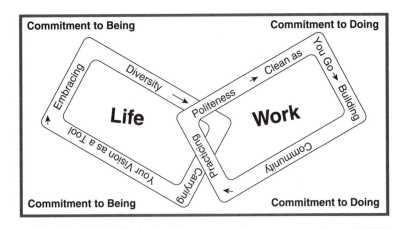

Figure 25.1   A Model of Personal and Organizational Transformation

As Helen's story and our model suggest, making the choice to see the glass as always full alters the meaning of those actions because each of them, while minor in scope, is now fraught with the potential for ongoing meaning and lasting legacy. As the famous Buddhist story goes, "A wise man approached two men who were hard at work, busily cutting stones. He asked them what they were doing. The first looked at him angrily and growled, 'What's it look like I'm doing? I'm cutting stones!' The second replied, his voice filled with happiness, 'I'm helping build a magnificent cathedral!'" (We need not ask which was named Smith and which Jacques!) It is up to each of us to carve our own responses to these tasks. As our next chapters on "doing" will spell out, cleaning as you go, practicing politeness, carrying your vision, embracing difference, and building community each can also have an animated, transformative power in the special way you and those around you come to view those demands.

At the same time, Figure 25.1 makes clear that these actions are not linked hierarchically, as if one action must precede another. They instead are woven through the day, with shifting degrees of duration and emphasis as the day's events unfold. Taken together, they weave an infinite configuration that joins them through the active choices you make to see them as new examples of why the glass is always full. Sometimes that fullness will be based on the joy of a client's or a student's success. Other times that fullness will be expressed through your own internal effort to meet a challenge caused by your own mistakes and miscues, whether missed appointments, a moment of irritability and anger, or failure to follow through. As the inner circles connecting these actions suggest, lifework—the carrying forth of your daily commitment to seeing the glass as always full as you engage in these tasks—goes on within them all, no matter the hardship *or* the success. As Austin and Hopkins (2004) documented elsewhere on learning organizational culture, by consciously joining your own effort to your agency or school's events, personal and organizational transformation will continue together through the day, every day.[1]

We will now show you how others have gone about their own work of personal and organizational transformation.

The Commitment to Doing

As with your commitment to how you will be in the world, your commitment to doing requires the development of small behaviors applied to large habits that will later determine how much you get done each day, the way you approach your work and that of your team, how you are remembered by others, and the leadership shadow that you cast. Those actions are *carrying your vision, practicing patience and politeness, embracing diversity, cleaning as you go, and building community.* Each is told through the stories of remarkable men and women and their "small" actions that came to have a very significant influence on their transformative leadership.

Note

1. Austin and Hopkins (2004) documented literature that suggests four dimensions to a transformational leader that will be found in our following examples: (a) idealized influence (high standards and a commitment to excellence); (b) inspirational motivation (people who communicate expectations in ways that motivate others); (c) intellectual stimulation (creative coaching that rethinks issues, seeks reflection and not just reaction, and has a willingness to approach old problems in new ways); (d) individualized consideration (people pay attention to each person's need for achievement and growth through ongoing, constructive feedback and coaching).

26

CARRY YOUR VISION AS A TOOL

Nicholas Scoppetta, former commissioner of the New York City Administration for Children's Services and present head of that city's fire department, is a powerful man, with great influence over the city's affairs. When he was commissioner of the country's largest child welfare agency (8,000 workers serving 40,000 children and families, with a $2.1 billion budget), he was known to have direct access to New York's mayor, Rudolph Giuliani, and a guarantee that child welfare reform would remain at the center of the city's reform efforts throughout his administration. Spearheading an unprecedented reorganizational effort that had both national interest and intense involvement of such influential foundations as the Annie E. Casey Foundation, as well as Mayor Giuliani's commitment of $562 million for the new agency, he brought in and promoted some of the best and brightest talent in the child welfare field, including future commissioners William Bell and Linda Gibbs. When he spoke, significant players across the city and nation sat up and listened.

But none of this is what truly impressed us about Scoppetta. Far more remarkable was the degree to which the line staff in his agency sat up and listened as well. We worked with more than 2,000 line supervisors and managers in child welfare throughout the duration of the Scoppetta administration. When we began, early in his tenure, we were confronted with the traditional cultural response of public sector employees to their new boss: "Reform? Sure. Whatever. He'll be gone soon, and we'll still be here. We'll wait these 'reforms' out, too." This staff response of immense caution and resistance to change was borne of years of commissioners coming and going, their reform plans begun and later scrapped, their initial stated commitments flagging with shifts in the mayoral winds of public opinion.

But a funny thing happened with Scoppetta. He didn't leave. He didn't want to leave! He actually addressed the rumor of his imminent departure—first heard about a year into his 7-year tenure at one of our training's graduations. "I hear there are a few people who think I'm leaving soon," he calmly addressed the crowd of 200. A notable nervous tension ran through the audience as its members waited for his announced exit. "Why would I leave? I didn't take this job to do it halfway. . . . This is about the children, not those of us on this stage. . . ."

A surge of energy went through the room again, this time far more positive. Scoppetta continued to speak, weaving into his announcement examples of work he had heard about in various trainees' earlier speeches. The rest of his speech contained two themes. The first and more complex one related to various managerial mandates and reforms that were moving ahead under reform plan initiatives. The other, more simpler theme was his vision: that the children of New York, especially the most vulnerable, would be safe and secure under his—and his staff's—watch.

His vision was a tool to make those otherwise complex mandates remain alive for everyone in the room. He had rooted that vision in himself personally, staking claim to values that mattered regardless of the type of mandate: court-ordered compliance data, timely visitations of families, assessments of children at risk. What was startling to his line staff was his personal stake in what happened to the children under his and their care.

His commitment was in part borne from his own stay in the child welfare system as a young child. But a valuable commitment doesn't necessarily translate into the concreteness and specificity that make it real to line staff who only occasionally come in contact with an executive. Staff believed Scoppetta's vision because it appeared in forms that embodied that commitment: a thoughtfully designed children's center for those entering the system emphasizing colors, size, and scale that appealed to children, explaining the importance of immediate actions on behalf of children in terms of a child's perspective on time (where a month of separation in a young child's life is an extraordinarily long period of time).

To be a usable tool for the work you do, a vision must contain three parts:

- It must be rooted in values that matter to you.
- Those values must be expressed in a concrete, actionable form.
- They also must show an engaged relationship between you and others.

As with Frankie Lee Chan and his story about "Smithie" in Vietnam, a vision is best rooted in a story from your own life that expresses all three elements. In this way, it is possible for your vision to be incorporated into the presumably minor things of the day as it is "added in" throughout your work.

Because Scoppetta's vision was a tool to be used to make the actual work better, he wasn't afraid to include it in directly addressing points of longstanding organizational resistance ("He's leaving, so we don't have to buy in"), as well as in the complicated professional realignments embedded in redesigning such unique child welfare procedures as 72-hour investigations or family-to-family conferences. *In doing so, he forced others to rethink their own commitment to their vision as well.* The result was a surge of enthusiasm and interest in his reforms that had not happened before.

By seeing his vision as a tool, Scoppetta did what Robert Heifitz (1994) identified as a hallmark task of true leadership:

> [He] create[d] a guide to goal formation and strategy [within the agency's work environment and] . . . in doing so . . . consider[ed] not only the values that the goal represents, but also the goal's ability to mobilize people to face, rather than avoid, tough realities and conflicts. (p. 23)

Scoppetta did not use his vision unattached to the work. *It was a part of it* and the enormous reform plan he and his executives initiated. It was thus possible for others to see this vision appear in what they did as well. The resulting alignment between executive leader and front-line staff was based on a unity that previously had not been experienced deep within the agency. Using your own vision as a tool to do the work may take practice, but Scoppetta's example shows that it can and does happen.

Because he was clear in his vision as well as the results that he expected to accomplish, Scoppetta carried the twin responsibilities of an executive well: managing and leading. However there is one fundamental difference between managing and leading that makes developing your own vision all the more important: A manager requires a stable and resourceful work environment to be fully effective; management is an externally focused position. A leader, on the other hand, may or may not thrive under stability and a resource-rich environment because a significant part of his or her effort is *internally focused on the vision* he or she is putting in place. Scoppetta kept his vision in his work whether with aligned fellow executives or doubtful line workers.

To use more historical examples on leadership, historians uniformly rank only three presidents as "great": George Washington, Abraham Lincoln, and Franklin D. Roosevelt. Likewise, Martin Luther King is recognized as our nation's greatest civil rights leader. All four were leaders during times of our nation's greatest instability. *Their leadership greatness did not happen because of the stability and plenty in their external worlds.*

The challenge of leadership is never one of external resources; that is primarily a management issue. As Heifitz (1994) wrote regarding leadership in unstable times, when "answers" are not easy:

> Leaders [in crisis] have to address and diminish the gaps between the values people stand for and the reality they face . . . it requires leaders to [help others] create a change in values, beliefs, or behavior. They help expose and orchestrate conflict—internal contradictions—within individuals and constituencies that can provide the leverage for mobilizing people to learn new ways. (p. 22)

These four men's visions began to appear in what they were *doing* even while others did not accept or believe in them. Washington had to convince America's new citizens that he would neither be the king they wanted nor simply administer to the 13 separate republics they desired. Lincoln never lost sight of "one nation, undivided" even when significant segments of his cabinet were decidedly less certain. In 1932, Roosevelt began his presidency with the nation's first federal deficit, huge unemployment, skyrocketing inflation, and business advisors drawn from the same set that Herbert Hoover had used. King had to convince a nation of the rightness of his cause of racial equality well before most White Americans knew there was a problem.

In short, both the objective circumstances and people's perceptions of "what could be done" were so out of alignment between executiveship and membership that management techniques alone would have failed these four men. As with Scoppetta and his line staff, the gaps between Washington, Lincoln, Roosevelt, and King and their followers began so chasmlike that managing the crises alone would have changed little.

What allowed them to not only survive but also thrive as leaders was their internal vision of what the world was and could be. It was this internal vision, used as a tool to moor them to what they truly wished to accomplish, that kept them both part of and removed from the environment around them as they went about their work. Day-to-day tasks were managed. And, often unbeknownst to those with whom they worked, elements of that vision would begin to appear in the way those tasks were carried out.

This internal capacity to use their vision as a tool allows leaders to be fully engaged in the world as it is while never succumbing to all its pressures, demands, and short-term expectations. On the small stage of our story, Oliver Trumbull made certain that flowers appeared on staff desks each week and that his gardens were looked after through the seasons as markers of beauty for all to enjoy. King preached his message of bracing but compassionate love from within the confines of the Birmingham jail and on the world stage in front of the Washington Monument. Security guard or national leader, these men's visions took concrete form regardless of the circumstances around them.

Developing this inner strength to use your vision in what you do is important, for you must remember something else about these great leaders. At the start of—and often throughout—their tenure, many of those around them thought them failures or soon-to-be failures. King was seen as a vacillating figure by many activists inside the civil rights movement (Branch, 1989). While he was a war hero, Washington's commitment to his federal vision so enraged Jeffersonians that Thomas Paine wished him to leave his presidency in a pine box (Ellis, 2004). Lincoln was viewed within his own cabinet as weak and indecisive, so much so that some considered opposing him for the presidency in his second term (Kearns Goodwin, 2006). Roosevelt was considered shallow and "intellectually unfit" for years by the majority of the nation's editorialists (Schlesinger, 2003).

Their success as leaders emerged with so much power later because people reinterpreted their earlier actions as signs of greatness rather than weakness or indecision. Because the leaders' inner vision began to be more and more externally recognized, the people around them had a "paradigm shift" in how the world could be: civil rights for all Americans, a federal nation, a reunited country, a revitalized economy . . . or a child welfare agency that truly made a difference in the lives of children.

Remarkably, over time each of them gained far more authority than others around them—many of whom were seen as "more effective" in the short run—because they were always leading even while they managed. By *being centered within,* they could allow their internal vision to take shape a small "bit and a piece" at a time until the emerging picture shifted to an entirely new view.

One need not be as famous as a president, our nation's leading civil rights figure, or the head of a $2.1 billion child welfare agency to work with a transformative vision that inspires others.

We have used the legacy icebreaker that Helen Jacques referred to early on as her initial inspiration for change with thousands of people. With just one exception (the nationally recognized former president of Morehouse College), every person named has been a modest figure: a homemaker, a cabinet maker, a grade school teacher, or a front-line supervisor. The people Helen mentioned to Nick Costello are based on real men and women: Otis Bledsaw Crawley, beloved grandfather of Roger Newman, commissioner of the New York City Mayor's Office of Veterans' Affairs; Wilfreda Peterson, the stern and inspiring teacher to Melanie Atkinson, grade school teacher; and Richard Harrey, skilled craftsman and house intellectual to Rodney Pride, child welfare executive.

While created in smaller venues, their legacy through their vision that others embraced as their own has been truly lasting. People remember these men and women so clearly—and with such emotion—because their mentors carried their vision in their concrete interactions. The *joining of a genuine value stance with what they did with others* left a powerful imprint far after the actions were over. What more profound legacy could one leave?

Carrying your vision into what you do turns it into a tool that grows more finely honed with time. Scoppetta did not overly dwell on his vision as child welfare commissioner. He rarely spoke at length, if at all, about his own past inside child welfare. *He lived it through what he did, asking and inspiring others to join him.* In a very different context, so did Roger Newman's grandfather Otis Crawley as he sat in his wheelchair during a long summer many, many years ago. His grandson had been forced to spend time with him because he, too, was house ridden (albeit with childhood asthma). Young Roger, a vital boy of 7, laid low by the painful constriction in his chest, would grow frustrated as he imagined his friends outside playing without him. At the lowest point of his young life, he soon found time with his aged grandfather a surprising place of consolation. Instead of sharing in the bitterness of his own confinement, Otis shared stories of hope and excitement that fired young Roger's imagination.

Without knowing it, the little boy was being told fishing stories that joined patience with the pursuit of excellence, stories of taking his time to bait a hook the right way to guarantee the trophy waiting for him in the nearby pond. By holding to his own integrity of excellence even at his most physically challenged, Otis inspired his grandson to live a life of integrity borne of patience and trust in others, even as his own sharply limited circumstances might have dictated otherwise. The frailties of old age that left the elderly Otis in a wheelchair did not deter him from acting on his vision. Whether in an overcrowded school or a service agency facing another round of cuts, you can do the same.

What follows are concrete activities to help you develop your vision. Others will be found at the end of each chapter that follows. As we make clear throughout the book, these activities and those that follow are to be done over time, as you move consistently through the day. Some will be easier to do than others; some you already do; others will require genuine effort to remember. There is no linear order to them; there *is* an expectation that these kinds of activities will occur throughout the week.

Likewise, as with the activities we mention above related to meditation, diet, and exercise, for every activity we describe here, countless others are as worthy. *What is important is that they be framed within the transformative model we have created, using these practices in a daily, circular, and open-ended approach that keeps alive your commitment to being and doing throughout your life as the sacred acts that they are.*

Carry Your Vision as a Tool Exercises

Developing your own vision as to how you wish to be remembered and embodying it in concrete terms so that it is usable and actionable takes practice. Anyone can say he or she has a vision. It is far harder—and far more important—to be able to translate that vision into the concrete actions of the day, both in words that resonate with others and in the small actions that deepen the meaning behind those words. What follows is a clear exercise to help you develop a vision that you, too, can carry in your pocket.

Personal Reflection Exercise

In what ways are you leading and not just managing at work?

_____

_____

_____

In what area of your work are you most able to hold an internal vision of "what is and could be" that connects to your core values, even when times are difficult?

_____

_____

_____

"What is and could be": What is your present state of leadership, and what is the desired state you want to see emerge?

_____

_____

_____

Core values to your vision (list at least three):

_____

_____

_____

How do you express these core values concretely through actions and behaviors that others can identify? For example, how do you associate "excellence"? How do you associate "support"?

_____

_____

_____

Reflect on these distinctions as you go about your work over the coming weeks ... and in fact, for a lifetime! Please keep them "handy" so that you can refine them as you test them in the real world.

(Continued)

(Continued)

One of the most profound challenges in leadership is to reflect on and draw the inner strength from that vision so that you can bring these qualities into all parts of your life and work, rather than a few.

Your Most Important Teacher or Mentor Exercise:

One of the ways you can become clear on your own vision is to remember your most significant mentor or teacher. Take a minute to reflect on him or her and why he or she remains so important to you:

Name of teacher or mentor:

_____

Why he or she remains so inspiring to you:

_____

_____

Values he or she embodied (attach a concrete behavior to each value):

_____

_____

_____

Real leaders, whether family mentors or presidents, grade school teachers or charismatic national figures, do more than keep their vision. *They use it as a tool to shape how they act upon the world.* That others may not notice it until later does not mean it is not always present. Often, only upon reflection do others realize its presence.

This is why a leader is also a coach. With his or her vision as a tool, a leader builds reflective capacity in others, even as the work is getting done in the humdrum beat of everyday life. This is why it is so important for your vision to be crafted as a tool as well.

Your Vision as a Tool Matters
Most When Things Are at Their Worst

As a tool, your vision is accessible to you to use as you go forward, pulling it out of your tool kit when roadblocks occur, when others are stymied, when the reasons for "keepin' on keepin' on" seem most distant. Like your own identified mentor or teacher did, you will find *its value as a tool greatest when times are difficult, not when they are easy.* That's why it is so important for each member of your team to have your vision at the ready.

Sometimes one's vision becomes a useful tool in situations outside of work, even seemingly minor ones. For example, your vision of a "perfect vacation" keeps you motivated when you get hit with roadblocks along the way: When the plane arrives late and you miss your connection, you don't go off to another destination. You "keep on" problem solving and seeking a solution because the "perfect vacation" is tied to the images at your destination, whether a relaxing beach, a thrilling mountain view, or a breathtaking cathedral. You don't give up and go somewhere else. The vision holds you there, seeking answers that may not be immediately present.

Even as your frustration grows when your hotel loses your reservation, you don't give up: You resent the confusion, but you refuse to let the hotel's problems "ruin your vacation." You get the hotel to figure out a new solution for you and those you're with.

Why? Because the image of what matters is not tied to the plane or the hotel but the actual destination and what it means to your definition of "a perfect vacation." It is a mix of the outcome and the values you associate *concretely* with that outcome—the spiritual beauty you find in a religious place, the relaxation the beach creates, the vigor of the mountain trail itself.

The roadblocks along the way are still roadblocks, and roadblocks cause tension and irritability but do not define what matters. *You have used your vision of what matters for that perfect vacation to keep you on track to arrive and to not let the obstacles ruin your 2 weeks.*

Your vision has served as a tool that balances your perspective without denying the need to keep pushing ahead, frustrations and all. Without that, the obstacles become the focus and the vacation gets ruined, even when you finally arrive.

It is the same regarding your vision of yourself and the work you do within child welfare. The obstacles are many and daily, the frustrations real. Without a vision that seeks to locate the important parts of one's vision in one's work, an executive, a manager, or a supervisor can only operate on the obstacles. Over time, those obstacles become almost insurmountable. They also frame the focus of work. Who can remain inspired by that?

A leader does not deny the obstacles (and their frustrations). But it is at the point of the obstacles that the vision becomes an invaluable tool—what is then pulled out to keep the leader going.

"Ensuring the safety and well-being of the child," when deepened by your own values and deepest commitments as a human being, turns your concrete work into true legacy building even when the work has been the hardest.

It is in this way that you lay the basis for the legacy you are leaving tomorrow. Like your mentor, you will be remembered far more for the way you handled day-to-day work and its demands than for spoken pronouncements or occasional acts of greatness.

If you wish to be well remembered tomorrow, your reflective practice today will determine whether that will be so.

27

PRACTICING PATIENCE
AND POLITENESS

In the 50-plus years of Hunter College School of Social Work history, there have been just three "standing-room-only" retirement parties at its social work school. Two were for retiring deans, complete with major figures from the city university system, city agencies, and the social work profession. Only one, however, had every member of the social work school community in attendance: the retirement gala for Esther Rohatiner, supervisor of the school's word processing unit. Typist extraordinaire, massager of academic egos, reader of penned hieroglyphics, and unruffled respondent to all immediate priorities and unforeseen grant deadlines, this sweet, unassuming lady managed to be admired by every member of a community in which uniform admiration was rare indeed.

"I just do what my mother taught me, years ago. She said 'always be polite to your elders.'" The 60-plus woman laughed. "I just make believe everyone is an elder, even if they're 20 years younger!"

But don't confuse politeness with acquiescence. Asked about those academics who come to her with their last-minute requests each and every time, she replied, "First I ask them when it's really due. Sometimes people come in all upset, so I just try to calm them a bit. I try not to get ruffled. That doesn't do anybody any good. If I can help them relax, the work for both of us goes smoother."

Behind Rohatiner's politeness are two other "Ps": patience and perspective. She embodies what Ryan (2003) discussed in her work *The Power of Patience:* "That calm inner steadiness in the face of what might otherwise annoy us is the gateway to empathy, the capacity to be aware of the feelings of others . . . 'enough calm and receptivity so that the subtle feelings from another person can be received'" (p. 45). Like Senge's (2006) Personal Mastery capacity for holding creative tension, this master typist maintained her patience in the face of others' anxiety because she worked with a calming focus, rather than a reactive tension, on what she wanted to create with others. In being able to respond nicely to others' torrent of words and requests that would otherwise intensify both needs and demands, her polite focus on what needed to be done calmed generations of grant writers and scholars made frantic over looming deadlines.

Not that she has lived a work life of equanimity. A former work mate drove Rohatiner to distraction through his unfocused, disinterested approach to the job. After a few fruitless attempts to modify his performance through example and appeals to share their workload equitably, she decided, aware that job protections insulated him from supervisory mandates, on a far more effective course of action: She changed herself. "I realized he would never change. I wasn't going to fight with him; he would have loved that. It would have been another excuse not to do the work. So I put up a large calendar over the window separating us so I couldn't see him fooling around anymore. As soon as I did that I stopped being upset. Why waste all that energy on what I can do nothing about? It made it so much easier to do my job."

Rohatiner's wisdom focused on her energy and its impact on her performance. Like so many behaviors people note as "special," her politeness stemmed from an inner capacity to seek equilibrium and balance, especially in the face of adversity. As she related, she sought ways to find the patience within herself to return to the politeness she had been taught years and years ago by her mother.

In her modest, unassuming way, Rohatiner modeled a fundamental quality of leadership that Bennis (2003) identified years ago: "a desire to live as a fully integrated human being" (p. 16). She did not waste time, energy, and resources in a protracted battle to change the unchangeable (somebody actively disinterested in and protected from changing his work habits) or lower her own standards of performance through workplace gossip or grumbling impatience with others' demands. Rohatiner instead focused on what she could change so she stayed true to how she wanted to be. Her Personal Mastery of *expanding her inner capacities to hold to her own vision regardless of external forces* maintained her remarkably personable and supportive style with those whom she served. Rohatiner unfailingly practiced politeness with others because she developed the patience to stay true to who she wanted to be.

Of course, it could be argued that politeness and the patience it requires in the face of adversity are more qualities of disposition and temperament than they are acquired habits. In fact, as books like *Vital Lies, Simple Truths* (Goleman, 1996) and *Chained to the Desk* (Robinson, 1998) suggest, the higher one goes up the organizational chart, the more such qualities encumber rather than enrich one's effectiveness. The truth, however, is perhaps the opposite. Being a "fully integrated human being" with a lasting legacy doesn't emerge from a lifetime of irritable—and irritating—exchanges with others. As Ryan (2003) wrote, "Patience is a human quality that can be strengthened. . . . We're just not always aware of what helps, . . . what triggers our impatience, or what to do when our patience runs out" (p. 7).

In fact, developing the qualities of politeness and patience can and does occur among powerful executives . . . if they choose to do so. In some ways, it is as admirable to see this effort among executives as it is among those lacking formal authority like Rohatiner *because* executives have enough external power to ward off internal personal examinations for self-improvement. Why take on what might be an uncomfortable internal process of changing ingrained habits when nobody who works for you will dare to complain in the first place? What Helen Jacques lamented—that the hardest part of the struggle to change was within herself, taking on new practices that weren't comfortable—are the words we have heard echoed time and again by powerful executives with too much to do and no external demand to change. It is very, very easy for such people not to bother to look inward at all.

But some do. In fact, we have often found that the more consistently successful the executive is, the more open he or she is to improving those subtle areas of performance that may never show up on a yearly outcomes spreadsheet but are fundamental to his or her lasting legacy. One who has done so is Linda Gibbs, the present New York City deputy mayor for human services, formerly the commissioner for homeless services and considered the city's most successful homeless services commissioner in more than a generation. When we first met Gibbs, she was Scoppetta's deputy commissioner for policy and planning at the Administration for Children's Services. Brilliant, hard-charging, and unafraid to push the commissioner's agenda, she had a powerful impact on anyone she worked with. That in itself wasn't surprising: What powerful executive doesn't have impact?

Nobody would have called her patient, including herself. Many people from outside the agency were intimidated by the very mention of her name. However, we saw that the closer someone on her staff worked with her, the more loyalty she created. In fact, any time she had direct presence with people, the warmth of her personality and personal concern for others' well-being softened the laserlike clarity she brought to often contentious and conflictual reforms underway across child welfare services. The problem she confronted was not that she lacked such personable qualities; it was that many others didn't know they existed.

The result was that at times her laserlike intensity could create its own tensions, especially with those whose programs would be changed significantly by her focus. It became clear that the further they were removed from her personal presence, the more intimidated and resistant some child welfare actors would be to needed reforms.

The revolution that Scoppetta and his first lieutenants had underway in child welfare had to cause upset from tradition-bound agencies unchanged in years. Because of his established reputation and closeness to Mayor Rudolph Giuliani, the commissioner was more difficult to attack. Easier to criticize was a younger woman who had moved over from the Office of Management and Budget. While she had the inner strength to deflect criticisms' sting and the external support of her boss to maintain her focus, it was an added burden to carry a fearsome reputation into her daily encounters across the child welfare world.

People with the degree of power Gibbs has can choose an easy response to such a reputation: Ward off the short-term dissonance by becoming fiercer still. After all, it's easy enough to locate the "problem" in others not quite as smart and not quite as quick as you are, especially if in the end they must defer to the formal authority of your office. Such people are replete in human services and education, going on to retire with lavish dinners, heartfelt speeches, crystal bowls, and a legacy that lasts all the way to the door.

But Gibbs decided to choose a different path, one that is all the more admirable because it was not easy *and* she didn't have to walk it. Informed that a significant part of people's perceptions of her "intimidation" was a function of whether or not they had had personal contact with her, Gibbs initially responded, like Helen Jacques to Gloria Samuels, with consternation. The simple fact was that the "campaign" part of an executive's job was the most personally difficult for her: Temperamentally, she preferred analytical problem solving in small groups to meeting and greeting lots of people and speech writing to making speeches.

However, it is within the consternation itself that Gibbs demonstrated core elements of Senge's (2006) Personal Mastery. Personal Mastery is not about the powerful use of force but about how you handle the internal effort to hold the creative tension between the "current reality of 'what is'" and the image of yourself and how you are acting on the world. That tension is most powerfully expressed when you confront a current reality that is dissonant with what you truly want to be like (and perhaps think you are!) within that reality.

After all, what tension is there when the alignment is easy, the agreement is ensured, and the assumptions are the same? All of us can be "great" on those tasks and projects we love to work on, laboring with people whose presence we enjoy. Such activity requires little Personal Mastery. Internal effort on the external work matters most when we don't like the work, are uncomfortable with the people working with us, or are uncertain that we are equipped to handle the tasks at hand. But it is within those arenas that the greatest growth can occur . . . if we have the courage and fortitude to make that effort.

Gibbs made the effort. After she was appointed commissioner for homeless services, one of her first projects was to take a tour of her shelter facilities. She later traveled monthly to make certain she met with shelter providers under contract with the city. In both cases, morale and respect followed. She is no less demanding in her results focus. As one of her direct reports commented, "Sure, she's demanding of us. She's so smart it can be overwhelming sometimes. But seeing her as a person makes it easier. She's a human being, too." *The simple external act of "walk-around management" with shelter providers and other agency staff took place because of the far larger internal effort Gibbs made to meet a challenge within herself.*

More significantly, Gibbs made this internal effort while embarking on the most ambitious reorganization of homeless services since shelters were first created in the early 1980s. The outside political pressures and public scrutiny of the department had never been greater, especially because the economic downturn of 2000–2003 increased the homeless ranks to record numbers. In short, "the current reality of 'what is'" in her world had been at its most daunting at the very time she took on the internal challenge to expand her personal contact and engagement with more and more people. Pausing to meet with line staff, listen to shelter facility personnel, and take lunch with advocates could easily drop off an executive's demanding schedule, but in Gibbs's case it did not.

What Gibbs began modeling for other executives is something often in short supply in their board rooms . . . and something she herself might be surprised to see: patience.

However, it is not the patience of an Esther Rohatiner. It is the patience *within herself* that is required if she—or any other powerful and successful person, for that matter—is to confront and change those areas of inner struggle that are less easily mastered than many of the outer markings of success. Remember how Helen Jacques discussed her frustrations within herself to "stay the course" on her own change. An executive must confront and then live within that personal struggle to change. Gibbs would be the first to tell you this kind of internal effort, as valuable as it is, is hard. *That is why it is so admirable.*

Gibbs already has plaques on her wall and has been honored with numerous awards. Less publicized, however, is the observation of a shelter facilities assistant director for programs who had the opportunity to meet her leader a few times during her first year: "I heard she was mean, really tough on people. . . . Well, she's tough on what she wants done, I'll grant you that. But she's not mean; she's nice! She listens; I can tell she actually cares. She took the time to listen to me. That makes it easier to do the work. A person down here in the trenches doesn't forget that."

What better legacy could two very different women leave? Whether an executive secretary or a public executive, these two women have taken on the challenges of meeting the tensions of the current reality and their vision of how they want to be. Esther Rohatiner never let her lack of formal power cause her to be less than polite and helpful, regardless of who anxiously walked through her door. Linda Gibbs has not allowed the trappings of her formal authority to impede her own personal development, even though those walking through her door could never demand she change at all. One woman, nearing the end of her career, will never be forgotten by those whom she touched. The other, not yet at midcareer, can expect as much.

Such memories are created regardless of whether or not you have power. Simply start with the underlying secret to Rohatiner's outer politeness and Gibbs's surprising effort for inner patience. If you want to leave lasting memories with others, begin with the patient commitment to change yourself. If it takes hold within you, others are sure to notice.

Here are some steps to developing inner patience and outer politeness:

Practicing Patience and Politeness Exercises

Politeness is a state of being that is often a reflection of inner patience *and* an adroit tactic designed to smooth the turbulent waters of daily exchange between all-too-busy and often frazzled friends and colleagues. A simple smile joined with a genuine "please" and a well-meant "thank you" can go far in developing authentic good will between people who otherwise view the common currency of daily exchange as more burden than it's worth. Through politeness, one reinforces connection, not isolation. Over time, politeness helps instill the desire for reciprocity between people that is the hallmark of all good relationships . . . and with it, a true sense of community is nurtured and deepened.

Of course, it is far easier to keep our patience and to practice politeness with those with whom we already get along, not those who drive us crazy. With those with whom we are not in alignment, we find ourselves easily impatient, ready with an inevitable excuse for why politeness is neither needed nor desired. With this in mind, we are reminded of the wise Lakota saying from about 300 BC: *To practice patience, you need a real rascal to help you. It's no use practicing on gentle and kind creatures, for they require no patience.*

So who in your community is your rascal? Who irritates you simply by speaking? Whose approach to things causes you to think of nails on the chalkboard? With the Lakota saying as your guide, consider the following:

1. What is the quality, whether a personal quirk or a point of view, in that person that bothers you?

   _____

   _____

2. Why does that quality bother you when it appears in that particular person but not in other friends or colleagues?

   _____

   _____

3. What blocks your politeness when you are able to forgive others so much more easily?

   _____

   _____

4. Is there something unresolved within you that causes you to react so strongly?

   _____

   _____

   Are you sure? _____

   Ask a good friend or close colleague who knows you both.

   _____

   _____

5. What do you gain from holding on to your impolite, impatient stance here?

   _____

   _____

6. What would happen to your leadership stance if you practiced patience and politeness with this "rascal"?

_____

_____

I commit to developing my politeness by practicing patience with the following rascals, from whom I have much to learn:

a. _____

b. _____

c. _____

d. _____

28

EMBRACING DIVERSITY

Florida State Representative Al Lawson's campaign team was in an uproar. Running in a hard-fought primary to become the first Black state senator elected in northern Florida since Reconstruction, the eight-term representative from Tallahassee and his team had been counting on the financial and political support of absence of the lobbyists financial support powerful lobbying groups that had often sought Lawson's legislative expertise while he served in the Florida House of Representatives. Since he did not have the financial muscle of his two closest White rivals, the absence of the lobbyists financial support had been a real fiscal blow to the campaign's prospects. The press, looking to stir things up, kept calling Lawson's office for a comment: Didn't the absence of serious money smack of racism?

Some campaign members hoped for a blistering attack from their leader. After all, Lawson was the most senior member of the legislature in the district, and he had worked hard for the constituents. Throwing financial muscle behind White candidates who already had two times the funds had to be racism! Hurt and angry, the campaign team looked forward to Lawson's powerfully worded response.

His response, however, was a 5:30 a.m. walk around the Florida A&M University track. Walking with one of us (Willie), he admitted he was hurt, as he'd hoped for the political and financial muscle in what was clearly going to be a hard-fought campaign. But was it racism? When is a racial difference simply a difference and not something more sinister? By the third lap, he'd thought out his answers to those difficult questions. While he was Black and his primary opponents were White, in this case the lobbyists choosing to back White rivals was a political calculation, not a racist choice.

Looking back, being able to make the distinction between "race" and "racism" was a crucial factor in then-Representative Lawson becoming State Senator Lawson. "If I'd labeled the association's choice as racial and not political in a three-person primary," he told us, "what room did I give anybody who chose any candidate other than me? For me to put that racist label out there was to say the same about a lot of White people who I knew weren't racist. If I backed them into a corner, then they could never vote for me if there was a runoff. I wasn't going to let that happen."

Lawson never responded to the press with the race card it was searching for. "It's not a racial issue," he said. "It's a political one. Now let the people decide who's the best for them."

It was boring copy for the newspaper reporters but made for an interesting response in the urban and rural White areas of the Florida district. In the ensuing two-person runoff, by keeping the campaign focused on political issues and his distinguished record of service, Lawson received more than 40% of the White vote. As a result of his not labeling others, scores of White people responded in kind: They labeled him the most qualified candidate in the field and elected him easily to the Florida Senate. For the first time since the 1880s, a Black man represented Tallahassee and its surrounding counties in the Florida Senate.

While it's exciting to retell the story of his historic victory, what matters here is Lawson's capacity to distinguish between "racism" and "racial difference." "I've been living and working with White, Black, and Latino people all my life," he said. "When you're with enough different people long enough, you can tell who's genuine. It's not always a matter of the color of somebody's skin."

Lawson's wisdom came from a lifetime of embracing diversity and living the credo "all as one." Being comfortable with difference, however, is not as easy as it may seem. In fact, one of the most difficult barriers to embracing diversity that so many Americans of every race and ethnicity confront is the *marked imbalance between what people believe about multiracial and multiethnic relations and how they feel when trying to act on that belief.* Countless polls show Americans support the idea of multiracial communities and oppose segregation, while our popular culture embraces a wide social array of movie, TV, and musical stars that would have been unthinkable 30 years ago. However, in day-to-day practical experience, no barrier remains wider to cross than that of social diversity. Whether evidenced by the segregated lunch tables of our children's schools or the lack of people of color and women in executive board rooms, embracing ethnic and racial diversity "up close and personal" is still moving at a snail's pace that frustrates some and flusters us all. Why have we come so far, yet so many of us still shy away from the personal and team closeness needed if leadership is to fully engage in the hard-fought give-and-take that brilliant problem solving requires?

Elaine Pinderhughes, a professor of social work at Boston College and a national authority on diversity, pinpointed a key answer to this gnawing problem in her 1989 book *Understanding Race, Ethnicity, and Power.* She came to her answer after she had been called upon, again and again, to work with agencies under siege and with numerous students and alumni troubled by the difference in what they believed to be true about racial and ethnic groups but rarely could act on. How could good people who were committed to racial and ethnic equality still be so nervous in addressing the issue when it surfaced where they worked? Like Rachel Borenstein and Angelina Browne, the women arguing over a seemingly average case in Chapter 9, why do so many well-meaning people stop talking as soon as even mild disagreement occurs? Similar issues continue to affect the gender, sexual orientation, and disabilities divisions we experience as well.

A skilled clinician, Pinderhughes began to explore what had happened developmentally in the lives of both agency personnel and her students to make them afraid of even the mildest disagreement between racial and ethnic groups. Her research, centering on developmental history of her respondents, revealed that an overwhelming majority of people's first remembered experiences of difference were negative (Pinderhughes, 1989). The initial events that would trigger an awkward awareness of difference later on in life did not have to be socially significant to have lasting impact: They ranged from skin color, height, or eye color to being the new kid at camp, the only Jew or Muslim in a classroom, or the child with the most toys.

What mattered, Pinderhughes (1989) found, was not the nature of the event but how one interpreted the discomfort it triggered. Faced with discomfort, the child, often assisted by well-meaning and supportive adults seeking to soothe his or her pain, would compare it to *his or her initial experience of difference,* which heightened the child's *personal discomfort with all difference.* As Pinderhughes explained, "In conveying the meaning of unequal value [between two characteristics such as skin color or height], of being 'more than' or 'less than,' 'differentness' [for the child and later the adult] evokes the notion of power. This becomes particularly clear when one party in the comparison comes to symbolize 'good' and the other 'bad,' pushing the comparison to a more polarized meaning" (p. 32).

Children's cognitive development necessarily intensifies their interpretations of difference into polarizing opposites, filling them over time with emotional meaning of "good" and "bad" as a way to order their understanding of the world. Left unchecked by experience or alternative interpretations from adults around them (most of whom have had the same responses to difference), the vast majority of children likewise grow into adults who feel uncomfortable in social and work settings, which is all the more unsettling because their beliefs tell them to feel otherwise.

Part of Al Lawson's success in northern Florida came from the fact that difference has been a constant part of his life. Growing up in rural Gadsden County, he fished and played with almost as many White kids as Black. As it was a time of great social transformation in the South as well, this consistent interaction with "other" helped the young Black boy see those who crossed his path not as archetypes and symbols to defend against (or for) but as flesh-and-blood people with their own idiosyncrasies, abilities, and interests. On the campaign stump, his staff marveled at his relaxed ability to travel into the backwater rural areas of the senatorial district and sit and tailgate in a small town like Eastpoint, Florida, with the White regulars, sipping Coca-Cola and eating boiled peanuts. Asked by his own staff how he could be so calm with people so different, Lawson looked surprised and then smiled. "If all you see is difference, you can't see how much we're alike. I may be Black, and they may be White, but I *like* sipping Coke and eating boiled peanuts. *See us as one.* They know I'm the only candidate who does, too."

It was no accident that later that day one of those White regulars approached Lawson, his hand outstretched. "You're getting my vote, Al. You're the candidate of the working man!"

Lawson's comfort with difference allowed him to embrace diversity. Instead of "difference" being powerfully attached to the fear of *other,* his comfort with diversity led him to relate comfortably with *another . . .* and then another. Seeing "another" is to sit comfortably with the variability of human experience; reacting to "other" is to uncomfortably feel the power of old categories that separate us into "those like us" and everyone else—that is, those who appear to be "less than" us. The mental map that screens people into such rigid boxes creates the same rigidity in our interactions. Feeling the rigidity as discomfort results in a formalized engagement that allows for superficial interaction but never the practiced give-and-take that creative problem solving truly requires.

To embrace diversity is to be able to live with the "two truths" of difference and sameness, denying neither nor dwelling on one or the other. As Pinderhughes (1989) noted, although "a stance of [only] nondifference and 'all people are alike' may seem to diminish anxiety related to differentness, it also creates real problems in that real differences cannot be acknowledged, sameness may be overemphasized, and distortion and misunderstanding may be reinforced rather than avoided. . . . [Likewise] to focus on difference without attention to similarities can also be anxiety-provoking and defeat the goal of understanding" (p. 115).

Pinderhughes's (1989) work sought to help Whites and people of color alike work to expand their perspective so that, like Lawson, they "can recognize that responses to difference can be understood and managed and, at the same time, similarities to others must be accepted but not overemphasized, feared, or avoided" (p. 116).

This capacity to hold the "two truths" of sameness and difference we refer to in Chapter 20 is not specific to only one racial group. It is possible for everyone, regardless of background. Someone who grew up under conditions far different from Al Lawson's who nevertheless has embraced an equal commitment to and comfort with diversity is Megan Nolan, a former South Bronx community organizer now working for Settlement Housing Fund, an innovator in housing redevelopment in New York City.

White and Irish, Nolan grew up in a working-/middle-class community on Long Island. Her closest girlfriends from kindergarten through high school happened to be an Italian American and an African American. "At 5 years old," she told us, "I didn't think of skin color but who I liked. When either of my friends visited me at my house, there was never anything said. I never got mixed messages from my parents when I was little."

Like Lawson, Nolan at an early age came to see different types of people up close without the social interpretation of race or class that can so often happen in a child's early years. The resulting personal comfort was a foundation on which she, as well as Lawson, could build future professional success.

The defining areas of difference in Nolan's life were not race or class. "I came from a home where my mother was very liberal and my father conservative. We'd be sitting at the dinner table, and I'd hear my father say, 'Respect your elders,' followed by my mother saying,

'Question authority,' and it was no big deal. I grew up knowing that difference was real and that it was healthy."

Nolan paused as she reflected on her childhood. "At the same time, I came from a traditional Irish American home in a lot of other ways, especially gender. My brothers' needs came first."

She ruefully smiled, reliving an old memory. "It may seem small today, but as a little girl my brothers' extracurricular activities came first. Every weekend my mother would take my brothers to swim meets, while my father worked. My sister and I were left at home alone. My mother fought at my school for my right as a girl to do anything a boy could do. I knew she believed in us as equals. But her daughters were getting a mixed message, too. I understood pretty early that you found meaning about difference in the little things, too."

Nolan's respect for difference that she picked up at the dinner table, joined with her acute dislike for how easily perceived difference on the basis of race, class, or gender can sabotage that respect, is a large part of what led her to community organizing. Over time, her vast experience working in the neighborhoods of some of New York's poorest communities helped her learn to comfortably confront perceived difference before it escalated into unresolved problems beyond her control.

The week we met for this interview, Nolan had just finished helping move a young man's belongings into his dorm room upstate. She had met him 6 years earlier, on a street corner, where he and his friends were hustling drugs. When she took her daily walk over to the local bodega to pick up her lunch, the young drug dealers were always on the corner, their beepers on, phone calls being answered. Rather than be intimidated by their comments and the obvious social differences in their backgrounds, she walked over and introduced herself. Within a month, some of the young men were escorting her to the subway when she worked late, admonishing the community organizer to leave the neighborhood before it got too dark. Neither afraid of them nor ignoring what they were doing, Nolan began confronting them as well about going back to school. Because of her easy humor and genuine affection for them as people, a few took her up on her offer to join Bronx Helpers, a youth advocacy program she was running at the time. Returning to school on a permanent basis was the next step. Such success never would have happened if the young Irish American woman had looked at that group of young Black and Latino men and seen only negative differences bred from fear.

But what happens to children who are raised in worlds where difference is either less acute or less positive and thus, ironically, more problematic for them as adults? Nolan was as emphatic as Pinderhughes.

"Everyone can become comfortable with difference, but it takes time," she said. "I may have been basically comfortable with lots of different people and issues, but I had to work on my anger at gender inequality before I was as effective as I wanted to be. What people have to do is find their own experience with difference and how they handled it [and] then use that to learn from and struggle with. It's something you commit to every day.

"The secret, if there is a secret, is you have to want to do this, because at first it's hard. Guilt and anger come up pretty easily when you first surface issues like difference and our discomfort on race or class or gender. But lots of people from very different experiences do just fine. When you create space for voice after people have been silenced, great things can happen."

Nolan paused for a moment, thinking about her work up in the South Bronx. "You know, the other side of struggle is freedom. You get to enjoy a lot more people in your life. You raise the issues you want to and need to before they become a big deal. You get to laugh more. People get to joke around and not have it matter. That helps a lot when you do this kind of work. If we're not in it for the money, we sure ought to get to laugh along the way!"

Nolan's quiet joy in laughing on the street corner with Black and Latino guys whom she eventually recruits to her youth leadership program and Lawson's simple pleasure in small talk with a few White regulars over Cokes and peanuts are two moments of "lived experience" that could happen to anyone engaged in the multiracial, socially diverse workplaces that all agencies and businesses of America have become. Nolan and Lawson embrace diversity as richness with "we are one" as their unifying theme for working together because, paradoxically, they acknowledge the two truths of difference and commonality at the same time. Indeed, it is this developed internal capacity that makes them better equipped to handle the demands of difference that still exist, whether economic and racial disparities in school funding in New York City or the grievous health care for poor rural Black people of Gadsden County, Florida.

For those who did not grow up with the lived experience of difference of Lawson or Nolan, there are clear ways to genuinely embrace diversity. The most important place to begin is with Pinderhughes's (1989) insight, as referred to by Helen Jacques in Chapter 21:

> *For most of us, when race shows up, it's different, with "different" and "problem" meaning the same thing.* Later on in life, we *think* we're fine because by now we're well-meaning people out to save the world. Unfortunately, as soon as the group becomes mixed we still *feel* anxious. *That old childhood anxiety leads us as adults to feel any social difference as a negative, even when we don't think that way about a group.* Left uncovered, people say the right things while acting stupid. Our past trips us up, even while we try to do the right thing in the present.

In short, to begin truly embracing diversity, people must begin with what we have described elsewhere as becoming comfortable with discomfort (Burghardt, 1982). By openly naming differences in the room, whether racial, gender related, or ethnic, you will create initial discomfort in people (including yourself!) as the unspoken "otherness" of rigid difference is acknowledged. In doing so, however, a sweet paradox will occur: Like Helen

Jacques casually acknowledging Nick Costello's Whiteness and her Blackness, you will *lay the foundation for "other" to move to "another,"* for people to be able to see the two truths of difference and commonality as resources to be worked with as opposed to denied or misunderstood.

Nolan and Lawson's inherent understanding of these truths throughout their lives allowed others to experience the same with them: drinking Coca-Cola and eating boiled peanuts among Blacks and Whites who were committed to the "working man"; a White woman organizer and a few Black and Latino young men engaging in discussions that led some to a youth leadership program and entry to college.

Becoming "comfortable with discomfort" refers to another dimension of the internal effort that is the hallmark of leadership excellence. It speaks to the challenge that Pinderhughes (1989) presented to all professionals:

- Surface the social differences in your agency.
- Do not run from the age-old awkwardness that will initially ensue.
- Allow yourself and others to admit to the discomfort as a necessary step in your internal growth and development and not as a mark of shame or "political incorrectness."
- Move on to use all the talent in the room now at your disposal.

In this way, the social differences that do exist will become assets to your problem solving. To take the example of educational reform, working-class parents and their children in urban schools face pressures and demands that are different from those faced by White educators. At the same time, those White educators have a body of knowledge and expertise on curriculum reform to share that will enrich those parents' and children's lives. Those real differences, joined with the common pursuit of quality education and safety for all children, make grappling with how to achieve such excellence all the more valuable. The same two truths of experience and expertise can be found in mental health reform, child welfare advocacy, and youth leadership. Allowing the discomfort of social difference into the early discussions will free you to do this more serious work far sooner and with far more positive results than can otherwise be expected.

Lawson and Nolan used their lived experience from socially diverse worlds to transcend the "otherness" of difference and embrace diversity in ways that have led others to their side. But they are not unique. As anyone who makes the effort to hold the two truths of difference and commonality knows, as one lives and works with "another," a richer and more humane world begins to emerge. Hard work remains, whether fighting for Food Stamps for unemployed oyster men in Eastpoint, Florida, or educating children of color in the South Bronx. However, if you embrace diversity, the work will seem far lighter than perhaps imagined. For once "the elephant in the room" will leave, and so will its shadow.

To embrace diversity so you can see people as one, use the following exercises:

Embracing Diversity Exercises

It is commonplace in every organization in the United States to have issues of cultural competency that all staff members wish to address and improve upon. The cultural competency questions most commonly raised include:

> Are people across racial and ethnic differences able to comfortably disagree with each other?
>
> Are all levels of staff comfortable with hiring and promotion procedures?
>
> Are men and women comfortable working closely with each other?
>
> Are straights and lesbians and gays comfortable working closely with each other?

That said, it is of vital importance in a world as multicultural and globalized as ours that each workplace be an environment for open discussion, no matter how painful or difficult, with the objective of supplanting mistrust with trust and resentment with improved morale. Only in such an environment can concerns be raised without labeling or blame being measured.

To create the building blocks of communication, you must first remove the stumbling blocks. Here are a few suggestions that you may want to use as you bring this activity inside your own workplace. People need to commit to the following:

1. **Do not characterize statements as based on intentional bias or prejudice.** Accusations should always be avoided, as should terms like *racist, sexist, hypocrite,* and so on. Avoid sentences that solicit anger: "You are a _____ist or a _____ite," for example.

2. **Do not respond without understanding.** If you disagree with another's statement, first ask for clarification before responding.

3. **Do not reproach; instead, respectfully disagree.** If you still find a statement problematic, reframe it in terms of "if you said . . . , then it comes across to me as a problem because . . ." Then explain why you feel this way.

4. **Do not rank oppression.** Strive to respect differences in experience without creating a "hierarchy of oppression" (in which one form of bias, discrimination, or oppression is automatically worse than another).

5. **Do not belittle a concern.** No two people experience the same thing exactly the same way.

6. **Do not add fuel to fire.** There is nothing wrong with a heated discussion, but an attitude intended to inflame will be counterproductive.

Equally important, it is not possible to cover the range of issues touched on under the rubric of cultural competence. What we can and will do is provide you with an exercise to do by yourself and another to do at a later time, perhaps with your team or another work group. Worked on consistently over time, these exercises—Your First Experience With "Difference" and Locating Your Commonalities in the Midst of Difference— can help you become culturally competent enough to work with your "others" on issues of race, ethnicity, sexual orientation, age, and other social dynamics in a way that builds unity rather than tension.

While the first exercise can also be done with a group, begin it when you are in a clear and reflective mindset. It is important that you take the time to do the exercise thoroughly and honestly.

Begin with a small notebook and jot down your answers to the following. After you ask each question, please take at least 3 minutes before answering so that you have had an opportunity to relax and reflect on your answers. Do not hesitate to rewrite or rethink your answers as you uncover more material through your writing.

Your First Experience With "Difference"

We have learned that an effective way to begin addressing *how to embrace diversity as an asset throughout your life is to develop cultural competency as a skill.* Making a list of current complaints or issues may increase emotions and thus prove less effective; instead, begin well before you were employed—way back when you were a child.

Recall the first time that you—before the age of 10—experienced "difference."

1. How old were you?

2. What was the setting?

3. How did you respond to feeling different?

4. What effect, if any, did this experience have on you later in life?

Implications to This Exercise

1. While there are exceptions, almost all of us remember our first experience with "difference" as a negative one: a telling moment in which the world's axis shifted and altered our perspective. Your moment of difference may have revealed your skin as darker than that of your classmates, or it may have shown your peers that you're the only one who has to translate English for his or her parents. Difference may have revealed your attraction to persons of the same sex or perhaps that your love of basketball would remain unrequited because you're too small to make the team. Maybe you were the only person with a single mother or father.

2. As children, we almost always do not know how to respond to this sense of difference, except with confusion, fear, and isolation. These first experiences are the foundation of a social psychological *response of awkwardness and unconscious fear* to difference that is separate from any cultural connotations (that may be and are added later). So, quite often, we all begin our cognitive understanding of difference as a barrier between us and the proverbial "others" with whom we work today. Indeed, "difference" often translates into "not good enough" or "not fitting in." It is no surprise, then, that we almost always respond with confusion, fear, and isolation. Understandably, our perceived "difference" may be the source of lifelong patterns of behavior—for instance, mistrusting White authority figures or dismissing or diminishing Black colleagues' capacities and skills. Our training in cultural competence helps us understand how our particular moment of "difference" casts a light that can blind us to the true intention of others.

3. If we reflect on them over time, we come to see that these powerful feelings of difference affected our behavior for years to come. We thus can now reinterpret actions in a new light. For example, awkwardness around "newness" and in new situations with unfamiliar connotations of appropriate behavior is to be expected. *When we surface this expectation, we no longer have difficulty becoming "anxious about being anxious!"*

4. Understanding the power of difference helps us in our practice by allowing us to become *comfortable with discomfort*. We have done this work for years. It is always the most charged for us, and it will be for you when the issues come up inside an agency. If you feel uncomfortable, that is normal. By seeing this added discomfort as normal, you can relax into the comfort of helping others become aware of this state as well, thus allowing everyone to move more easily to the substance of *the topic or topics at hand*.

The first prong of embracing diversity as an asset is to recognize that people's first experience with difference created feelings of awkwardness and not to flee that tension: Over time, your practice of becoming comfortable with discomfort will help others stay with the issues as well.

Locating Your Commonalities in the Midst of Difference

As Elaine Pinderhughes wrote in her 1989 classic *Understanding Race, Ethnicity, and Power,* focusing on difference alone can create barriers where they do not exist. That said, as there are real differences and genuine perceptions of difference that affect all school and human service environments, it is equally important to understand how much commonality we share as well. For example, everyone who works with people shares deep humanistic concerns for a better society.

To *feel* our commonalities with others, however, in our daily work requires some experiential practice to remind us of that twofold lesson. If possible, try answering the following questions with a small group, although this exercise can also be done by yourself:

1. What is your name, and how do you like it pronounced?

2. What is your racial and ethnic identity?

3. What family value that you had as a child still matters to you as an adult?

4. Describe any experience of discrimination that you have encountered.

After you have completed this exercise, reflect on the following:

Note how profoundly similar we are in our underlying approaches to what we want and what our families have wanted, *no matter how socially distinct we seem to be.* We have no difficulty understanding where "someone is coming from" when we are guided by that awareness!

The second prong to effective cultural competence is to always operate from the assumption that you share commonalities in values and aspirations with those with whom you work and whom you serve.

Culturally competent practice operates from the fundamental basis that we start with more similarities than differences and that the differences that do exist are overwhelmingly positive, not negative. From serious "similarity/difference" issues like life goals, quality-of-life concerns, and education for our children to more prosaic ones like our favorite sweets or baseball player, fundamental commonality underlies most of what we do. We can use this awareness in understanding how to approach others, especially when perceived differences seem to dominate in the early stages of a relationship.

Demonstrating awareness of commonalty and difference occurs through small, consistent acts and behaviors, not "large statements" or political stances. *Taking the time to learn and pronounce another's name correctly is one of those small yet significant acts that can build bridges between people who assume bridges exist.*

Race shadows and undermines America, and perhaps it always will. Given the United States' long and painful history of dealing with difference, one of the key skills in cultural competency is "becoming comfortable with discomfort." In social service and educational work there is always a tension between ignored or exaggerated cultural differences. Neither denying racial experience and history nor unnecessarily emphasizing them is helpful. It is better to make certain that both *commonality of purpose* and *difference in opinion* are acknowledged—not dwelled upon.

Summing Up: The Steps to Embracing Difference as a Transformative Leader

From Understanding the Response to Difference to Handling the Dynamics of Power

1. You may use your leadership position to help end perceived negative social differences. This does not include giving up your authority to do a job well. It does mean you must be open to interpreting "daily living" from multiple points of view that you may or may not know about.

2. By being open to multiple perceptions of daily activities and events in cultural terms, you give up power in a positive way by not forcing your own reality as the only reality. It is a sharing of power in a new and positive manner.

3. In doing so, you lay the foundation for culturally competent practice.

4. This also means that issues of culture are woven into all areas of practice and program as "add-ins," not "add-ons."

5. Work on this with *consistency, not constancy.* In this way, issues of culture and positive difference are raised regularly,

not every minute of the day. They become a *normal part* of the work, not the *focus* of the work.

6. Recognizing that your response to difference is in part a social psychological phenomenon, you can practice developing "comfort with discomfort" as new cultural issues and unrecognized social differences emerge over time. In this way *everyone*—White or a person of color, Jewish or Jamaican, gay or straight—has areas to work on and change.

7. The willingness of a person to openly submit to this difficult process of adaptation and change is another building block of transformative leadership that establishes trust in multicultural, community-based settings.

8. This leadership framework that embraces diversity and difference does not require you to know all things about all cultures. No one does or can. It does expect you to be open to keep learning about the positive differences and experiences of various ethnic or racial groups that can and will inform your work.

9. This openness to new cultural material will grow over time as you practice sharing perceptions and power. The vulnerability of admitting to "knowing less" has the paradoxical effect of allowing you to learn more over time!

In short, people develop cultural competency by understanding how powerfully they are influenced by their past experiences with "difference" in their lives. Knowing this can help you relearn and practice seeing difference as a healthy and positive part of your life and work.

Likewise, you can use the commonality in your value systems to moor yourself in working with others in community-based work. Such commonality creates a foundation that can help you work through "the comfort with discomfort" that is a core dimension in transformative leadership.

29

CLEAN AS YOU GO

Annie Burris was the cook for a very demanding clientele. They were the 11 residents of Ivy House, a halfway house for formerly homeless, severely mentally ill people who were too fragile for the single-room-occupancy housing in another wing of Brooklyn Community Housing and Services (BCHS), a multiservice agency in the Fort Greene section of Brooklyn, New York. These residents were the segment of the homeless population most everyone feared or avoided: the young woman dressed in rags who smelled of urine from 10 feet away; the hulking teenager who screamed obscenities at demons only he could see; the frightened, cowering older gentleman who couldn't stop moaning. So ill they avoided almost all human contact, they were placed in Ivy House so that they could be stabilized on their medications and learn the basic routines of daily living that the rest of us take for granted.

Burris helped these people learn how to put cereal in a bowl before the milk, then how to make muffins, and then how to make fried chicken and mashed potatoes, complete with gravy. Along the way, they learned that the kitchen had to be clean before, during, and after the cooking. Some learned these lessons in a few weeks; for others, the time between pouring milk in a bowl and making fried chicken batter might have been 3 months. Interestingly enough, by the time most learned to cook, they had learned to keep their rooms clean as well. What had spilled over from Burris's lessons wasn't milk but the sense of systems and order it takes to make a decent meal . . . and live a normal life.

Burris was hired to be Ivy House's cook, not the trainer and counselor that she indirectly became. "At our team meetings," she told us, "our supervisor was asking people if there were programs for clients we could do. I noticed people coming up to me at breakfast and watching me work. Some asked me if they could help make lunch. It seemed like the right thing to do."

Her approach was as basic as her meals. "Show them the routines; let them make mistakes; reward them when they got it right; don't punish them for getting it wrong but help them see how to do it right."

And never give up on people on whom others gave up a long time ago. "Some took to cooking right away, but a lot of people in Ivy were scared all the time. Their meds were so strong that their hands would shake. Some felt so bad about themselves they had no confidence. When they got it wrong," she explained, "I'd correct them but not yell at them. Pretty soon people could see how much flour went into that batter [for fried chicken]."

Burris had learned how to work with the mentally ill as a child growing up in Rock Hill, South Carolina. Her grandmother, Annie White, had a lifelong friend who became mentally ill in her later years. As the larger White community provided next to no services for its Black residents, her grandmother's friend stayed at home, nearly a recluse because so few neighbors would visit. "Not my grandmother," Burris said. "I'd go with her on Sundays. She'd come into her home and go over and sit with her, talking with her in a quiet voice. I'd see that the lady would get calm when she was treated that way. Helped her eat better, too."

Burris took the same approach with the residents of Ivy House. She joined her steadying, direct approach to people with neatness and order in the kitchen, which also had a calming effect. "I always made sure the kitchen was spotless before I began my day. Only when that was done would I get out pots and pans to start preparing meals. People had to see order beforehand. You know, people who are mentally ill feel a lot of chaos sometimes. They can't learn new things like how to cook if they see a mess."

Like *Doña* Carmen in Chapter 17, Burris has a no-nonsense manner about her. The first time people meet her she can seem a bit standoffish, even gruff. But that gruff exterior is just a cover for an innately intelligent woman practiced in motivating others to do what they don't think they can do. As Doris Clark, BCHS's former executive director, warmly described her, "You think Annie's a drill sergeant until you notice her speaking quietly with an Ivy resident. Do you think people as damaged and hurt as Ivy folks would work with somebody mean?"

Like *Doña* Carmen's demand for excellence, Burris has hers, too. "I keep my standards the same for everybody," she said. "After all, fried chicken's fried chicken. It's either good, or it isn't. But you've got to be patient with people. They're not gonna make the batter right the first time. You have to have patience. Just like my grandmother did. When they spill, they have to clean it up before they move on. Spills make a mess; they could end up hurting somebody. So I'm serious about cleaning. But that doesn't mean people have to be yelled at."

Burris's attention to teaching systems and not just making meals had the same ripple effect W. E. Deming, the grandfather of quality improvement, predicted years ago: "Once people understand the power of systems . . . it transforms their approach to all relationships in their lives" (Walton, 1988, p. 6). Whether to manager or mentally ill, the same principle applies. Burris explained what happened at Ivy House: "I saw the other changes happen first with Danny. He had the worst room, full of stale, dirty clothes and enough cigarette smoke that the walls and floors reeked. He'd gotten good down here in the kitchen, so when I noticed the mess upstairs [in his room], I told him his room should look like my kitchen. If he could help me downstairs, his own room could be that way, too."

She laughed warmly at the memory. "A few hours later, his room was better than it had ever been. Stayed that way, too."

Others under her care followed suit. A year into Burris's cooking program, Doris Clark, the executive director, paid one of her midmorning visits to Ivy House. She was surprised that no one was around the TV, a frequent pastime in halfway programs like Ivy House. After asking Burris where the residents were, she soon learned that most of them were cleaning their rooms.[1] Having learned not only to cook but how to clean as they go, Ivy's residents were cleaning where they lived as well.

Annie Burris made sure Ivy House residents had clean pots and pans before, during, and after their cooking. It was her way of helping people who often had trouble getting through the day take care of themselves so that at day's end they would be as safe and secure in their rooms as they were in her kitchen. She kept focus on her systems in the present so that the future of those under her watchful cook's eye would be filled with more success than many others had once thought possible.

Barbara Byrd-Bennett used systems in a similar way, only the future she was focused on was that of the 100,000 children under her care. The former chief executive officer (or chancellor) of the Cleveland Municipal School District, Byrd-Bennett arrived in Cleveland with a school system in disarray. Only 22% of fourth graders had passed the reading test, with sixth-grade scores just as low. Great capital improvements were needed for schools that were admittedly crumbling, making them unsafe for students, let alone inviting environments that stimulated learning. With then Mayor Michael White having to use real political capital to gain her the autonomy to make genuine reform, Byrd-Bennett began her tenure in a seat as warm as Annie Burris's stove.

The team she assembled under her trusted, long-term chief of staff Myrna Elliott-Lewis was a sharp, capable group of school administrators from within and outside the Cleveland district. They knew their chief executive was as demanding as she was brilliant and expected her to drive them hard. Like Annie Burris's kitchen helpers, they knew they'd be expected to perform well on each part of their job. What they hadn't expected was the learning environment she set about creating inside the executive team. They were shocked to find out they were going to read books together.

Like all good executives, Byrd-Bennett had a vision statement complete with six strategic focal points that helped set the district's course as well as directed each team member's work.

What truly elevated her efforts, however, was the *system of long-term learning and leadership she and Elliott-Lewis began and hoped would continue after they were no longer in the district.* For them, "clean as you go" was about preparing for the continuity of their team's success well before their team had achieved it. Just as Burris had people cleaning up before the fried chicken ever arrived so they could fully appreciate what they had accomplished, these two educational leaders created systems for executive learning among their team members so their lessons would take shape as the reforms moved forward (Allen, 2001; Blanchard, Johnson, & Johnson, 1982). "I needed a system for our own team learning so the team would keep the lessons alive years later," Byrd-Bennett said. "You don't prepare for the future by working hard today and just hoping for the best tomorrow. I wanted my executive team to think of themselves as leaders carrying on the work for the children regardless of who sits at the front of the table. That kind of learning won't happen through a farewell speech 6 or 7 years down the road."

The system for leadership development that Byrd-Bennett and Elliott-Lewis decided to use was deceptively simple: They put Cleveland's school district executives into a book club. The list of books was as varied as *Leading With Soul* by Bolman and Deal (2001) and *The Corporate Mystic* by Hendricks and Ludeman (1997). Two books were read per month, and the team committed to coming together at monthly executive leadership retreats for a day and a half to explore the books' lessons and how they could be incorporated into their work within the Cleveland school system.

"The books were the vehicle we used to create my system of leadership," Byrd-Bennett said. "What I was looking for was in the future: people able to carry on this work of reform for years to come. I wanted the retreats to be the first learning environment where people talked with each other. The books helped people talk out ideas. They began to learn how to converse with each other as human beings. As that starts to happen, people can more easily work with each other later on with the hard management problems that remain."

Some were resistant to the idea. After all, educators are hired to manage issues, not talk about books! Early on one executive was adamant in his opposition. "What does reading these books have to do with results? I wasn't hired to share thoughts on the place of my soul at work!"

An outcome-focused and hard-charging manager used to looking at the bottom line, he found the initial retreats very discomforting. However, as with any good system in place, Byrd-Bennett's system's effective workings over time caused him—and others—to rethink their own approach to how things get done. Six months into the retreats, this same executive began to share his own ideas and thoughts within the group. "I had to change my mind," he told us. "Seeing people open up like they did in these retreats made things go better than I expected. I got a lot from this."

Byrd-Bennett had the confidence in ongoing systems improvements because she knew the underlying secret to what at first can seem like annoying diversions from the "real work." She had confidence in her systematic approach to leadership because *some of what she wanted to accomplish would occur after she saw results in the short run.* "I needed test scores to improve, of course. We're proud that in 2003 59% of fourth graders [passed their tests] as opposed to 22% in 1998. But those results need to be sustained," she stressed. "That means there must be people here for years to come with the leadership capability and the desire to work things out as new academic challenges appear. What good is it if we get these scores for 1 or 2 years and then things fall back to where they were? Taking the time at these executive leadership retreats to learn how to talk things out and see one's own leadership in this work is how we'll guarantee these results stick. Sometimes, the longer way is the only way."

Cleaning as you go and sharing books at retreats are concrete examples of the systems framework you can use to diminish the crises so many human service directors respond to. Instead of fighting the never-ending and often exhausting battle of "running to catch up" that we describe in Chapters 4 and 5, Burris and Byrd-Bennett chose to "pause" in their work to keep and improve systems in place that allowed for both immediate results and lasting lessons. Each has developed the ability to handle two systems at the same time: one managerial system designed to meet shorter-term needs (good fried chicken and better test scores) and one leadership system focusing on internal lessons of responsibility and personal accountability that could be applied elsewhere on another day. As Rilke (2000) wrote long ago, good, ongoing systems development means "the future enters you long before it happens" (p. 75). Having developed their own ability to handle spills along the way, whether batter on the floor from a frightened resident or resistance to indirect learning by executives, Burris and Byrd-Bennett prepared others for a future they never thought possible.

You can do the same, using some of the following activities:

Clean as You Go Exercises

"Clean as you go" is the skilled chef's answer to systems improvement, where to do otherwise might diminish the satisfaction of a well-cooked, delicious meal. Who can fully enjoy a meal with a room full of dirty pots and pans waiting to be scrubbed? It is no different for the executive, manager, or school principal trying to achieve great things. Those test scores might go up, and that grant might be funded, but the outcome might not be worth it if the organizational havoc left in its wake has been too great. Transformative leadership gets things done without undoing the relationships and depleting the resources of all those affected by the effort. Careful attention to the details of systems improvement—cleaning as you go—can go far in helping moor you and your program to the long-term demands of a resource-strapped, demanding world in which you and your staff work.

There are innumerable quality improvement tools, skills, and exercises that you can employ for quality systems improvements. Mary Walton's 1988 book on the father of quality improvement,

W. E. Deming, remains one of the best for accessible, useful tools for quality improvement. We will instead focus on two tools that you can personally use for managing the quality of your day so that your priorities are maintained and your goals achieved.

David Allen (2001), in *Getting Things Done,* brilliantly identified the core principle in "clean as you go": the 2-minute rule. Like every good cook, he asks you to answer one simple question: *Can you get it done in 2 minutes or less?* If the answer is yes, do it! He then quickly asks two other questions: *Can it be delegated to someone else for immediate action? Or should it be deferred until later?*

By asking the initial simple question, a chef gets a far cleaner kitchen and a well-prepared meal. The tasks of the day unfold far more easily than they would with the frenzy of an overwrought cook and an overly messy kitchen. The same applies to grantsmanship, project maintenance, and staff development. Applying this to two areas—grant development and e-mail leadership—that often otherwise seem overwhelming can greatly improve both work performance and overall systems improvement.

Grant Development

1. Can you answer this item in 2 minutes? Can someone else find the answer? Should you do this later when there is more time?

2. Go through each part of the project. Can a staff member provide the boilerplate on the school or agency? Can you write a quick e-mail that gets the answer elsewhere?

3. Are there parts of the grant prepared by others that you can review quickly?

4. Which design person can make the final product look terrific? Have you spent 2 minutes making expectations clear, as the school or agency has done these before? Or will it require a half-hour?

Finding the segments to do in 2 minutes and those to delegate can free you up to focus on the complex, innovative, and demanding parts of the grant that otherwise end up being underdeveloped. A great chef doesn't stop and wash that huge pot when the soufflé must be prepared so that it rises perfectly. But getting a few spoons out of the way while the rising begins starts to make a difference when it is repeated 10 or 12 times over the entire meal's preparation. The same is true for projects like grants.

E-mail Leadership

1. People often e-mail more than they talk with each other. Sometimes this can be helpful, providing information that otherwise might be missed. Sometimes the e-mails are so much clutter, used to cover one's tracks or simply out of insecurity. And, of course, there are those who use e-mail to write things that might never be said in person! It is clearly an arena where leadership is practiced as well.

2. So begin knowing that you are carrying your leadership vision into your e-mails (see Chapter 26, "Carry Your Vision As a Tool"). Likewise, the tone and politeness of your message carries deep into your work with others. Adding the name of the person, a touch of humor, or a warm "Hi!" takes less than 10 seconds. Don't let the speed of the Internet fool you into believing you have no time to be polite on your e-mail as well.

3. E-mails do not have to be long to mean something. A brief reply crafted with 10 seconds of care can make a huge impression on a staff member.

4. E-mails build up. Don't let them! Apply the Two-Minute Rule three times a day, and most e-mails requiring a response can be answered. Be clear, and as Allen (2001) suggested: Some don't require a response . . . so dump them!

Practice the Following

    A. Review the last 30 e-mails you sent. Where is your vision in any of them—that is, where do you concretely express what matters to others? (*Remember: Your vision doesn't have to show up in all of your e-mails, all of the time—just some of them, sometimes!*)

    Part of my vision that showed up concretely in the e-mails:

_____

_____

_____

    What can and needs to be added in the future:

_____

_____

_____

    B. What is the tone of your e-mails? Are you "practicing politeness"? What you can add/continue to use for a good tone:

_____

_____

_____

    C. In looking at e-mails you have received, how many could have been dumped and not dealt with?

_____

_____

    D. How many e-mails required more than a 2-minute reply?

_____

    Was there someone else who more legitimately could have answered them?

_____

E. Have you held or asked someone else to hold a meeting that outlines the kind of e-mail leadership you are trying to create in your program, school, or agency? If not, can you include it on the agenda of your next meeting?

_____

_____

_____

Other, more detailed systems work can be developed through the application of Deming's and others' tools that can be found elsewhere, including the Five Whys, Ishikawa diagrams, and other important analytic tools (Peters, 2002; Walton, 1988). That said, remember that in the critique of both total quality management and continuous quality improvement processes and reengineering programs (two variations of systems development), the programs consistently fail to work not because of the tools but because of three mistakes in application: (a) not consistently utilizing front-line staff for ongoing feedback, (b) not driving out fear in order to give honest feedback, and (c) impatience with long-term improvements leading to short-term solutions at the expense of longer-term quality improvements. *All three of these problems are those of leadership itself, not the value of systems frameworks* (Coffee & Radin, 1993).

Notes

1. It is important to note that the turnover at Ivy House meant that there was a constant number of new residents who functioned at very low levels and did not participate in the kitchen. These examples apply only to those whose medications had been stabilized so that other issues could be addressed.

30

BUILDING COMMUNITY

A quick two subway stops past Yankee Stadium on the Lexington Avenue 4 Line is 170th Street. A long walk up the hill takes you to the majesty of the Grand Concourse, its spacious three-bedroom apartments home to upwardly mobile folks for five generations. A stone's throw away is the ever-busy New York State Supreme Court building, its marble walls home to a different kind of mobility. No one is ever bored on 170th Street.

Walk back down the hill a bit toward Jerome Avenue and the elevated trains, and you know you're in the South Bronx. The streets bustle with activity, from street vendors selling papaya cut like jungle flowers to the latest CDs burned for pennies and sold for five bucks. You can wash your car, cut your hair, place a bet, buy a wig, shop for food, or simply hang out. There's a little too much garbage on the streets from the overflowing containers found too infrequently along the way, and the exhaust from older cars and worn-out-looking trucks may fill your lungs with a sickly blast and cause you to turn away. The potholes crisscrossing the streets slow the two-way traffic to a crawl. But overall, it's a fun street, noisy and vibrant the way commercial streets in the South Bronx are. Poor and working-class folks of every color are on the move, getting on with the tasks of their day.

Things get interesting in a different way up the side streets. Turn south back toward Yankee Stadium, and you're on a block less quiet than foreboding. Ugly brown gates, their faded paint peeling like so much overgrown ivy, stand like sentinels in front of every huge apartment building. Peering inside, you see the lobbies are dark and shaded, the sidewalks leading up to them cracked and broken. Every once in a while a couple of teenagers, their adolescent rituals interrupted by your presence, stare back at you sullenly as you move along. And move along you do: The street action, save for those few guys with beepers on the far corner, has disappeared. There is no sense of community here, only a growing uneasiness. On this street, one is alone, and safety is as far away as the roar from the famous stadium.

You would do better to turn north off 170th. Walking up Townsend Avenue, you find the same buildings framed with the same colored gates. But this time they are painted a snappy green. The lobby areas look inviting, with small walkways framed by lovely blue and yellow flowers. A few folks smile as you walk by, and some simply nod. By the time you arrive at your destination at 172nd Street, New Settlement Apartments, you realize there's no litter anywhere. No one ever will mistake Townsend Avenue for Park Avenue (at least the Park Avenue below 96th Street in Manhattan), but the street leading up to this settlement house has a clean and airy look. The sense of security that comes from traveling through a well-tended place has made your arrival almost as pleasant as the small garden you spot thriving inside the local school's playground.

Nicely painted gates. Walkways bordered with tiny flower arrangements. Well-lit lobbies. A local school's playground surrounded by touches of green. No litter in the streets. How could one city block be so different from the others? The income of the people who live there is the same, their racial and ethnic makeup just alike. Their families face the same struggles in getting through the day: They drive over the same potholes, ride the same crowded trains to work, and breathe the same sticky, humid air in the summer. What makes Townsend Avenue feel like it's part of an embracing community?

There is no one answer, of course. After all, as Helen Jacques made clear, "Community is built through all the little things," not one big thing. It's surely not one person, either. Keeping litter off the streets and flowers well tended takes a lot of willing hands. But if you want to find a few of the answers as to how to build community where resources are few and needs are great, you'd be wise to get to know Jack Doyle, executive director of New Settlement Apartments.

Doyle, a tall, lanky Irish American, the son of a cop and a homemaker, has worked in social services throughout his career. But you're not going to learn about Doyle's vision of either community or leadership by only talking with him. A modest man who is more comfortable expressing himself through his actions than by expounding his ideas (although, when pressed, he can), Jack Doyle demonstrates his beliefs through daily engagement in the small tasks of community building, not talk. One of us (Steve) first met him when he was the executive director overseeing three Red Cross homeless shelters. Having been asked to facilitate a management retreat, Steve arranged to meet Doyle for the first time as the senior team prepared for an upcoming celebration at the shelter on 41st Street and 10th Avenue in Manhattan. Steve asked for the executive director in the administrative offices, and the secretary directed him to the dining room. Inside the hall, there was Jack Doyle, working alongside the custodial and recreation staff to unfold chairs, move cafeteria-length tables around the room, and string crepe paper from the ceiling. If Steve hadn't been told what Doyle looked like (more than 6 ft tall, thin, White, with khaki pants and a white shirt), he wouldn't have known who the executive director was.

As Steve got to know him, it became clear why Doyle could easily get his hands dirty, no matter the tasks at hand or with whom he worked: *His actions are guided not by the authority of his external position but by his internal vision.* Equally important, Doyle's vision of how the world can be is constantly finding expression in the deeds of the day, not the words of the week. No task is too menial to avoid if it fits within that vision. "Pitching in," whether with dining hall setup or a school gardening project, is just as important as grant writing or board development. While he spends far more time with the latter than the former, the everyday tasks of agency maintenance and those who do them matter as much to Doyle as anything else.

Others who work for him sense that respect for all parts of agency life and in turn come to value their own daily work. How does a custodian know his or her work is valued if an executive never gets his or her hands dirty? Most street cleaning projects at New Settlement will find Jack Doyle involved, partly overseeing what needs to be done, partly picking up litter. Asked why he pays so much attention to these little details, Doyle spoke to the core of his vision: "It's not just cleaning to be clean. People deserve a place to look nice. It shows them respect."

Doyle's response to his cleanup work frames what we mean by "values consecrated in action." Those who toil in the world of public and nonprofit social services, education, and health all espouse strong values. Such values are found in every mission statement and professional code of ethics. The work of leadership is to turn such values into the concrete experience of everyday life. Doyle's lasting legacy has grown so great because such essential community values as *respect, support, and excellence* can be seen through the "little things" of how New Settlement Apartments operates, whether its staff members "clean as they go" in keeping streets litter-free or "practice politeness" for those who enter its offices.

On a more theoretical level, one can see how leadership connects to community building by applying Doyle's "little things" to the framework of community-building engagement that Fabricant and Fisher (2002) developed in *Settlement Houses Under Siege*. After documenting the decline of settlement houses' democratic influence within their communities over the last 30 years due in large part to many executives' reactive response to the state's cost containment demands for cutbacks, the authors argued for a model of "citizen engagement" as a key mechanism for rebuilding the social capital of poor neighborhoods and the institutions that serve them.[1]

Fabricant and Fisher (2002) pointed out, however, that such engagement in the world cannot begin inside agencies simply with an offer of more services and programs. People in neighborhoods like those of the South Bronx have become too estranged from the crisis-driven and reactive climates of most agency cultures for such engagement to happen easily. Instead,

Fabricant and Fisher argued, agencies and schools must be run by people committed to rebuilding that sense of relationship in every aspect of their organizations. For these researchers, creating a meaningful relationship between agency and community, it's all in the little things, too.

Having examined the decline of engaged relationships inside community-based agency life, Fabricant and Fisher (2002) posed four stages of relationship building that must go on between neighborhood residents and agencies before one can expect an agency to be perceived in the neighborhood as a space conducive to building neighborhood social capital. Those stages are welcome, engagement, participation, and citizenship.

Fabricant and Fisher (2002) made clear that each stage is necessary as part of *a strategy of engagement* as people are won back to participation in everyday life as citizens of their communities. As such, this strategy is a framework of implicit leadership because it poses a series of actions that must be accomplished over time if people are to willingly embrace the responsibilities that democratic experience requires.

Without a developed sense of reciprocity between people and the organizations they are a part of, there is little likelihood that the goal of social capital formation can occur. At the same time, Fabricant and Fisher (2002) argued, one cannot simply ask for or demand something as all-encompassing as "reciprocity" between agencies and clients and expect it to be embraced by those whose previous experiences in agencies and schools have been far more like those inside Allison Smith's agency than those inside Helen Jacques's.[2]

By looking at Fabricant and Fisher's (2002) stages of engagement through the prism of Doyle's work, you can see how "the little things" of practicing politeness, cleaning as you go, embracing diversity, carrying your vision, and building community are in fact the core elements of leadership that lead to lasting executive excellence.

Welcome

When you walk into the lobby of New Settlement Apartments, the first thing you are struck by is the burst of color. The walls are painted a cheerful red, the floors a sparklingly clean and well-waxed white. While the chairs are institutionally bland and boxy in shape and hardly new, they are neither frayed nor wobbly. One's eyes quickly are diverted by the art covering the walls: extraordinarily colored African and Native American masks, made in papier-mâché in all sizes and shapes, the latest art project of New Settlement's youngest and oldest members. The artwork, a burst of yellows, oranges, blues, and reds, gives the lobby an energy lacking in most social service agencies. Doyle's staff members learned long ago that the art projects their groups create are part of the fabric of agency life. At least twice a year, participants in New Settlement's art programs (for elders and schoolchildren) create the art for display throughout the agency, starting with the lobby area.

Such work is the perfect counterpoint to those institutional-looking chairs: free-flowing, not functional, and mythic, not utilitarian. The art of the neighborhood residents has been used to create a sense of warmth as others from the community walk through the doors for whatever services they require. The color of the walls and the art on them transmit a silent message of welcome: People sense they matter enough to sit in a well-lit and attractive space.

The color and the art are the most striking examples of New Settlement's welcome, but perhaps they are not its most respectful. Doyle and his staff practice politeness in more subtle ways, too. "You have to set the tone" is Doyle's point of view regarding how people deserve to feel inside the agency. Sometimes a respectful tone is simply a few words of explanation. For example, when people work with limited resources, as staff in schools and agencies do, there's often not enough time to finish one project before having to handle other needs of the day, whether another group to see or paperwork to file for the latest audit. Art program directors at New Settlement often can't get a new bulletin board up before attending to their next group or meeting with their interns for a brief training program.

What do you do with so much happening and not enough time? In Allison Smith's agency, you drop what you're doing and come back to it when you can. With a touch of whimsy, exhausted personnel interpret the ensuing sloppiness that appears in leftover projects as simply a sign of how much people have to do and how hard they are working. Rather than seeing it through the eyes of those who enter the program, they evaluate it only through their own professional point of view. At New Settlement, such interpretation is not acceptable. It's OK not to be finished; Doyle just wants his staff to let people know, for example, that the half-done bulletin board is a "work in progress." A small sign appears on any unfinished public project so that those exposed to it have the information to interpret it correctly as a work under construction, not another mess to avoid. For the people in communities like the South Bronx, who live with potholes and burned-out streetlights far longer than most other citizens, that small sign on the bulletin board is a form of politeness signifying far more than what will appear in its space later that week.

Through Doyle's leadership, his staff has learned how to turn an unfinished project into a polite sign of respect. "Providing information," especially on actions that otherwise can be interpreted as marginalization that people may have experienced elsewhere, is a polite, understated way for people to have a sense of power before they have met a staff member. The work is no less demanding, but entering New Settlement's welcoming lobby means that people's relationship to it will be different. "Support" and "respect" are mutually there for everyone: busy workers, worried community members, and overextended executives. It's right there on the walls for everyone to see.

Engagement

Feeling welcome is not the same as having a desire to participate. As Fabricant and Fisher (2002) suggested, agency leaders have to create experiences in which participation can be entered gradually and meaningfully before local residents consider such participation worth the added effort. The respect and support consecrated in how people feel welcome in an agency must be deepened in other ways. Clients, parents, and students must find that their encounters with others carry the same kind of respect.

Like other real leaders, Doyle understands that the only way such encounters can occur with regularity is if they are also experienced among staff. But how can a staff member empower others if he or she feels little power? The power won't be coming from being paid a six-figure salary. There are no bonuses for doing exceptional work. How does an executive inspire often overworked staff members to believe they have the potential to connect people in transformative ways? For Doyle, one small way was through stick pins and a map of the world.

The Mt. Eden section of the South Bronx in which New Settlement is located teems with the immigrant crosscurrents of our globalized world. The staff and clients who walk through the agency's doors are as much a part of that mix as any other place in the community. Such difference, of course, can sow confusion, turning diversity into distance as people from around the world encounter each other warily, not wanting their own cultural identity to be diminished. Doyle noticed just this kind of encounter as housing coordinators consistently confused the African country Ghana with the Caribbean nation of Guyana.

Rather than use the mistakes in identity as a chance for didactic learning, Doyle put up a huge wall map of the world and asked his 137 staff members to stick a pushpin in their native country and connect it with a colored piece of yarn to New York. The ensuing mosaic across the map became an opportunity for staff and clients to see the cultural exchange of their community as an exciting part of the change going on in the world. Any new encounter was embraced as a chance for a richer mosaic, not an embarrassment leading to later avoidance.

Such engagement among staff and clients carried over into concrete commitments to support differences as people engaged in other parts of agency life. Spanish translators are a part of every large group meeting. After all, people can't participate if they don't understand what is going on. The agency's commitment to the bilingual reality of its staff members' and residents' lives further signifies support for people to engage more fully in the community life of the agency.

The success of New Settlement's active programs grows from its leader's interpretation of the world through others' experience rather than his own. "I know who I am," Doyle told us. "I don't pretend to be something else. I try to be respectful of other people and their experiences and expect the same from the staff."

By working to interpret the current reality of what others are going through as they are involved with his agency staff, Doyle has practiced a key tenet of Senge's (2006) Personal Mastery: *He has discerned reality as it is from what he might otherwise imagine it to be.* Having embraced diversity as an asset, Doyle sees such breakdowns as the mistaken confusion of staff members' homelands as an opportunity for staff and clients to learn from each other, not him. His leadership has modeled how difference, when embraced, can enrich rather than diminish the encounters of one's experience in organizational life. Further engagement becomes a more active possibility for staff and clients alike.

Participation

As people find that their participation is welcomed into agency life, the possibility of membership becomes more real as well. Membership, that sense of belonging to a group or community, emerges over time in any agency. Of course, as Fabricant and Fisher (2002) pointed out, each level of engagement carries with it not only the possibility of greater civic involvement but the risk of greater responsibility as well. If people are welcomed to and desire to participate in agency life, they also can expect more visibility in the larger world. As they move toward membership, the challenge for leaders is both to maintain the standards that real membership requires and to support people in the growth those new standards require.

At New Settlement, there are various programs for young people to be a part of, including Bronx Helpers, a leadership group, and the Young Artists program, a computer literacy group. At some point in each group's development, those who have participated as active group members are acknowledged through agencywide events. Quite often, the young people receive a chance to write what they have experienced and to share their words with the New Settlement community.

To hear one's words in an auditorium of one's parents, friends, and neighbors for the very first time is a powerful experience. In many ways, it models what Paulo Freire (2000) stated when analyzing key moments in the development of a person's sense of capacity to act fully in the world as a citizen: "To name the word is to transform the world" (p. 73). As Freire, one of the world's most famous theorists on educational pedagogy, noted, this process is a gradual and demanding one, occurring only as the teachers and the taught join together in learning from each other in genuine dialogue. It is perhaps the most difficult stage of development in learning, either as a student or teacher or as a democratic citizen.

As Doyle attended these community-wide events at New Settlement, he noticed what many would have missed. Young people, invited to read their words, were so nervous at speaking in front of such a large group that the experience was almost painful for them. Trying to handle their nervousness and find their speaking voice at the same time produced results that were often less than satisfying for the young people.

Witnessing their discomfort, Doyle and his staff came to a different decision that in fact created more voice, not less, and more desire for future membership, not later avoidance. At the year-end celebrations, the students' words were read by others. Freed of that burden while standing next to the readers, participants could hear their name attached to their story while actually listening to the world they were a part of. As the speakers gave full expression to the words' meaning, the authors then saw their impact on the audience. The result was an expanded sense of the power that their actions had on others in a positive and meaningful way. Such potency in a public arena then opened them up to even more possibilities of participation and membership in their community.

This is not to say that everyone participates in everything, all the time, up on Townsend Avenue and 172nd Street. They do not, any more than people elsewhere in the world do. But what does happen is that far more people at New Settlement, compared with those elsewhere, attend large meetings, street cleanups, and community forums. Because people feel they belong, such attendance becomes a matter of choice rather than coercion. Such choice for a person is the true mark of membership that all communities (and the agencies of which they are a part) require for engaged citizenship to occur.

Citizenship

As stated earlier, no one "little thing" in our transformative model occurs at a time. Because transformative leadership is an internal process consecrated through small actions in the external world, it occurs in seemingly spontaneous activities at any one moment in time. As such, its measurement is over time, not at one predetermined deadline. Because of this, any executive or staff member who embraces this model will still devote far more time in the day to the tasks of management: grant writing, attending meetings, and resolving budgetary items, for example.

With almost 1,000 units of renovated housing spread throughout the neighborhood and 20 different social service programs to oversee, Doyle's day is packed with the same managerial demands of any overstretched social services administrator. In fact, New Settlement staff members would tell you that their boss—all too often the first person at the agency in the morning and the last to leave at night—does too much. Doyle is aware of this lack of balance as well, and he has worked harder in the last few years to spend more weekend time with his large extended family and to go on hikes and excursions into the country more often as a way to replenish himself. The birth of his grandchildren and their frequent presence at home has added more joy to his life as well.

But there is another place where Doyle experiences joy of a type that is all too often lacking in many professionals' lives: the Mt. Eden community of which New Settlement is a vital part. Not that he planned for it; who can "plan" for joy? You can't. *But you can experience joy when the vision that has guided your life manifests in how people live and act in the world of which you, too, are a part.* For Jack Doyle and his staff, this happens with a frequency that cannot be accounted for through either organizational mandates or a funder's expected measurable outcome.

However, a clue as to where this joy emanates from can be seen in New Settlement's frequent celebrations, whether the festive holiday parties or a program's year-end celebrations and ceremonies. The agency's budget is hardly larger than that of other social service agencies and schools nearby, yet these events happen far more often at Townsend and 172nd. Why? For Doyle, the answer is simple: Each budget request, whether a million-dollar request for proposal or a $5,000 grant, has a line item called "staff good and welfare." Its purpose is to provide a small amount of resources for staff and community members to plan an event with a few resources more than their own extra work.

The value of the few dollars added to each celebratory effort cannot be underestimated. As a line item per budgetary request, the amount can literally be the equivalent of pennies. But the difference in catering a meal for those used to only doing the catering is incalculable. The respect toward others signified in being served instead of serving transcends a simple formula. It is a quiet, unstated example of the respect, responsibility, and reciprocity between a committed agency and now-engaged clients that are the hallmarks of citizenship so often sought but so rarely experienced in modern American life.

If you ask Jack Doyle if he set out to be a democratic leader capable of inspiring citizenship through his work and the programs he helped create, he will look at you as if you have lost your mind. He might tell you about the legacy his own mother, Helen Doyle, inspired in him as he grew up. Living in a one-bedroom apartment, his family of (at that time) five didn't have a lot of money. "It mattered to my mother that our home looked good. We didn't have a lot, but I felt we lived in a place with dignity. Our folks involved us in that dignity. . . . We had a small bathroom in the apartment. My mother wallpapered it and then let us kids take the stars on the wallpaper and paste them on the bathtub. We couldn't have real wood paneling, but we had wall paneling paper that made us feel like we had it. She'd place those oil painting reproductions on the wall. For a kid, it always felt like a place we could be proud of. . . ."

Doyle went on to talk about the Saturday cleaning ritual, and at times a bemused smile crossed his face as he relived the memories of his childhood. "Even if it didn't need it, every Saturday was cleaning day at the Doyle house. I guess I was a little better at it than my brothers. . . . You see, my grandmother, Mary Kiernan, had come over from Ireland at 17 and got work as a domestic. She worked for rich families up at Newport, Rhode Island, and the Dorset Hotel, where only the best service was expected. She passed that on to my mother. . . . We didn't just make up the beds with fresh linen; we turned over the mattress once a week to keep it fresh. Dusting in every corner. . . . We had a Formica kitchen table; each week it was my job to polish the chrome legs until they shined. My mother set an example that you could be proud of your home. . . ."

Doyle may no longer polish much chrome, but he sets an example that mirrors his mother and grandmother's legacy from long ago. To his own life experience, Doyle applies "the little things" of his own leadership model that keep New Settlement "always full." Figure 30.1 demonstrates how he does it.

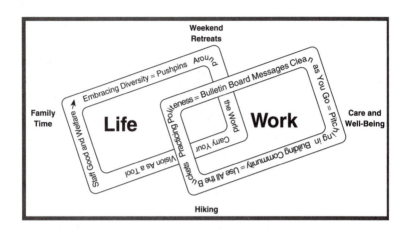

Figure 30.1   An Example of Transformational Leadership: Jack Doyle

A final story perhaps captures the joy that can appear through "doing the work" of transformative leadership. In May 2004, the leaders from New Settlement's Parent Action Committee were about to hold a rally to celebrate their successful year of working within the local Public School 64 (that school down the block with the well-tended plantings around its borders). Such engaged, local leaders—entering the final stage of citizenship that Fabricant and Fisher (2002) noted as critical to social capital formation in a poor community—wanted others to join them in the combination rally and cleanup around the school. How could the leaders get others to turn out on a beautiful Saturday morning?

Doyle remembered that the building staff had a large number of buckets left over from various maintenance projects. There also were a lot of old cardboard poles that had held various materials (paper, cloth, etc.) that could be decorated with streamers. He asked the maintenance director if he could find the buckets and poles. A little while later the buckets appeared, cleaned up and ready to use.[3]

With holes drilled in the buckets and colorful streamers stapled to the located cardboard poles, a potentially listless rally was transformed into a community celebration. Smiling kids pounded on their newfound drums; as people looked from their windows at the colorful sight below, complete with brightly decorated signs inviting them to join in, more and more members of the Mt. Eden community left their morning chores and joined the rally. By the time the rally began, 150 community folks were involved with the leaders of the Parent Action Committee in acknowledging the improvements in their local school: green gardens, for example, and an involved and committed principal seeking to work with the parents, not avoid them.

Early-morning drums inviting residents to come together in citizenship boomed down Townsend Avenue. With each new arrival, a stage of engagement was deepened, from new welcome to deeper participation and membership in the community. Along the way, the small leadership tasks of genuine transformation were occurring as well: Staff good and welfare were extended to all; brightly colored banners of welcome were hung; signs in English and Spanish invited everyone to join; and the settlement house community became a welcome part of PS 64, just as the school community had become a welcome part of New Settlement.

As theorists might say, the rally was a wonderful example of social capital creation. As we might say, it was a living example of how transformative leadership can affect an agency and a community in profound ways that others can learn from. Jack Doyle? He probably wouldn't say much. Instead, you'd find him elsewhere, perhaps banging one of those drums or picking up a streamer that fell on the street. He'd be cleaning up along the way, maybe shouting a chant offered by a parent leader at the head of the line. He'd be living his legacy one small, consecrated act at a time, demonstrating that respect, support, and excellence are for the many and not just the few (Weil, 2004).

As we stated at the beginning of this section, the secret to trans-formative leadership capable of building a learning organization culture as Austin and Hopkins (2004) detailed is a simple one: Use small actions that express your values in concrete, real ways to transform over time how you feel about yourself and act on the world. If you do so, the secret underlying this model will emerge: *Done over time and framed in this manner, such reciprocal leadership gets back as much as it ever gives.* The ease in Doyle's request to his maintenance director sprang from the effort made years before. Having shown respect and support, he received it in kind: As Stephen Covey (1989) wrote elsewhere, the win-win in this exchange is 100%=100%. The work is still there: That rally needs organizing; the banners need to be strung. This model doesn't promise less work. It simply offers you a way to lead and learn and see *your* glass as always full.

You can develop transformative leadership, too, by using the activities from the earlier chapters as well as the following exercises for building community:

Building Community Exercises

Points for Reflection

Authors as different as Parker Palmer (1999) and Michael Fabricant and Robert Fisher (2002) have nevertheless agreed that building community demands more, not less, leadership if that sense of belonging and connection is to occur. That said, they also remind their readers of what it means to be involved in a genuine community-building process. We offer some of their insights for you to reflect on as you engage in community building throughout your work:

1. To build community is to be engaged in building a relationship but not necessarily a personal one. All people in a community cannot be expected to like each other. They can, however, be expected to work together well on common goals and needs that they come to see they share. *Are people invited to be together, not love each other, in your community?*

2. As we make clear through this book, the leadership required for community building is deeply internal but expressed in concrete actions. As such, those actions most importantly are found in "creating spaces for common connection" whereby people feel more able to relax and relate with each other. Attention to detail in the lobby,

meeting rooms, and common spaces help support the building of that connection. *Are the spaces of your agency or program inviting enough for that connection to occur?*

3. Community occurs in bits and pieces of an agency or a program, in parts of a school or city bureaucracy, not in some romanticized Shangri-La that is always out of reach. *Where do those moments of connection occur? How are they created? How can they be sustained?*

4. Genuine community does not deny leadership or power. Instead, democratic community building redefines both so that as others with less authority in the community gain power, no leader loses it. Working to reconfigure authority as something to be shared and grown requires ongoing diligence, not indifference, to the small ways others come to gain a sense of mastery in their lives, as leaders simply deepen their own. Like the master potter who effortlessly creates art at the kiln, community-building leaders do not ignore their capacities but instead seek to impart them over time for others to choose to take on or not. It is this effortless, non-fear-based form of leadership that community building seeks to grow. *When is the last time you shared power? When did you last let others share the limelight? When did you last let others correct you on a point of fact or an approach to the work?*

5. Building community over time leads to an outward, not an inward, focus. While relationships may be closest and longer-lasting within the smaller circles of those with whom you work most often, building community over time creates a sense of connection to those in other communities as well. Each member of your defined community has other relationships outside of it, whether with the school principal down the block or the neighborhood clinic director a car ride away. *In what ways does your community extend to and overlap with other communities? How do those interactions build as opposed to diminish community building?*

Building Community Through Conversation

Community building happens in many ways: for example, through the attention to detail that makes a shared space conducive to a relationship, through common activities that build trust and support, and through celebrations that acknowledge victories and support us through the hard times. Through them all, the moments of connection that make a sense of community real occur in conversations, those moments of connection that are different from standard supervisory sessions or strategic planning reviews.

Meg Wheatley (2002), in her illuminating work *Turning to One Another: Simple Conversations to Restore Hope to the Future,* made clear what distinguishes conversation and its power for connection from other forms of interaction:

- People acknowledge each other as equals *(we share power).*
- People try to stay curious about each other *(we break free of preconceived notions of each other so no one is "boxed in").*
- People recognize that they need each other's help to become better listeners *("what is" and "what we perceive to be what is" change as we speak).*
- People slow down so they have time to think and reflect *(there may never be a problem to solve as much as an issue to confront).*
- People remember that conversation is the natural way humans think together *(there is no win-lose or zero-sum game in a conversation).*
- People expect it to be messy at times *(being open to your own doubts and issues is both honest and vulnerable . . . and vulnerability can be scary!).*

When is the last time you had a genuine conversation with others? With whom can you do so?

Write down his or her name: _____

What do you wish to have a conversation about?

_____

Can you be curious and open to another's point of view?

_____

Have you made enough time and are you in balance enough to be reflective and not just reactive?

_____

_____

Will the discussion be win-win and not win-lose or win-at-any-cost?

_____

_____

Can you remain open to doubt in your point of view?

_____

_____

Building Community:
Campaigns and Alliance Building

Sustaining community requires transformative leadership, genuine conversation, the creation of spaces for common connection, and ongoing reflection and relating. It also requires sustained strategic awareness of the larger world, whether your world is one of foundations for grants, political alliances for legislative support, or neighborhood churches, synagogues, mosques, and other community-based organizations for neighborhood improvement campaigns or school safety zones. Fabricant and Fisher (2002) went into detail about this strategic focus:

With whom are you building a broader alliance?

What are the short- and long-term objectives in this alliance?

What parts of your vision are in accord? Where do you differ? What impact will those differences have on your goals? What impact will they have on your work together?

What are the tradeoffs in this alliance or campaign? What are you gaining? What are you losing?

Can you sustain your vision, or will it be permanently compromised?

Will your vision be lost if you do not engage in this campaign?

Notes

1. Social capital, defined by Robert Putnam and others (Putnam, Feldstein, & Cohen, 2001, p. 16) as "a set of reciprocal relationships between individuals, groups and organizations that build the trust and solidarity necessary to gain access to larger forms of capital formation and labor market access for its members," is seen as a key measurable outcome to community building. As such, it is of value for both social service and educational institutions, such as schools, settlement houses, and public sector institutions, including hospitals, mental health clinics, and welfare offices. (See also Anton, Fisk, & Holmstrom, 2002; Fabricant & Fisher, 2002; Saegert, Thompson, & Warren, 2001.)

2. For a more thorough discussion on the strategies of engagement and social capital formation, see Fabricant and Fisher (2002, Chapters 6 and 7).

3. While Doyle didn't mention this, it is significant to note the ease with which this request and exchange occurred between an executive director and a maintenance staff member. Such a task, including the cleaning, the spontaneity of the request, and the time of day (early morning), are "out of title" and easily could have been either dismissed as "not my job" or passively acquiesced to in an overly deliberative manner, causing other staff members to "run to catch up" as they scrambled to work on the rally and locate the buckets and poles. Such ease can be created not at the time of the request but only through one's demonstrated actions and commitments well before that request is ever made.

REFERENCES AND BOOKS OF NOTE

Allen, D. (2001). *Getting things done.* New York: Bantam.

Anton, A., Fisk, M., & Holmstrom, N. (2002). *Not for sale: In defense of public goods.* New York: Monthly Review Press.

Austin, M. J., Brody, R. P., & Packard, T. R. (2008). *Managing the challenges in human service organizations.* Thousand Oaks, CA: Sage.

Austin, M., & Hopkins, K. (2004). *Supervision as collaboration in the human services: Building a learning culture.* Thousand Oaks, CA: Sage.

Bennis, W. (2003). *On becoming a leader: The leadership classic.* New York: Perseus.

Berube, M. (Ed.). (1999). *Webster's II: New college dictionary.* New York: Houghton-Mifflin.

Blanchard, K., Johnson, C., & Johnson, S. (1982). *The one minute manager.* New York: Harper-Collins.

Bolman, L., & Deal, T. (2001). *Leading with soul.* New York: Wiley & Sons.

Branch, T. (1989). *Parting the waters.* New York: Simon & Schuster.

Burghardt, S. (1982). *The other side of organizing.* Cambridge, MA: Schenkman Publishers.

Centers for Disease Control and Prevention. (2009). *Division of Nutrition, Physical Activity and Obesity statistics.* Atlanta, GA: Author. Available from http://www.cdc.gov/nccdphp/dnpa/

Coffee, J., & Radin, B. (1993). A critique of TQM: Problems of implementation in the public sector. *Public Administration Quarterly, 17*(1), 42–54.

Collins, J. (2001). *Good to great.* New York: Harper-Collins.

Covey, S. (1989). *The seven habits of highly effective people.* New York: Wiley & Sons.

Ellis, J. (2004). *His Excellency, George Washington.* New York: Knopf.

Evans, S. M., & Boyte, H. (1992). *Free spaces: The source of Democratic change in America.* Chicago: University of Chicago Press.

Fabricant, M., & Fisher, R. (2002). *Settlement houses under siege.* New York: Columbia University Press.

Freire, P. (2000). *Pedagogy of the oppressed.* New York: Continuum.

Goleman, D. (1996). *Vital lies, simple truths.* New York: Simon & Schuster.

Heifitz, R. (1994). *Leadership without easy answers.* Cambridge, MA: Harvard University Press.

Hendricks, G., & Ludeman, K. (1997). *The corporate mystic.* New York: Bantam-Doubleday.

Hill, L. A. (2003). *Becoming a manager.* Boston: Harvard Business School Press.

Jansson, B. (2001). *The reluctant welfare state.* New York: Wadsworth Publishers.

Katie, B. (2007). *Your Inner Awakening: The Work of Byron Katie.* New York: Simon & Schuster.

Kearns Goodwin, D. (2006). *Team of rivals: The political genius of Abraham Lincoln.* New York: Simon & Schuster.

Krugman, P. (2002). *The great unraveling.* New York: Norton.

Loehr, J., & Schwartz, T. (2003). *The power of full engagement.* New York: Simon & Schuster.

Moore, T. (2002). *The souls' religion.* New York: Harper-Collins.

Palmer, P. (1999). *Hidden wholeness: The journey toward an undivided life.* New York: Wiley & Sons.

Peters, T. (2002). *Reimagining: Business excellence in a disruptive age.* New York: DK Publishing.

Phillips, K. (2003). *Wealth & democracy.* New York: Broadway Books.

Pinderhughes, E. (1989). *Understanding race, ethnicity, and power.* New York: Simon & Schuster.

Putnam, R., Feldstein, L., & Cohen D. (2001). *Bowling alone: The collapse and revival of the American community.* New York: Simon & Schuster.

Putnam, R., Feldstein, L., & Cohen, D. (2004). *Better together: Restoring the American community.* New York: Simon & Schuster.

Rilke, R. M. (2000). *Letters to a young poet.* Novato, CA: New World Library.

Robinson, B. E. (1998). *Chained to the desk* (1st ed.). New York: NYU Press.

Ryan, M. J. (2003). *The power of patience.* New York: Broadway Books.

Saegert, S., Thompson, J. P., & Warren, M. E. (2001). *Social capital and poor communities.* New York: Russell Sage Foundation.

Scharmer, O. (2007). *Theory U: Leading from the future as it emerges.* Cambridge, MA: Society for Organizational Learning.

Schlesinger, A., Jr. (2003). *The politics of upheaval (1935–1936): The age of Roosevelt.* New York: Houghton-Mifflin.

Senge, P. (1990). *The fifth discipline: The art and practice of the learning organization.* New York: Bantam-Doubleday.

Senge, P. (2006). *The fifth discipline: The art and practice of the learning organization.* New York: Doubleday.

Senge, P., Cambron-McCabe, N., Dutton, J., Kleiner, A., Lucas, T., & Smith, B. (2000). *The fifth discipline resource: Schools that learn.* New York: Doubleday.

Senge, P., Jaworski, J., & Scharmer, O. (2008). *Presence: Human purpose and the field for the future.* New York: Doubleday.

Senge, P., Kleiner, A., Roberts, C., Ross, R., Roth, G., & Smith, B. (1994). *The fifth discipline.* New York: Doubleday.

Senge, P., Kleiner, A., Roberts, C., Ross, R., & Smith, B. (1994). *The fifth discipline fieldbook: Strategies and tools for building a learning organization.* New York: Bantam-Doubleday.

Senge, P., Kleiner, A., Roberts, C., Roth, G., Ross, R., & Smith, B. (1999). *The dance of change: The challenge of sustaining momentum in a learning organization.* New York: Bantam-Doubleday.

Tolle, E. (2008). *A new earth: Awakening to your life's purpose.* New York: Penguin Group.

Trattner, W. (1999). *From poor law to welfare state.* New York: Simon & Schuster.

U.S. Government. (2004). *Interactive diet and exercise sheet.* Washington, DC: Author. Available at http://www.nutrition.gov

Vidal, G. (2000). *Lincoln.* New York: Vintage.

Walton, M. (1988). *The Deming management method.* New York: Penguin Group.

Weil, M. (2004). *The handbook of community practice.* Thousand Oaks, CA: Sage.

Wheatley, M. (2002). *Turning to one another: Simple conversations to restore hope to the future.* San Francisco: Berrett-Koehler.

Zukav, G. (2006). *The seat of the soul.* New York: Simon & Schuster.

INDEX

ABOUT THE AUTHORS

Steve Burghardt, PhD, a professor of social work at the Hunter College School of Social Work and vice president of the Leadership Transformation Group, is a recognized expert on organizational development, leadership, and community organizing and planning. Over the past 20 years, he has consulted extensively on long-term leadership dynamics and training needs of the workplace for human service executives, staff, and community members. The author of six other books and numerous articles, he has taught courses on community organizing and planning through popular education, political economy of social welfare, and theories of social change.

Willie Tolliver, DSW, an associate professor of social work at the Hunter College School of Social Work and president of the Leadership Transformation Group, is a recognized national leader on diversity in the workplace, the role of spirituality on the job, and the dynamics of leadership in crisis-based organizations, as well as a noted motivational speaker. His most recent speaking engagements on healing and the workplace focused on chronicling lessons learned from birth in the Jim Crow South, appointments in majority White institutions, and extensive travel in West Africa. He has taught courses on human behavior, spirituality, and organizational development and change, as well as social policy.

Supporting researchers for more than 40 years

Research methods have always been at the core of SAGE's publishing program. Founder Sara Miller McCune published SAGE's first methods book, *Public Policy Evaluation*, in 1970. Soon after, she launched the *Quantitative Applications in the Social Sciences* series—affectionately known as the "little green books."

Always at the forefront of developing and supporting new approaches in methods, SAGE published early groundbreaking texts and journals in the fields of qualitative methods and evaluation.

Today, more than 40 years and two million little green books later, SAGE continues to push the boundaries with a growing list of more than 1,200 research methods books, journals, and reference works across the social, behavioral, and health sciences. Its imprints—Pine Forge Press, home of innovative textbooks in sociology, and Corwin, publisher of PreK–12 resources for teachers and administrators—broaden SAGE's range of offerings in methods. SAGE further extended its impact in 2008 when it acquired CQ Press and its best-selling and highly respected political science research methods list.

From qualitative, quantitative, and mixed methods to evaluation, SAGE is the essential resource for academics and practitioners looking for the latest methods by leading scholars.

For more information, visit **www.sagepub.com**.